The
Painted
Message

Color plate 1 *Hunting charm; Korewari River, New Guinea.*

The Painted Message

Otto Billig

B.G. Burton-Bradley

SCHENKMAN PUBLISHING COMPANY

Halsted Press Division
JOHN WILEY & SONS
New York—London—Sydney—Toronto

Contents

Preface

. . . Madness was . . . opposed to reality, where reigned an implacable light . . . leaving no space for shadow; an immense space without boundary . . . flat . . . this stretching emptiness . . . I am lost in it . . . I am terrifyingly alone.[1]

The Painted Message attempts to gain an entrance into the distorted world of the schizophrenic—a world in which the orderly sequence of deductive thinking is severely disrupted and where the influx of many simultaneous and unstable thoughts becomes alarming. The schizophrenic hides his inner turmoil behind a mask of aloofness. His lack of affective expression is often seen by others as indifference, or even as an air of superiority. Yet behind the mask the patient suffers from an inability to make his feelings known. The frustration over not being able to convey his feelings is enhanced by the lack of cohesiveness of his speech. The fragmentation of his thoughts interferes with the sequential order of verbal language, leading eventually to a breakdown of communication and to frightening isolation. Everything surrounding the patient appears unreal; in some advanced cases, he feels that he has ceased to exist and that he functions as a robot. To heighten his confusion, he may feel that he is controlled by the thoughts of others, and at the same time, that he himself can control other people and even the forces of nature.

In my student days, I was captivated by the outstanding lectures of my teacher in psychiatry. Coming early in my medical education, his lectures influenced me profoundly in an interdisciplinary approach to human behavior. They were full of literary and historical references, sound in their approach, and scientific by the standards of their day. But still I went away wondering. I was puzzled about what was going on in the patients' inner thoughts. The patients were obviously disturbed; their world seemed different from ours. When I made my first attempts to talk to a schizophrenic patient, I discovered that I could hardly understand him; it was as if he talked in a different language. It was only later that I realized that his thought processes followed different rules from ours.

When I became a resident in a private psychiatric hospital, I was impressed by a patient who presented me, somewhat ceremoniously, with his crayon drawings each day when I saw him. He had a persistent, flat smile as he handed me these

1. From Marguerite Sechehaye, *Autobiography of a Schizophrenic Girl* (New York: Grune and Stratton, 1951).

drawings, which were made up of figures in rigid postures drawn on any material that he could obtain. Some were on torn newspaper; most were sketched on laundry cartons. His persistent attempts to give me his sketches made me realize that he needed to tell me something. Obviously, he felt unable to communicate his ideas verbally. His thinking was highly disorganized, his speech was fragmented, and the sentences were half finished; some of the words were neologisms. Since he could not express himself with words, he tried to communicate through his drawings, which remained consistent.

In subsequent years I treated other patients who drew and painted on their own initiative. Most of them had never had any previous interest in art—it was their psychotic condition that made them paint. The content of their graphics seemed bizarre: it was obviously meant to be symbolic even though its meaning was obscure. As their clinical condition improved and their verbal communications became more orderly, patients no longer needed their graphics to express themselves, and they lost interest in speaking through their drawings.

When following the graphics that patients drew during the course of their illnesses, I could detect specific patterns. Motion depicted in the drawings appeared rigid and the spatial structure paralleled the disintegration of the patients' personality structures. As my experience was limited to Western schizophrenics, I wondered if the structural patterns I had noticed were a cultural attribute restricted to Western patients, or if they appeared universally among the mentally ill of all cultures.

At this point, I contacted B. G. Burton-Bradley, M.D., director of Mental Health Services in Papua, New Guinea. His active support and great enthusiasm opened the way for a close collaboration. New Guineans were of particular significance as the area had been one of the last large parts of the world that had been isolated from outside contacts until recent years. Many middle-aged patients had never seen any outsiders until they were in their late teens; their traditional cultural patterns had changed little during the first twenty years of their lives. They had lived in the seclusion of their villages, not knowing that life existed beyond a twenty-five-mile radius. Their cultural isolation is reflected in the lack of a common language: the 2.5 million inhabitants speak seven hundred different languages.

In many areas of New Guinea, art has played an intricate role in the traditional life of the people. Residuals of the local art forms can be seen in the graphics of patients who are not severely regressed. A patient's drawings must be examined in light of both his personal history and his sociocultural background. Certain repetitious designs may reflect the local art in some areas, while the same designs may be of pathological significance in the art of patients from other regions.

Graphics by schizophrenics from Western and non-Western cultures indicate very similar disintegrative spatial concepts. As with Western patients, the structure of space in New Guinean psychotics' graphics corresponds closely to the level of the patients' personality disorganization. The structuralization of space reflects the image of the individual's structure of reality. This structure is built upon a universal base from which cultural differentiation originates.

Our study made us aware that the patient's productions, like the artist's work, emerge from his particular culture and that the specific characteristics of both artist's and patient's work often reflect the attitudes of their time. The main difference between artist and patient is this: the mentally ill individual is solipsistic and expresses his own inner feelings; the artist's work has societal meaning that evokes significant reactions in his audience. The viewer's response may be heightened by a painter who suffers from deep inner conflicts. Van Gogh, de Chirico and Munch left a deep mark on their periods as long as their mental illnesses were not incapacitating. But Van Gogh's last paintings lost their meaning when the painter's personality became severely disorganized, and de Chirico's later art was halted in pale reproductions of his earlier works. Munch, on the other hand, put life in his ghostlike faces after improving from his mental disturbances.

Successful creation is a continuous struggle to keep constancies that have their roots in the past in equilibrium with experiences that venture out to find new forms. The motivation to explore new aspects of reality is not limited to the artist but is important to the growth of the individual as well. Extreme conservatism and resistance to change can become stifling rigidity, while rebellious denial of the past tends to produce chaotic uncertainties.

We have felt that long lists of acknowledgements are an imposition on the attention of readers. In putting this book together, there were many on whom we relied for their generous support and assistance. Not to tire the reader with numerous names, we included only the names of some of the people in New Guinea who made great efforts in our behalf.

We are particularly grateful for the help rendered by Professor William Beattie, chairman of the Art Department of Goroka Teachers College, and by Dr. Dirk Smidt, director of the Papua New Guinea Public Museum. Both aided us in collecting significant art material. We are also thankful to the administration and staff of the Laloki Psychiatric Center at Port Moresby. In particular, we would like to mention Dr. W. Moi, Sister Angela Horn, and Mr. Harrison Brown whose enthusiastic cooperation proved invaluable to us.

OTTO BILLIG

Color plate 3. Resurrection: *A ghostly figure floats from a graveyard, through a threatening landscape, and into the dark sky where a gigantic face leers menacingly.*

Color plate 5. *A skull grins in a moon-like wasteland as a bird cries atop a cross of human bones. Out in space spins the planet Earth.*

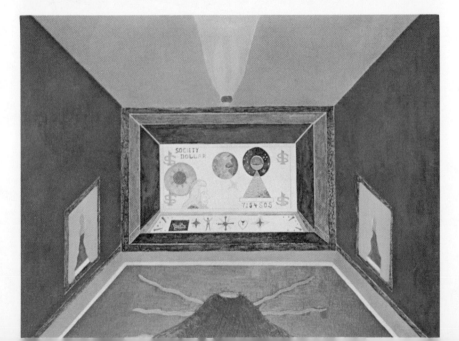

Color plate 6. *The walls slope inwards to exaggerate the distance to a flat backdrop, which is covered with monetary and religious symbols.*

Color plate 4. *As personality disintegration increases, the patient's world becomes increasingly empty. Details in his paintings disappear, distances increase, and figures are lost in the vast space around them.*

Color plate 8. *As a New Guinean patient recovers from his mental illness, his graphics show some characteristics of the traditional masks of his region (see also 8.30).*

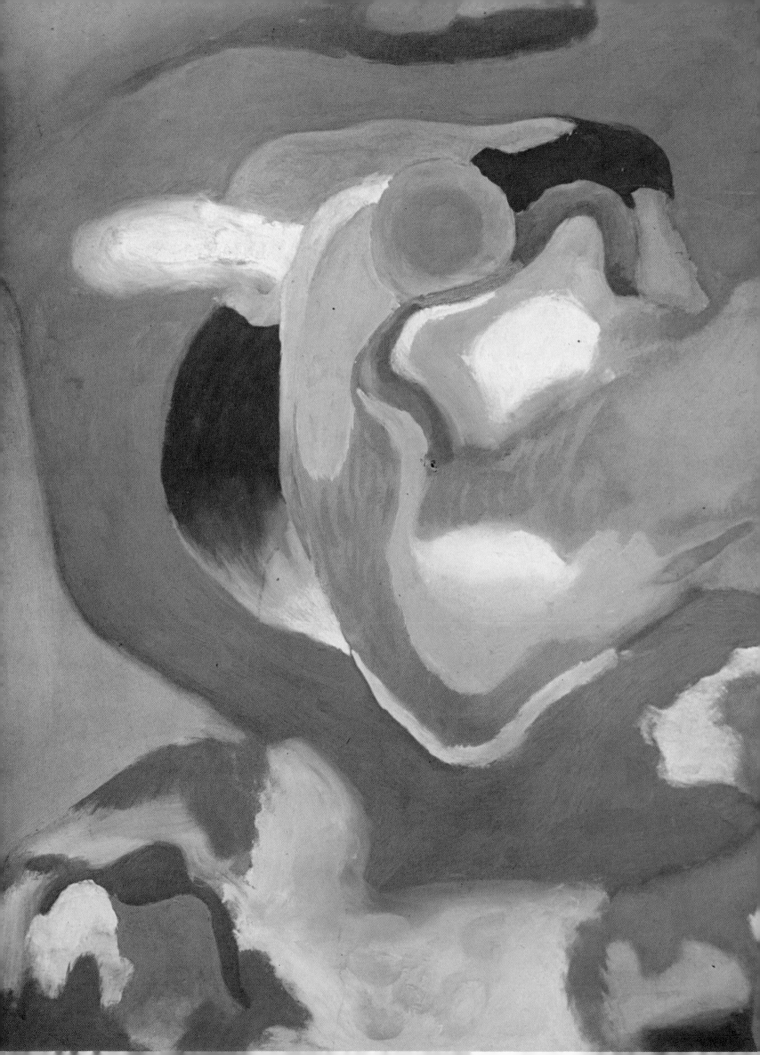

1

The Stage Is Set

A young man in his middle twenties entered the occupational therapy room of a university hospital to which he had recently been admitted. He had never been there before, but he was struck by a highly abstract oil painting (color plate 7) hanging on the wall; it was not readily identifiable. He, however, recognized it immediately as the portrait of the Department Chairman, "Dr. W . . ." The picture had been painted two years earlier by another patient whom he had never met. The patient who had painted the portrait had been a promising stockbroker who had lived in a prosperous part of a metropolitan American city. When he had become sick, he developed considerable difficulties in expressing himself verbally. His thought processes became disorganized and poorly integrated. When his ability to express himself verbally deteriorated, he began to paint to make himself understood. Apparently, his abstract painting was not a capricious or arbitrary expression without meaning to others. It immediately affected the newly admitted patient, who responded by promptly identifying the portrait though having no prior knowledge of its existence. One wonders if the two patients were able to communicate their needs on comparable levels of personality functioning as both had been diagnosed as schizophrenics of similar degree of disintegration.

In a small village on the coast of New Guinea, 12,000 miles away from the Americans, lived a young subsistence farmer, barely supporting himself and his family. His outlook on life was highly restricted culturally and he was hardly aware of life existing outside of his own village. He had always been considered a peculiar person by the other men of his village. When his wife was killed accidentally, he started to brood and act highly suspiciously. One day, he suddenly became excited; he started to run through his village firing arrows blindly from his bow. The incident provoked considerable uproar among the villagers. They overpowered him, but being aware of the grief that he had been suffering over his wife's death, they felt compassion for him. Instead of punishing him on the spot, as had been customary in the past, they called the police for help and he was sent to the psychiatric hospital in Port Moresby for treatment. While there, he began to paint; he produced numerous watercolors (illustration 1.2) in the style of traditional ceremonial plaques. He painted images of the powerful plaques to invoke protection against the spirit of his dead wife (see Chapter 8). Similar to the stock-broker patient, he attempted to make himself understood through his painting.

Both patients, American and Melanesian, had messages that they wanted to express. As they lived in diverse cultures, their messages differed. Following the local traditional custom, the Melanesian addressed himself to the ancestral spirit of his dead wife whom he believed was killed by a sorcerer; his watercolors served a magic function. The American, being influenced by his culture, painted the portrait of his psychiatrist on whom he depended for emotional support. The two patients, widely separated, living in entirely different cultures, expressed their emotional needs through graphics that were significant within their own settings.

While the verbal language of schizophrenics deteriorates due to its lack of cohesiveness and its abundance of *neologisms*,[1] nonverbal expressions by visual means may establish more successful ways of communication (see Chapter 3). The patients' messages may become comprehensible if an attempt is made to listen, to see or to understand the structure of their concepts and of their symbols that follow their own rules (71 a).[2] When a patient has regressed to severe levels of personality disorganization and his verbal communication is forestalled, his thoughts are still connected by links that can be comprehended, even if only with considerable effort.

Verbal language, the most significant bond between men, disintegrates in the schizophrenic, who often feels frustrated when he fails to make himself understood. As he realizes his limitations in communicating thoughts and feelings, the patient begins to paint and to substitute graphic images (an ancient mode of communication that may have preceded the verbal [102, 118]) for the verbal language which he can no longer command. Both the college-educated patient living in an American city and the patient living in a small village of New Guinea and leading the traditional life of his ancestors attempt to talk through their paintings, expressing visually what they cannot express verbally. The contents of the paintings tell the stories of their personal conflicts. The changing world of a disintegrating individual creates an outlook that is often desolate and deprived of significant relationships; psychotics feel that they stand alone, and are intensely aware of their frightening isolation. The graphics mirror the world that they see and their efforts reflect the way in which they structure the concepts of space around them (14 a, 130). During the beginning stages of their personality disintegration, the spatial structuralization of their paintings seems to deviate only slightly from the prevalent concepts that exist in their environment; but severely disturbed and disorganized patients, incapable of relating, produce only splotches or scribblings without understandable designs.

The structuralization of space in the graphics of Western patients seems to follow a consistent pattern; the level of disintegration corresponds rather closely to the degree of clinical regression. It seemed to be of interest, therefore, to determine if structural changes could be observed among non-Western patients and to determine to what degree they differ. Do cultural factors influence the content of the graphics and possibly their forms? Does the structuralization of

1. Technical terms are italicized the first time they appear; refer to the glossary at the back of the book. Illustrations, referred to by chapter and number, can usually be found within a page of the reference. Plates in color are in the front of the book. Numbered case histories are in Chapters 7 and 8.

space follow similar patterns forming a universal base for the development of specific concepts, and does this structure correspond to particular levels of societal organization? If such universal conceptions of space exist in psychotics and nonpsychotics from divergent cultures, would this support the hypothesis of a common foundation for the structuralization of reality?

Our plans to investigate the clinical aspects of "art" by schizophrenic patients raised many questions that led us into new areas, some of which were to be expected; some we did not anticipate. We had recognized that the significance of graphic expressions goes beyond an interest in the troubled and sick mind. Patients do not exist in a vacuum; they cannot live by their brains alone, but must interact with all aspects of the personal and sociocultural environment around them. Soon after beginning this study, our list of references began to grow, with subjects ranging from the Bible to comparative anatomy, from the influence of gravity on spatial concepts to art history. We realized that we had to consider man in his total environment and that we could understand him only within such a framework. Expanding the study to cover many disciplines could be rewarded by a more complete insight into the basic structuralization of human behavior and concepts of reality. Such a comprehensive approach places man, well-adjusted or psychotic, within the framework of history and each man in relation to his own and other cultures.

The relationship between creativity and mental illness has tempted some authors to conclude that both stem from the same source. We believe, as previously stated by the senior author, that graphics by the psychotic are not art (14 b), but that the great artist on the brink of psychosis may still be capable of producing important works. His illness does not enable him to create but does not necessarily interfere with his productivity if he is able to retain a level of marginal adjustment. It is possible that a slight loosening of ego control may reduce the artist's inhibitions and may allow him to produce more spontaneous, possibly more original, art forms; it is evidenced, however, that severe disintegration of the personality, as happened to Van Gogh, de Chirico and others, hinders the artist's creativity.

In the course of our studies, we collected productions by schizophrenic patients from Chile, Kenya, Senegal, Japan, Hong Kong, and Lebanon, in addition to our standard collection by patients from the United States and Europe (14 b and 16). These graphics seem to indicate no significant differences; many non-Western patients have had contacts with the outside, reducing specific cultural traits and making it difficult to differentiate between their indigenous experiences and the influences from Western culture. There seemed to be almost no region left in which the original sociocultural system had remained untouched. The only exception appeared to be New Guinea, particularly the more isolated mountain areas, the Highlands. This region was unknown to the outside world and was generally thought to be unpopulated until forty years ago. Many of our middle-aged patients were children then, and their personalities would have been established when the Europeans penetrated the region. Even younger patients who are in their twenties now, grew up under the influence of parents and parental figures steeped in the traditions of the past; their behavior is still dominated by the beliefs in spirit-beings and sorcery that continue to have considerable control over the people even today.[3] An additional advantage in moving our studies to New Guinea lay in the availability of an adequate sample of psychiatric patients that only a comparatively larger population could supply.

Our New Guinea material is drawn from over six hundred graphics by approxi-

2. Numbers within parentheses refer to the bibliography at the back of the book.

1.1. *A landscape by a young English nurse; nonpsychotic.*

1.2. *A patient's drawing shows severe regression.*

TABLE 1

Pathological and Nonpathological Thought Processes

	Deductive Thinking	Artistic Creativity	Magic Thinking	Schizophrenic Graphic Expressions
Personality Structure	Integrated	Integrated	Integrated	Disorganized
Personality Boundaries	Adequate	Adequate	Adequate	Defective; Disintegrating
Concept Formation	Cohesive, well integrated; Constant and stable but flexible; Deductive thinking accepts and integrates new concepts into existing images and is directed toward a goal idea	Cohesive, well delineated (even in non-representational art); Stable; Goal directed	Moderately vague, overlapping concepts accepting similes and identities; emotionally determined goal ideas; incomplete deductive thinking is rigidly maintained and supported by the individual or community.	Lacking cohesiveness; ill defined, fragmented; Unstable, lacking goal directed concepts; pseudoabstractive, concrete concepts
Creativity	Depending on new experiences; controlled by its own deductions	Determined by inner conflicts; conceptual fragments are linked in new relationships; often dependent on stylistin influences	Within traditional limits; rigidly controlled by its own system	Disintegration destroys creativity (except in borderline disintegration)
Defense Mechanisms		Primarily sublimation and identification	Compulsive rituals; repetition, omnipotence	Inadequate defenses; projection, omnipotence of thought processes
Symbol Formation	Goal Directed	Representative symbol formation	Culturally determined; societal or personal values	Solipsistic
Relation to External "Reality"	Can be authenticated by repetition	Dependency of societal acceptance or interaction	Shared, common acceptance within its own societal group; belief in the final solution, is accepted without question	Determined by inner needs of the individual; mostly lacking group acceptance

mately one hundred fifty psychotic patients. As we intended to make a comparative study of schizophrenics from New Guinea and the West, we had to be aware of the diagnostic problems. Not only was the influence of the cultural background on the individual an important factor, but the possible diagnostic bias of the psychiatrist (153) in making the diagnosis of schizophrenia also became an important issue. Although the basic symptoms of those diagnosed as schizophrenics seemed to be similar among New Guinean and Western patients, throughout this book we have used the less specific label of *personality disintegration* to describe the mental state of our patients. The term implies behavior patterns that deviate from those considered normal in the patient's own cultural group, and that are recognized as pathological by his peers. Personality disintegration leads to characteristic thought disturbances resulting in speech that is inadequately organized, disconnected, incoherent, slowed or interrupted in mid-sentence, and to verbal expressions that appear often purposeless, lacking a goal idea. An inability to relate to others adequately can be observed to varying degrees; patients may give the superficial impression of being indifferent, but may actually have strong underlying needs to relate to others. As they fear rejection, they withhold these feelings. They may appear puzzled and perplexed, not capable of understanding their changing relationships to others, which causes them to feel detached from the surrounding world. Appearing preoccupied with their own thoughts, they may suddenly exhibit unprovoked anger or rages that lead occasionally to unexpected violence. Delusions and hallucinations may assume magic or religious culture-bound trappings; more often, they differ in their actions from local customary behavior patterns enough to be considered bizarre. The intensity of symptoms varies with the severity of the illness.

The senior author made two field trips to New Guinea during which we interviewed patients and reviewed their hospital records at the psychiatric center at Laloki, outside Port Moresby, the capital of New Guinea and at the psychiatric division of the Regional Hospital in Goroka, in the eastern Highlands. We examined valuable data on each patient and important field reports supplied by nonmedical personnel of the area. The hospital at Laloki had a considerable collection of graphics since art therapy was introduced as part of the general occupational therapy program as early as 1959 or 1960 at a time when the psychiatric institute was still located in Bomana. However, some snags had developed in the occupational therapy program when the local patients did not accept it as part of their treatment; they considered the program to be work for which they expected to be paid. A system was devised that was based on an incentive piecework principle whereby patients would be paid for each day that they participated in occupational therapy, but would not receive any payment on other days. In time, however, the patients wanted to draw and paint, even without being paid. They, like their Western counterparts, found this activity to be a form of communication that enabled them to overcome their troubling isolation.

Many patients participated in the program on a voluntary basis. The art therapy building, being located in the tropics, was an open structure. The patients sat on a cement floor, painting on large sheets of paper, using paints and crayons of their own choice. The hospital at Bomana had no teachers to instruct them; patients could paint what they wished without interference.

---

3. See the appendix for a New Guinea newspaper clipping.

After the first hospital was closed, more advanced psychiatric facilities were opened at Laloki. A local psychiatric nurse, a young man, had been sent to Australia for training in occupational therapy. After returning, he expanded the art therapy program to include wood carving. He continued to emphasize spontaneous expression by the patients and was aware of its having greater therapeutic value than formalized art instruction could offer.

The other facility available to us was the psychiatric division in Goroka. Access to this part of the country is limited by its high mountain ranges which isolate the area and neighboring regions from the outside world. At the time of our visit, a young English nurse was in charge of the division. Being an amateur painter, full of enthusiasm, she encouraged both her co-workers and patients to participate in art work. Her own style influenced the local nursing personnel of predominately young men; they painted mostly Western style landscapes (illustration 1.1). The staff became very interested in art therapy; their interest was of great help in obtaining graphic material from the patients.

The patients' desire to paint overcame their reluctance to use the unfamiliar commercial paints, brushes and paper in place of the traditional clay paints, feathers and bark that had been familiar to them. A few of the patients might have painted in their home villages, but mostly they had been bystanders, watching local artists at work. Some may have assisted the painter by filling some of the yet unpainted spaces using black and white clay, yellow and red ocre that were mixed on stone palettes; painting was done with tail feathers from birds on tree bark. But the artist decided on the design and on the colors to be used (98). Cultural factors were evident in the graphics of many patients. They did not, however, influence the styles of other patients as association among patients from different areas was kept to a minimum. They maintained their kinship solidarity and the traditional separation was preserved even in the hospital setting unless a patient became so severely disturbed that he was almost fully unaware of his relationship to the environment. But at that point, his graphics had been reduced to scribblings devoid of cultural factors. In the villages, mainly the men painted; however, a few women did participate in the art program when they were in the hospital. Their personalities, being in general more advanced than the men's, allowed them to overcome the cultural prohibitions against painting. Being more regressed, their drawings were usually more severely disorganized (illustration 1.2). The women, like the men, were motivated by their desire to be understood in a world of emptiness and isolation.

2

The Conception
of Space

The development of a spatial structure is essential in order to act within the concepts of reality. As one of the basic functions, the potential to structure is formed early in life and finds its expression in shaping visual images long before verbal language has developed (118). Man, like any other being existing on earth, has to adapt to the space around him (82). As he lives in space, he must relate to it and to the objects existing in it. This requires the ability to differentiate between himself and his environment, a faculty that hardly exists during the earliest stages of infant development (137a). The lack of differentiation renders him at first incapable of establishing any relationship between himself and others. Reality has not yet formed for him. Being unable to recognize any limits of his personal world, he experiences a feeling of omnipotence. The first organized attempts to explore space result from a desire to satisfy biological needs—a desire with which the infant is born and without which he could not survive. Soon after birth, he moves in search of food, the innate biological patterns enabling him to locate its source: his mother's breast. He reacts intuitively to this stimulus by rotating his head horizontally as his face touches the maternal breast (*rooting reflex*). The horizontal motion developed out of a multitude of random movements; the infant has retained the successful movements while eliminating the unsuccessful ones. The basic spatial orientation is further developed as a vertically directed motion is added in the form of a head nodding (137a). During the infant's further growth, his movements are organized into more complex goal-directed patterns, creating the basis for the individual's orientation within his environment as he is beginning to conceive it.

Loeb (91) supports this opinion by concluding that "rooting . . . movements of the infant develop into elements of the adult's communication systems." The basic movement patterns have "a phylogenetically inherited, biological basis" and are performed from birth on, without any prior individual experience; the movements must be a "built-in innate behavior"; they later become endowed with psychic content by which they assume meaning and become an effective device of communication. As environmental objects are conceived, they are positioned within a spatial structure along the horizontal and vertical directions. Under the influence of subsequent socialization processes, they develop into more complex mechanisms which form increasingly intricate forms of communication.

The potentials for spatial integration and for the development of reality concepts can be traced to the first reflex activity of the fetus of vertebrate animals. G. E. Coghill (28) describes the first reflex activity of the fetus of vertebrate animals as a perpendicular or vertical bending of the head toward the body to which a "contralateral" (horizontal) movement is added. "Such simple movements form the building stones of behavior on which later action patterns are built . . . by addition of one 'simple' movement to another shaping the characteristic behavior of the organism" (66), of animals and humans alike.

The infant's early movements and his increasing contacts with his environment force upon him a gradual awareness of the existence of objects outside of himself. In order to avoid painful contacts, he must accept boundaries beyond which he cannot extend himself without experiencing discomfort. Such contacts make him more cautious and eventually lead to a controlled exploration of the surrounding space. Responsible environmental figures, represented particularly by his mother, aid him to an increasing recognition of the potent forces existing around him. The first orientation in the vertical and horizontal directions has a biological basis offering potentials which become activated by the environmental experiences of the maturing individual. The basic characteristics of early behavior patterns are duplicated in every individual of the species and appear chronologically at approximately the same age (86).

As the child matures psychologically and biologically, his relationships to the objects in his world become more clearly defined. He learns what to expect and he develops reaction patterns to cope with reality as it seems to exist. The conception of reality is highly personal, as it is shaped by the contacts with his surroundings. Personality patterns are formed by a complex multitude of selected and rejected experiences. He does not shape reality as a photographic image of what he sees; rather, he bases it on his perceptions as he experiences them in the course of the total relevant inner and outer events. The surrounding space, at first undifferentiated, becomes increasingly structuralized, and develops from "relative globality to a state of increased differentiation and hierarchic integration" (150). The developing structuralization of space reflects not only the integration of the personality, but also the individual's conception and adaptation to reality, forming a basis for his orientation and view of the world around him. Environmental influences and socialization processes such as feeding methods and early habit training, soon give way to complex mechanisms that a specific cultural group may exert on the family and eventually on the child. These mechanisms control attitudes and cultural beliefs, permissiveness and restrictions as they may prevail in a specific organization. The child who develops constant and secure relationships will possess different personality characteristics from one who has been exposed to an inconsistent, threatening environment.

Interaction between the environment and the individual affects not only the individual, but also societal structures. Small groups, loosely organized and without strong leaders, feel defenseless and unprotected as they lack an adequate authority figure. They seek safety within narrow borders and are not apt to ven-

2.1. *A New Guinean kneels in front of a ceremonial house.*

ture far beyond the security of their villages. Being loosely organized, wanting trust, and lacking the necessary mutual support, they cannot find sufficient strength within their own group to meet the dangers of the unknown. The absence of strong leadership creates a vacuum in which no one can assume the responsibility for exploring life beyond the immediate horizon.

The people of New Guinea formed such small groups enclosed in their own villages; they lacked a tribal organization in which the chief would have possessed a decisive leadership, a situation similar to that existing in many African societies. The Melanesians were primarily concerned with life within their immediate area. They hardly ventured more than twenty-five miles beyond their villages (40b). Having remained unaware of any activities that might exist beyond that limit, they rarely traveled further than a day's walk would take them from their villages, and they had to be able to retreat to the safety of their enclaves before dark. The fear of attack from neighboring groups caused them to be concerned with making their villages safe. In the Highlands, the villages were built on mountain ridges with a single access path limiting the entry of potential enemies but at the same time restricting their own expansion into surrounding territories (illustration 5.4). They walled themselves off physically and spiritually. The unknown outside world was believed to be occupied by potentially hostile spirits and men found it safer to huddle together. Ready to defend themselves not only against evil spirits but also against surprise attacks from neighboring clans,[1] New Guinean men lived together in the men's houses rather than being dispersed in individual huts. Since traditional beliefs made them apprehensive of women (women were held responsible for draining the men's strength—see Chapter 5), they sought security within their own group. Living alone with a woman was believed to leave them weak and defenseless. Young men were prepared against such dangers as they were initiated into the affairs of the clan, when they were warned against frequent intimate contacts with women. To be a warrior, a man lived in a community of other men. They built impressive ceremonial houses, the front of which was often fifty feet high; it served not only as a meeting place, but also as a stronghold for a more effective defense (illustration 2.1). These high, oversized structures, built with great effort and as a cooperative undertaking, became a symbol of supportive strength. The sacred images of powerful spirits used in rituals and ceremonials were kept in the dark interior of the men's houses. The initiated males were continually on guard so that no outside force could attack them by surprise and gain possession of their relics.

Concepts of reality, not being absolute, had to be adapted to their environment and to their societal organization. The individual had to conform to rigid societal demands and function within the existing structure; his society offered him, in turn, support to cope with outside dangers and threats. The rituals and ceremonials established a supportive system as long as the rigid rules were not violated and all demands were fulfilled; they offered to the clansman security only as long as their narrow borders which were limited to his immediate reach.

With the advancement of society, man is forced to step beyond his enclosed and protective space; doubts, insecurities and anxieties develop over the uncertainty of what may lie beyond the yet unexplored borders. Historically, whenever profound changes in spatial limits take place, subsequent crises are apt to follow. As the Roman Empire overextended itself, militarily and economically, waves of entire nations from the north and the east pushed against its borders, finally invading Rome in 410 A.D. leading to its collapse. Order in Europe was not established until the Carolingian Empire under Charlemagne was able to hold temporary power during the eighth and ninth centuries. After his death, constant invasions by large Nordic masses resumed, and they destroyed the foundations of European society. The economic system became paralyzed; city life disappeared as the king was no longer able to offer protection to his subjects. In his place, local lords provided safety in strong fortifications (105), building the massive castles and monasteries of the Romanesque period that supplied the needed protective stability. All existence centered in and around the feudal manor, and Manorial life did not extend beyond the borders of the estates. It was reflected in

1. Attacks came usually during the darkness of night when the attacker could not be seen and space seemed expanded; the attacker seemed hidden in his surroundings. Highlanders from the Mount Hagen area painted their faces black during battle (141) in the hope of making themselves invisible.

the narrow medieval scope and in the rigid religious system that built safeguards that were restricted to the confines of the castle.

Romanesque architecture and painting expressed the spatial limitations of the period's social system. The buildings were confined in structure and the paintings lacked perspective; like those of the earlier Byzantine period, they were two-dimensional (105). The figures stood on the horizontal baseline (illustration 2.2), and frequently lacked depth; pictorial space was handled arbitrarily by objects being folded over (illustration 2.3 [54]) or placed on top of each other in vertical projection (illustration 2.4 [54]).

As the Nordic raids ended, a firmer and more stable rule could be established in the West,[2] and with it came expansion. The Pope, the prevailing spiritual and also secular power, sought to extend his influence to the East. He inspired the holy wars against "the infidels," the Crusades between 1095 and 1291. They brought with them a change of the feudal system. The Pope's promise for abso-lution of all sins encouraged the feudal lords to fight the Islamics. When these promises lost their appeal, the threat of excommunication (20) persuaded many to engage in the voyages to the Holy Land. The long absences from their estates and the expenses of their travel often left the crusaders impoverished. Many who remained in the conquered areas found the new ways of life intriguing; they began to question their old biases and prejudices about the Muslims. When they returned home, they seemed more like Galileans and Palestinians than Franks or Romans. Westerners had become Easterners (47); Muslim ways were imposed on the West. Arabic words became part of Western languages; new products were imported, particularly foods and clothing. The Crusades had opened new vistas that were unknown before. The long journeys forced a change in the financial structure; bills of exchange, letters of credit, became a necessity and created a new social class, the bankers. The financially depleted nobility became dependent upon the bankers, who eventually replaced the feudal lords in social importance. The power of the feudal system declined; the protection of the manorial house was no longer needed. The oppressed peasants left and founded towns that came under the protection of the monarch (105); the royal might was reestablished.

The central power of the kings and Pope increased as the feudal system weakened. The Church used the threat of the Inquisition to wipe out opposition, calling dissent heresy. The stark and somber Romanesque monasteries that had been the bulwark against change had to submit to the new mysticism encouraged by the Church.

The societal events of the later Middle Ages, the period of the Gothic, coin-cide with the freeing from the immediacy of the feudal lords but not from spirit-ual restraints. It was a period of religious mysticism when men's activities were directed to the glory of God, when the Church controlled and penetrated all aspects of life, and when the Courts of the Inquisition began their work; charges of heresy were often unscrupulously leveled, instilling fears over deviating from the prescribed assumptions and precluding the acceptance of new discoveries that would disturb the accustomed way of life. The Church seized the exclusive right to formal education (20). As man's life on earth was restricted, he felt driven beyond his earthly existence to seek salvation in the next world, to probe upward, toward communion with God. The base of many Gothic churches was laid out in the shape of the Cross; the ceilings were lifted, striving toward loftier heights. Man's ingenious skills were placed in the service of the Church. He excelled in his

2. As will be pointed out later in this chapter, man feels challenged by the space around him, but before he can face this challenge, he must assert his security within his immediate area.

Three Byzantine mosaics show some of the ways medieval artists handled space. In the sixth century mosaic (2.2), flat figures are organized on a base line. Space in the twelfth century mosaic (2.3) is folded over: at least four directions could be called "down." In the fourteenth century mosaic (2.4) heavenly figures are placed above mortals, and the scene is rendered in vertical projection.

2.2.

2.3.

2.4.

new style when the vaulted cathedrals, the pointed arch supported by flying buttresses, appeared to soar toward Heaven. The open structure, the airiness, made room for a mystical bond between God and man.[3] The Gothic cathedral projected an upward, ethereal, otherworldly look (33), absent in earlier architerctural styles. Eventually, man overreached himself, his ambitions failed him. As the tower of the late Gothic church of Beauvais was being built, it collapsed.

The paintings of the period moved away from the restricting baseline and the two-dimensional space of Romanesque art and expanded into the vertical direction; depth appeared, although not yet in the realistic perspective of the later Renaissance period; the human body assumed a lifelike plasticity; landscapes (illustration 2.5) and views of towns (illustration 2.6) were painted in some depth by raising the horizon upward. The frozen pictorial images of the Romanesque changed to a sequential unrolling of events telling a story, mostly of Biblical events (illustration 2.7).

The final assault of the feudal system against paternalism came with the invention of gunpowder. It made a shambles of the previously safe feudal castles; knightly armor offered no protection against bullets fired from the muskets of commoners. The chivalry of knighthood became an empty illusion and even pathetically absurd, as vividly presented in Cervantes's *Don Quixote*.

New ideas found broader dissemination with the invention of the printing press in the early fifteenth century as the influence of the Middle Ages began to wane. Prior to 1400, handwritten manuscripts had restricted knowledge to a select few, but now the printed word could reach wide audiences, spreading new thoughts that often proved disturbing. An economic shift increased the power of the financial houses, and the new ruling families of the Medicis in Italy and the Fuggers in Germany emerged (67). As the established system of the early Middle Ages was destroyed, a concern with law and order fostered a powerful judiciary which made secure the position of the bankers and that of the large cities which had sprung up. The burgher or trade class again received royal protection, now against their former feudal lords. Merchant and craft guilds formed the basis of town government; town councils and courts of law guarded their rights. The new order may have freed the emerging scientists to look beyond traditional concepts. They explored areas that had been restricted for hundreds of years. The revolutionary theories of Copernicus and Galileo shattered Ptolemy's rules, which limited space to the supposition that the earth was the center of the universe. The Church reacted against Galileo's exploration beyond the established spatial limits: he was accused of heresy and spent the last eight years of his life under house arrest. A less distinguished scholar would have been burned at the stake. Still the Pope's control of science appeared broken and the scientist's influence could not be silenced.

As the center of culture moved from the isolation and protection of the medieval castle to the freedom of towns and cities, new vistas continued to open. Scientific discoveries, the wide dissemination of knowledge by the printing press, and the discoveries of new worlds widened the restricted spatial concepts of the past. Liberation from the narrow, circumscribed views of the Middle Ages became mirrored in the arts. Depth perception developed into a realistic, representative, three-dimensional perspective. During the Gothic and preceding periods, the feudal lords, the royal and papal powers had controlled the social system. The peasant, the tradesman, and the artist had been servants of the ruling class,

---

3. The Egyptian pyramid builders were motivated by a similar principle of bringing the Pharaoh close to the sky, but medieval man, regardless of rank, could reach God by upward striving within the setting of the Gothic Church, which by its very structure sent his prayers upward toward Heaven.

2.5. *Perspective is indicated in views of landscapes and towns in medieval painting by raising the horizon upward. French, fourteenth century.*

2.6. *Vertical projection; Gothic period; French, fourteenth century.*

2.7. *A medieval illumination tells a story as several layers of images unroll in a sequential order. French, thirteenth century.*

and their identities had been insignificant; the artist had remained anonymous, his name was of little importance. The new realism brought recognition to the individual, to the ordinary man; as the burgher assumed importance, so did the artist and his work. The artist of the Renaissance often became a giant. Kings competed for his favors and he could at times even defy papal authority as evidenced by the dispute between Michelangelo and Julius II, an incident that was afforded wide notoriety during the early sixteenth century (55).

The art of the Renaissance transformed the two-dimensional space of the Middle Ages with its spiritual asceticism into three-dimensional realism. The inner world of man that had controlled the conception of space, made way for a freed representation of objects in realistic proportion, imitating the appearance of nature. Adding the third dimension of visual depth was an important innovation of the Renaissance (105), made possible by expanding into previously unknown space, and this was reflected in the naturalistic art style of the Renaissance period; it allowed reality to be presented not as it was thought to exist but as it appeared, while during medieval times, reality was restricted within the confines of mystical idealism.

Changes of spatial concepts were not new and occurred at various times of history; figures in Egyptian paintings had appeared in rigid postures and were apparently associated with the highly structured beliefs of polytheism (14c). When Amenophis IV broke with the powerful Egyptian priesthood, he introduced monotheism and became Akhenaten (translated as "God is satisfied"). He led the worship to a single god, breaking the traditional multitudes. After Akhenaten's death, the priesthood regained its former power and reintroduced polytheism. Artistic expression, as had frequently happened in other societies, fell again under religious control (illustration 2.8). Myers (105) attributes the stereotyped rigidity to a desire by the priests to control reality through their well established and unchanging system of religion, conveying the eternal role of the Pharaoh and the power of his priesthood.

In an entirely different culture, in medieval Japan, a spiritual equilibrium

2.9. *The emerging mono-theism of Akhenatan freed artists from the necessity of depicting faces in profile. Faces are shown in full frontal view.*

2.10. *As polytheism was reintroduced, the rigid postures of traditional paintings reappeared. Tomb of Queen Nefertary, Nineteenth Dynasty.*

was maintained through the imperial system; the Mikado was considered the center of the universe and his power was thought to be so great that his bodily movements would shatter the empire. This belief required him to sit motionless on his throne for several hours each morning while receiving his nobles. Any motion during these official appearances would supposedly have caused a total collapse of the established ways of life.

Today, when man crosses the boundaries of cosmic space, entire nations witness and take part in the changes; television cameras bridge spatial boundaries in unprecedented ways. Everyone becomes a participant in important events many thousands of miles away. We witness the horror of wars, yet remain in the comfort of our living rooms. Such conflicting experiences lead to emotional reactions with which we are often unable to cope. We feel the threats and dangers to which we are exposed, yet our inactivity produces guilt and inner upheavals for which we cannot find adequate relief.

Crossing spatial boundaries has always fascinated man, as it leads to new experiences and brings contacts with ideas often in conflict with traditional beliefs. Man has vacillated in his desire to explore the dark unknown beyond his limits and in his fear of it. Often, the temptation to reach what is out of reach has an attraction for which man is willing to risk his life, while to some, the unknown is a source of anxieties and of confusion, filled with their projections and fantasies.[4] As man seeks protection, he attempts to find it by control of time and space; he seeks to manipulate reality either by magic or technology. Fantasies of suspending or speeding up time, of expanding space, seem to be of universal concern; but only divinity moves in limitless space and eternal time.

4. In unexplored areas, uninhabited for their harsh climate, or in periods of stress, animals of unusual prowess, creatures suspected of strange cunning are sighted on the horizon, always out of reach, not seen in clear daylight but under conditions when the observer's senses are not fully under control. He may see the tracks of the Abominable Snowman in the snow and ice of the Himalayas, the monster of Loch Ness in the fog of northern Scotland. Such monsters are envisioned under conditions when the sight or the attentiveness is impaired and the unclear image has to be completed by additional, often fantasied, elements.

We have put forth the assumption that the expansion of space brings on periods of stress. Man's entire history reinforces this theme. Apparently, man cannot tolerate limitless space and infinite time—it results in chaos. In man's most highly organized communal fantasies, in his mythologies, chaos must end before man can exist. The myths of creation date the beginning of the world by separating the earth from an unstructured, undefined chaotic state. In Indian mythology, the Supreme Universal Being, embodied by water extending to all quarters, puts forth a golden lotus in whose center sits Brahma, the God-Creator. The lotus is the highest form of existence (151). In the Judeo-Christian religion, God separated the heavens from the earth before he created any creature. In the religion of New Guinea, the sky and earth were originally linked together in infinite space. The female pantheon, also considered to be the earth mother, separated the earth from the sky with tremendous thunder (129b). When the first man appeared on earth, heaven and earth had been separated and he was forced to function within a world where limits existed.

It is a common concept in widely different civilizations that creation takes place when the supreme being separates the heavens from the earth out of primordial undifferentiated chaos, often out of water. To create reality, the divine unlimited cosmos becomes limited; unlimited space is a divine privilege. As space is limited, man's time on earth is not eternal. In the past, man was satisfied to expand space or to speed up time by meditation or by his collective fantasies reflected in his mythology, literature, and fairy tales. The witch in *Sleeping Beauty* avenges the social slight of not being invited to the party by making the king's household sleep for a hundred years. Goethe's Faust makes a pact with Mephistopheles by which he would lose his soul whenever he wants time to stand still.[5] If he attempts to conquer time, he can no longer exist; as he violates the divine privilege of expanding space, he must die.[6] Interference with time and space is accepted as a magical act threatening the basic order of events, a deed that cannot go unpunished. The continuum of time cannot be altered, and the setting aside of spatial limits cannot be tolerated if an adequate adjustment is to be maintained. Only god, the dreamer, or the psychotic penetrate the conceptual limits assuming an existence in an infinite and eternal world. The development of reality concepts experienced by the individual parallel mythological and religious concepts that originated from a state of primordial chaos.

When the personality disintegrates, the boundaries differentiating the individual from his environment break up. He withdraws the emotional energy with which he has endowed reality (38). If the disintegration becomes severe, the cohesive order of reality has disintegrated; the world resembles the mythological state of dreamtime that supposedly existed prior to creation. Space appears empty at first; as the illness advances, it becomes limitless, infinite, flat, and without depth (130, 22). Objects, including other people, existing in the environment lose their significance and their plasticity. Patients may become disturbed by the inability to relate to the receding and emptying world around them; they are frightened by their feelings of isolation and their inability to be a part of the world. They become detached observers rather than active participants; they feel utterly rejected and alone. This emotional wasteland appears in the desertlike

2.11. *Isolated, unrelated figures were drawn by an American schizophrenic.*

5. "If to the moment I shall ever say:
   Ah linger on, thou art so fair!
   Then, may you fetters on me lay" (52)

6. "And time itself be past for me!"
   And he continues: "as soon as I stagnate, a slave am I. . . ." (52)

1. Magdalenian period
Multidirectional space

TABLE 2
Art of a Culture:
Development of Spatial Integration

2. Geometric designs

7. Mixing of geometric planes

3. Baseline with vertical projection

8. Cosmic destruction with fantasies of regeneration (Indian philosophies; Shiva)

4. Need to fill in or obliterate empty space—"Horror Vacui"

9. Elongation
Spatial concepts not fully integrated

5. X-ray pictures; transparencies

10. Overemphasis of three-dimensional space

6. Vertical projection

11. Integrated three-dimensional space

1. Feelings of undifferentiated separation from the environment

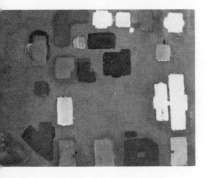

2. Severe psychotic regression

7. Inadequate balance between external reality and the self

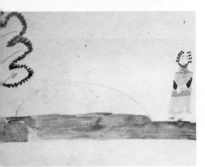

3. Severe psychotic regression

8. Moderate disintegration existing between the self and the environment

4. Advanced psychotic regression

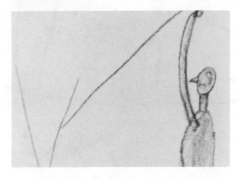

9. Early withdrawal of object relations

5. Inadequate balance between external reality and the self

10. Emptying space concepts; shadowy figures

6. Inadequate balance between external reality and the self

11. Reintegrated personality structure, possibly overemphasized depth conception

2.12.

2.13.

2.14.

The patterns of personality development reflected in children's drawings correspond, but are not identical to those reflected in the drawings of schizophrenics who are clinically improving. The children progress through scribbling (2.12, three years old), organizing figures on a base line (2.13, five years old), transparencies (2.14, eight years old), folding over spatial planes (2.15, eight years old), and elongations (2.16, ten years old).

paintings by a sophisticated American patient (color plate 2). Spatial relationships between objects cannot be visualized, and they appear unrelated to one another (illustration 2.11[130]). The ability to differentiate between objects is lost, as is the concept of depth and three-dimensional perspective.

The cohesive order of the world becomes fragmented, lacking clear-cut limits. The disintegrating personality can no longer conceive reality as it is, but distorted inner feelings and thoughts emerge into the "outside" world, filling it with the psychotic's own projections. Inappropriate and opposing elements are no longer repressed, while concurrent and supportive factors are not reinforced.

Disproportionate, unstructured, poorly articulated concepts appear and reach conscious levels (illustration 7.18); integrated, cohesive entities are lacking. The schizophrenic loses his ability to merge fragmented images into cohesive patterns; concepts are loosened and in a state of flux. He can no longer differentiate between himself and his environment. Often perplexed, he becomes afraid that others will be able to control him and know his intimate thoughts.

The changes in concept formation may be reflected more clearly in the schizophrenic's graphic production than in his verbal expressions (see Chapters 3 and 8). The graphics of the comparatively well-integrated patient remain fairly cohesive. As his personality disintegrates, his productions undergo more noticeable regressive changes until disintegration ultimately reaches a level at which he makes only scribblings and splotches. The spatial disintegration as seen in a patient's graphics parallels his level of personality disintegration (14a), and it illustrates the severity of his regression. As a patient improves clinically, the progressive nature of reintegration can be observed in consecutive drawings. Gradual changes from

2.15.

2.16.

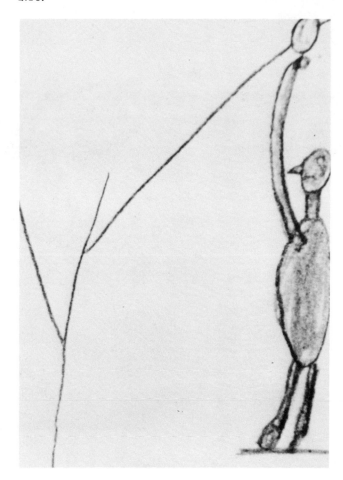

scribblings to drawings with three-dimensional space can be seen while the patient is passing through the various levels of the reintegrating structure (table 2).

A similar pattern can be seen in children's drawings. The ontogenetic development of the idea of space is represented in children's drawings, which exhibit a spatial structure that becomes increasingly organized as the children become older (92). At the earliest age, the scribblings of small children, as in the very regressed psychotic (illustration 2.12) are disorganized and without a definite pattern. The first attempts to organize space take place in horizontal and vertical directions; objects are erected on a "baseline" (illustration 2.13). At a later stage, children deal with space in a subjective manner; the child depicts what he knows exists regardless of its appearance. Objects are not limited by their outside surfaces; they become transparent (illustration 2.14); the geometrical planes of side and top views are mixed (illustration 2.15). Before reaching a fully integrated three-dimensional perspective, figures appear elongated (illustration 2.16), often shadowlike.

Giedion, the art historian, reaches very similar conclusions about the development of the spatial structure in the history of man. Space, being a psychic reflection of the visual world, undergoes significant changes which can be observed in the artistic expression beginning in prehistoric times (50). A pebble-stone of the Magdalenian period shows parallel and crisscross lines organized in groups but without any overall cohesive design. The spatial directions appear "multidirectional" (illustration 2.17). The seemingly sophisticated wall paintings of the Lascaux caves, presenting amazingly well conceived animals, consist of isolated figures, unrelated to each other. Each animal is well drawn (illustration 2.18), and is an entity in itself. The prehistoric painters were concerned only with their own immediate experience and ignored the paintings made before them; they often painted over them, superimposing their paintings on earlier ones. The lack of awareness of spatial relationships between objects is a significant characteristic of early spatial structuralization that is found not only in prehistoric art,

2.17. *This decorated pebble stone of the Magdalenian period suggests a conception of space as multidirectional.*

2.18. *The comparatively sophisticated cave paintings of Lascaux show an integrated "scene," but consist of isolated figures floating in space.*

but also in paintings by schizophrenics who have regressed to the earliest levels of personality integration (see Chapter 7).

Giedion considers the free-floating images of prehistoric art to be an attempt to bridge the limitations of time and space. In most primeval art, engraved animals appear on walls, ceilings, dark interiors of caves, or overhanging cliffs. They are isolated figures without connecting background and not bound by any spatial limitations; some appear upside down, one often superimposed over another. The outline of other rock engravings appears as if the contour of one animal continued into another (illustration 2.19).[7] The figures are seemingly suspended in space with an infinite freedom of direction and as if in perpetual change. In the flickering light kindled by paleolithic man, they must have appeared to be moving (50). they attained magic properties by which they seem to control frightening unknown forces.

Prehistoric hordes seem to have had no conception of eternity. There was no future and only a very immediate past; the present appeared to be their main concern. Australian aborigines or New Guineans whose concepts in our time are close to those of prehistoric man, do not worship their culture heroes who created the world in a distant past; they attempt only to placate the spirits of ancestors who have recently died. Even those fade away within a few months or in a few years. The magic, imbedded in their paintings, overcomes the limitations of space and time, and suspends the forces of gravity.

The society to which the primeval artist belonged consisted of small groups limited in their societal organization. They were without adequate defense and without stable food supplies. Being hunters and gatherers of food, they depended on the fortunes of their hunts. Animals, which assured man's existence, assumed greater esteem than these people felt for themselves. They accepted the wallaby and the antelope as their spiritual antecedents and revered the animals for the

2.19. *The contours of the animals blend into one another in this cave painting.*

7. Similar changing designs with borders flowing from one subject to another, and that are not fully enclosed are also seen in the drawings by a schizophrenic patient from Kenya (illustration 8.65).

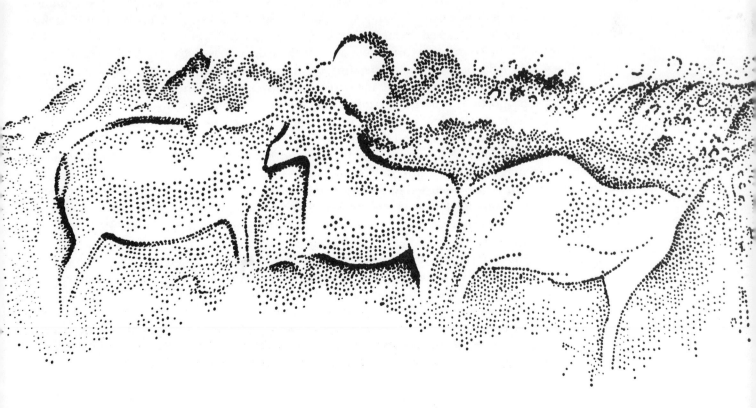

importance in their lives (50). Paintings of people seemed insignificant, and the human body is rarely seen; if seen at all, it is distorted in the form of symbols of fertility (illustration 3.1) or of a twisted mask. Primeval art reflects the poor self-image of its creator.

As the early high civilizations developed in Egypt, ancient Iraq, and Iran, men found security in mobilizing formidable masses under the protection of strong leaders who were endowed with divine qualities. A powerful priesthood supported the king-gods and ruled the lives of the people, establishing a rigid, hierarchic order. The magic practiced in the darkness of primeval caverns was replaced by rules laid down by a visible, divine king. Strictly prescribed rituals secured the supreme authority of the Pharaoh. His life and death were tied to an eternal cosmos. In contrast to prehistoric times, people were more concerned with the past and with a somewhat indefinite future; a continued eternity laid less stress on the present. The sociocultural concepts of ancient Egypt, as with most early high civilizations, built the future on the past, not so much on the existence of the present. The concern with the past was also expressed in the arts. It was the glorification of death that attracted the artist. The tombs were built with the greatest splendor, requiring superhuman efforts almost unbelievable to modern man.

When the Egyptians built the pyramids they expected that the Pharoah's body would ascend through the apex to join the sun god in the sky. The spiritual concept of the upright ascent into the sky was developed by the realization that the pyramids had to be built according to gravitational forces. With this new concept, the multidirectional aspects of the primeval cave paintings vanished. Space became controlled. It was a significant step from prehistory to the first high civilization when space became organized around the vertical; it became the stabilizing force, supreme in its significance, to align the segments of a structure into a functioning, cohesive entity; to find a true and realistic stability, the vertical came to rest on the horizontal. These concepts enabled man to move out of his caves into the open and to develop architectural designs unknown in prehistory (50). As he dealt with the force of gravity, he was able to erect imposing structures—his pyramids, cathedrals, and palaces. Even the structure of his simple huts was determined by the force of gravity.

In contrast to primitive art, which overemphasized some parts of the body or held back others, depending on their spiritual significance, Egyptian or Assyrian reliefs assembled the essential components of the human body in proper proportions. The facial profile was combined with a frontal view of the trunk and with a side view of the arms and legs. The various segments of the body were assembled in a vertical direction.

The development of the vertical and horizontal direction out of multidimensional space was not an isolated occurrence limited to the evolutionary growth in art. As we discussed in the beginning of this chapter, perpendicular and horizontal movements appear in the fetuses of vertebrate animals, and they develop out of random movements in the newborn infant in the search for food (28). They seem to be based on phylogenetic biological patterns, and as an adaptation to a force that affects all life on earth: the force of gravity.

Gravity, a constant and unchanging force, is screened from conscious awareness; it is usually not noticed and is disregarded. Nevertheless, it exercises an unescapable influence on all actions and behavior. It acts on a straight vertical line at right angles to the earth (123). The various parts and segments of the human body are aligned according to its control, drawing the gravitational center of each segment downward vertically. The body finds an adequate balance by moving in a horizontal direction, parallel to the surface of the earth. The various segments are interrelated and form an integrated structure which enables the individual to adapt in space and to function in his three-dimensional environment. The individual's integrated structure is sufficiently adaptable to align itself if changes occur in any one segment by setting off a series of compensations (134). Even the temporary suspension of the gravitational load does not result in any disturbance of the central nervous system's integrative processes. Experiments performed by astronauts during Gemini flights V and VII indicated that they were able to maintain their spatial orientation even when they were in a position near the horizontal line (6). Those experiments seem to confirm that gravitational forces have formed firmly established spatial constructs, and that peripheral changes have little influence on these ingrained concepts.

The individual functions within a spatial schema determined by the hierarchic order of time and space, forming basic coordinates such as up-down and self-other (44). The adequately integrated personality structures the relationship between the individual and his surrounding space so firmly that temporary changes in the sensory input do not affect the basic spatial concepts of the individual: he is able to compensate for the disarrangements of external cues (61). Only severe environmental changes interrupting most sensory stimulation lead to confused functioning. Experiments in sensory deprivation create an undifferentiated homogeneous environment in which external stimuli are almost completely eliminated; the subject is without any usable information for adequate spatial orientation, which precludes self-correcting measures that could reestablish a functioning equilibrium. Remaining more than twenty or thiry minutes suspended in a tank of near body temperature water and in a darkened room, he becomes confused, disoriented and unable to function effectively; he misinterprets spatial relationships and confuses his concepts of reality (152). Within a few hours after the experiment is terminated, the established pre-experimental temporo-spatial concepts return. Similar conceptual disturbances may be produced by transient societal stress and isolation, such as being cut off from outside communication in riots, during imprisonment, when at times of intense stress only incomplete distorted information is available. These disturbances are often caused by inadequate differentiation and emotional detachment. As the structured space becomes poorly integrated and the customary order of existing value systems becomes disrupted, the individual becomes dependent on others and on immediate external influences to supply him with data for his orientation and for the structuralization of his world. Being deprived of past and familiar experiences, he becomes susceptible to new information even if it is completely foreign to him and at variance with his accustomed standards.

Parallels exist in the ontogenetic development when the integration of spatial schemata is slowly learned by the infant (44). If early environmental contacts are inadequate and not supportive, he may have difficulties in relating to the surrounding structures. This seems supported experimentally by observations of newborn monkeys subjected to prolonged sensory deprivation, that subsequently developed poorly integrated concepts of space and reality (121); they became moody and unpredictable. Unable to meet environmental changes, they withdrew into the corners of their cages when anyone approached them. Similarly in man, lack of consistent relationships with an unpredictable parent or lack of "object constancy" created conflicts in the individual in forming reliable emotional constructs and may lead eventually to a disintegrated personality structure (22) and to disintegrated spatial concepts (44, 128).

3.6. *Horror vacui: the fear of empty space. A nativity scene is nearly obscured by the patient's obsessive addition of ornamental details to fill in all the blank areas.*

3

Creativity and Psychotic Disintegration

The process of creativity could be defined in broad, simple terms as the attempt to find original and uncharted experiences, searching for novel ways of expressing newfound forms. The field of creativity is so vast that we must restrict our topic to graphic expression. We will not attempt to make a judgment about the quality of the productions or their aesthetic value. We realize, however, that we have to differentiate inventive art forms from the purely solipsistic expressions of psychotics, which have little meaning to others. The artist is able to create reactions that he can share with others, while the mentally ill individual is limited in his efforts to the mere expression of inner feelings. The artist is able to give his work a societal significance, eliciting a response in others; the other is often aware of his inability to relate successfully (43, 111). The artist requires an audience for his work, the other is frustrated in his isolation and loneliness. According to the definition that we shall use, creativity has its roots in the past, leading to a basis for understanding between viewer and artist, as it ventures out to find new forms. It embodies a continuous struggle to maintain an equilibrium between constancies and new experiences. The motivation to explore new aspects of reality is essential for the growth of the individual, as it is for society as a whole. Without such motivation, a child is unable to grow and would remain on an infantile level, just as adult society would remain stagnant, fearful to move forward. Extreme conservatism resisting changes becomes stifling rigidity, while rebellious denial of the past produces chaotic uncertainty.

In a previous publication, we attempted to contrast the creativity of the integrated artist with schizophrenic expression (14b). This issue has never been clear-cut, and widely divergent opinions have existed since Lombroso (93), who viewed genius and insanity as closely related. He attributed the artistic genius to mental degeneration, supporting his findings by pointing to supposedly similar physical symptoms and personality patterns of great thinkers and the mentally ill—a theory that has been proven wrong. More recently, Navratil (109) put forth a more usable concept, as he wrote that "the psychic dynamics of creativity are the same in the healthy and in the sick . . . the healthy creativity has a restituting quality for the ego of the creator. . . ."

Any artistic era, regardless of how accomplished, eventually reaches the height of its creativeness and finds itself at a point of dilemma: it seeks to maintain the style of the period as it had been successful; but now that the style has lost its meaning, it has become shallow. The spiritual bankruptcy of a period, affecting its arts, may precede and substantially contribute to coming historical events. The established schools of art cannot successfully cling to the customary forms, which have become empty and without meaning, and so new forms develop to fill the vacuum. The religious, spiritual and political changes culminating in turmoil during the early sixteenth century (20), made the prevalent High Renaissance style highly vulnerable. When the sacking of Rome in 1527 made the final impact, and scattered the last important Renaissance school, that of Raphael, the new Mannerism emerged (105). The distortions of manneristic art appeared as a reaction to the conflicts of the Church that reached their crisis during the Reformation. Human bodies became elongated, often distorted; unearthly figures seemed suspended in space; discordant colors created a restless appearance. "Manneristic" styles, however, have appeared often in history when traditional art styles have become excessively constrained and empty, when they have lost their original freshness. At such times, conventional standards and views, including art forms, are treated with contempt. The artistic heritage, which is identified with the newly disavowed societal structure, is ridiculed and condemned (5). Ideas hostile to the established tradition and its art lead to new values and new approaches. Hocke (64) extended the meaning of Mannerism, applying it to any period in history when art becomes anticlassic and antinaturalistic. A preoccupation with the bizarre and the unusual dominates; death and destruction, distant and distorted space, fragmented and grotesque figures are as much a part of Bosch's and Breughel's sixteenth-century paintings as they are of Dali's and the art of the twentieth-century Dada movement. Dubuffet's paintings and James Joyce's writings were intended to shock bourgeois society (131).

In modern Western society, the comforts of a complacent society tolerate new art forms as nearly insignificant within the total societal structure; such complacency may overlook the fact that the new art forms may signal developing societal stresses and tensions. During periods of crisis, however, society is not nearly so tolerant of free artistic expression as it may be in stabler periods. At times when social unrest comes actually into the open, the underlying symbolic meaning of art, otherwise ignored, emerges and can no longer be denied. It is then that art is met with the violent actions usually reserved for powerful provocations.

As the historical pendulum swings to authoritarian regimes (the specific political orientation does not seem to matter) the potential impact of unconventional art may prove a great threat to the strict and rigid concepts of the system. Such art cannot be ignored by the new regime; it becomes the symbol of heresy, treason, or the decadence of the epoch just past. Historical events, such as the auto-da-fé of heretic works during the days of the Inquisition, the book burnings, or the ridicule and quarantine of "degenerate art" to restricted showplaces in Hitler's Germany, bear witness to the emotional impact of the arts. In Russia during the days of Stalin, bourgeois art of the late nineteenth and of the twentieth centuries was hidden in the museums' storerooms. Art is recognized in periods of stress as a potential catalyst of underlying unrest.

Art is usually concerned with having a societal orientation. The prehistoric painter of Lascaux, the medieval mystic, the Renaissance and early nineteenth-century naturalists, the allegoric escapists Boucher and Fragonard, as well as the twentieth-century artist, all produce works significant to their immediate societies. The artist may distort, condense, elaborate and fragment the appearance of objects, but he creates according to prescribed cultural rules existing at various periods of history. He always creates a cohesive and denser unity, a new substance which becomes his essential reality, and "he always retains a controlling hand" as he produces (131). It is the artistic control that maintains a cohesiveness, making the art work meaningful and a part of the creative process; without it, the work has only a personal meaning.

The artist, like the psychotic, is motivated and driven by inner conflicts, disturbing his emotional equilibrium. Without such motivation, he would not create (31). The artist, in contrast to the psychotic, structures his impulses; his efforts are directed toward a formalized goal: he wants to appeal to an appreciative audience. The artist seeks a communicative response; he clamors for recognition of his creation and the acceptance of his message by others. The expected response may come from a not yet existing, but future audience, or only from a small band of followers. The communication takes place on a preconscious level (53) and it is often difficult to recognize consciously. A few experts, art historians and critics, may be capable of determining the technical aspects and values of a creative work, but even they are not equipped to substantiate its emotional appeal and impact on an audience. The affective component of creativity communicates meaningful symbols that free the observer to respond to his own inner fantasies, and conflicts that he would otherwise repress (103). The creative artist channels and integrates these symbols into a controlled structure with fixed rules that are established by the society and by the period during which the art work is created. Through this structure, the appreciative connoisseur identifies with the fantasies and conflicts of the artist. He responds intuitively to the affective needs that they may have in common. Having his unconscious needs satisfied, couched in a socially acceptable manner established by the aesthetic rules of the period, he acclaims the artistic creator and respects him far more than do most other members of society.

In western civilization, particularly since the days of the Renaissance, the artist is identified with his creation, and receives praise or scorn for it. In tribal societies the carver of masks and of ancestral figures is often the medicine man or the tribal chief who is feared for his unusual creative powers. In nonliterate societies that have no definite social stratification, as in New Guinea, the role of the artist is not distinct, but some individuals are recognized for their artistic ability to design the more complex artifacts (78). Gombrich (53) and Kris (75) distinguish the aesthetic and ritualistc aspects of an art work from its value in fulfilling emotional needs. The art styles of primitive and Western societies may appear highly divergent on a conscious level; however, the motivation creating them may differ little. In both cases a fantasized image is created that satisfies and controls the unconscious desires and needs of the individual and his societal group. Only the forms and styles—the distortions, condensations and elaborations-change in various artistic periods, from Western to non-Western man, from prehistoric to modern art. Creating an idealized woman has, for example, been an ever-returning theme preoccupying the fantasies of mankind. In prehistoric times, this theme appeared in fertility symbols. Notice the Venus of Willendorf (illustration 3.1) with her exaggerated feminine endowments—large breasts, abdomen and buttocks. In classic art, the idealized woman has the perfected beauty of the Venus of Milos.

Westerners, accustomed to classical art, may view the art of New Guinea as naive, or even distorted. What we may fail to understand is that these "distortions" are forms of an intentional, culturally determined style. Moreover, the art of each region of New Guinea displays its own particular and consistent style. To the Melanesian eye, these styles are as distinctly different as Greek and Victorian art would be to a Westerner. Thus, even though these tribal works appear distorted to the Western eye, they have a strong appeal within their own cultures, and any of their distortions are acceptable and significant.

A work of art has to be "plausible" (31) to the generation for which it was created; yet what is plausible varies from one area to another, from one period to another. Furthermore, what is plausible in art might not be so in life. Devereux (31) mentions that while a centaur was plausible in Greek mythology, an ancient Greek would have been shocked to find such a creature in his own back yard. Mythological figures are produced as a response to the needs of their respective societies, even if they appear implausible to the outsider. The splendid religious works of art decorating Western churches, like masks, plaques, and ancestral figures, have met the emotional needs of the culture that formed them. Later generations will respond principally to the aesthetic qualities of the art work that may have lulled the critical abilities of the original observer as to its unrealistic content and made him accept the fantastic creation of a mythological creature.

All art has to meet definite rules in order to be accepted by its own society, for the artist cannot isolate himself from the society in which he creates. Picasso, in introducing African concepts into his creations, was not free from the influence of contemporary thought or of his own environment. He used African forms to surface unconscious symbols in an attempt to give new and deeper directions to art. But he was building on a groundwork laid by nineteenth-century philosophy (58), and particularly Freudian psychiatry, which placed emphasis on the unconscious mind, in order to find the motivations for human behavior. Even before that time, Bosch and Breughel had painted disturbing and distorted figures, pointing an accusing finger at the vanities of their society (illustration 3.2), their works growing out of the spiritual revival of the Reformation.

Art functions as a safety valve for expressing desires and needs which may be otherwise unacceptable. They may be acceptable in one setting but offensive in another—the sexual practices displayed undisguised in the stone carvings of Hindu temples may be offensive to Western eyes; the phallic representations in Mexican or Melanesian art were so disturbing to missionaries that they forced the local people to destroy them—yet all these works served purposeful roles in their society. Ancestral plaques, such as the Hohao boards of the Papuan Gulf, embodied powerful, fearful forces which could not have been faced without their carved presence. The religious paintings of the Middle Ages and the Renaissance were not mere museum pieces when they were created; they evoked deep religious feelings and generated an atmosphere of holiness for the worshipper. By representing the deities in his art work, the worshipper could deal with the fearful aspects of his gods and spirits. The sacred images established a presence that became personal and intimate. They helped the believer to fill the gap between

3.1. The "Venus of Willendorf" is a prehistoric fertility symbol.

30

himself and his gods, and he became able to reach his gods directly or to bring sacrifices on the altars of their temples.

We may be deeply touched by a staged tragedy, our aroused feelings lasting for hours after the end of the play. A few years ago, I attended a Japanese Kabuki theatre at which several plays were enacted during the four to six hours of performance. The audience seemed caught up in the drama, and at times participated in the action directly by shouting warnings to the endangered hero. During one of the plays, a middle-aged man called admiringly to a beautiful woman who was played by a male actor (only men act in the Kabuki theatre). In spite of knowing that "she" was portrayed by a man, he was entranced by the beauty of her makeup; he accepted the representation for what it was meant to be, not for what it was. It is easy to assume that the representation had become reality for him and that he had channeled his feelings and emotional needs toward the substitute; the male actor became his Galatea. He admired "her" openly, and he could safely express unfulfilled feelings which he would otherwise have had to repress. If he had approached a beautiful woman on the street with such intensity of emotion, he would have been slapped in the face. His identification with the actions on the stage saved this individual from "jeopardizing" himself (103) and allowed him a safe discharge of repressed feelings. He became a participant in the play.

Art enables the knowledgeable connoisseur to repeat the artist's imaginative performance (53). But to do this, the participant and the artist have to be part of the same societal institution, and capable of understanding the same symbolism. As a Westerner, I could follow the Kabuki performance and the audience's re-action with great interest and fascination, but I remained detached; the plays failed to have the same emotional impact on me as they did on the local audience. Being of a foreign culture, I could only admire its aesthetic quality; I could see but not feel.

3.2. Vanity *(detail) by Hie-ronymus Bosch.*

In more recent times, art concerns itself with social conflicts. In dealing with the fears arising from disturbing inner needs, art may become a powerful tool as it mobilizes the forces of protest. At first it may seem curious that works of art often anticipate social unrest, but as soon as the upheaval is accomplished and political control is established, art becomes controlled by the powers it helped to create. It becomes excessively realistic and restrained, prostituting itself, losing its aesthetic values, and becoming an obvious propaganda tool, as in Nazi Germany and Soviet Russia. It is reduced to a vehicle for the ideals of the regime, just as pornography presents sex undisguised and without subtlety.

The walls of Persepolis depict long processions of gift bearers (illustration 3.3), not simply to record important historical events and to demonstrate the sophisticated artistry of the period, but mainly to reflect the power of the Persian kings and to induce visitors paying homage to submit to the royal might. In Egypt, vast treasures in the tombs of the Pharaohs were protected by wooden guards. These guards were not just wooden objects of art; they were considered to be royal guards who successfully kept any potential grave robbers away; they were an effective deterrent against robbers who belonged to the same societal group and shared the beliefs of the tomb builders. During subsequent dynasties, however, the tombs were robbed repeatedly by thieves who were no longer part of the society that had buried the Pharaoh. The spiritual power of the guards vanished, and they became nothing but wooden figures, no longer endowed with their original protective power. The loss of the magic power of art does not imply that art created by other societies does not appeal to us, but that the appeal takes place on a different level. We appreciate its aesthetic values—the colors, the composition, the perfection of its lines and balance—but the work is deprived of its magic. We may be in awe of the magnitude and beauty of an Egyptian pyramid, but, lacking the worshipful devotion of the period, we remain detached and miss the full impact of the tomb. Even art considered timeless, art which depicts the basic human conflicts that transcend centuries of social change, remains in some ways culture-bound. Not only art works of another culture, but also those of an earlier period of one's own culture, are perceived differently. Greek tragedies as well as Shakespearean drama have an impact on today's Western audiences. Touching on universal themes, they may have social appeal, but the Elizabethan language alone puts distance between the listener and the playwright, reducing the power of the play. Sophisticated audiences may transpose themselves temporarily into the original setting, but even then, the art of a different generation loses some of its original meaning.

As foreign contacts increase and cultural difference become less clearly defined, the value of symbols may be transferred from one culture to another. Still, adjustments have to be made to avoid destroying a work's impact on foreign audiences. In recent years, *Macbeth* has been produced in a Japanese setting with Japanese actors. Macbeth becomes a feudal lord of twelfth-century Japan, deposing the supreme warlord MacDuff; the conspiring witches who entangle Macbeth in his ambitions become wood spirits. This transformation makes the play more palatable to oriental audiences.

As already discussed in Chapter 2, artistic creativity assumes social significance by transforming the personal and private needs of the artist into works that have significance to others. Great art subordinates the technical aspects of composition to this end. It maintains its aesthetic values beyond the immediate period for which it was created, yet it expresses the needs of its time. The great artist, involved in his own conflicts, can free himself from the immediacy of their personal significance and transform them into a format that evokes consonant feelings in the observer. Cohesive and meaningful, his work avoids being excessively personal or literal as it reaches corresponding conflicts in the observer that he may have repressed as unacceptable. By acting out solutions in front of the spectator, it permits him to identify with them without taking any action himself. The spectator attains satisfaction by reexperiencing the artist's creative act, by repeating the imaginative performance of the artist in his own thoughts, and thereby becoming creative himself (53). As there is less and less distance between creator and spectator, the observer becomes a participant in the art work.

During the creative process, the artist's personality functioning and his concepts of reality undergo significant changes. Reality has a multidimensional spatial structure which verbal language dismantles. Language takes the multidimensional and simultaneous spatial concepts and aligns them in linear, sequential order, forcing one throught to follow another. Concepts that exist side by side in space are arranged, through language, into sequence. Because language cannot deal with objects of equal significance simultaneously, it must force them into a hierarchic order, obscuring their original multidimensionality. Verbal language, in turn, stabilizes and preserves the intellectual entities necessary for logical deductive thinking (4b).

Creativity requires access to mental processes and fantasies which are ordinarily repressed by our linear way of thinking, and of which the individual is not consciously aware. As the artist contemplates the conflicts that motivate him to create, he shuts out environmental stimuli (103). Though he may appear withdrawn while contemplating, he always retains control of his functioning.[1] The boundaries between inner and outer reality are reduced, but not dissolved; control is loosened and made flexible to permit the realization of concepts beyond the immediate level of consciousness; habitual conceptual patterns and the linear sequence of thought processes are interrupted (4b). In this creative state, customary limits of concepts that exist in logical thinking become de-differentiated; images become fragmented and less articulated, opening the way to new, original rearrangements of concepts.

The state of artistic contemplation, with its fragmented concepts and changed levels of awareness, its reduced cognizance of surrounding events and heightened awareness of one's inner imagery, produces subjective discomfort and often *dysphoria*. This discomfort motivates the artist to reestablish his emotional equilibrium by linking his fragmented concepts, an important defensive reaction during the second phase of creation. A creative *ego rhythm* (35) scans the fragmented substructure, picking up multiple links and merging them into new cohesive entities. It alternates constantly between undifferentiated fragmented structures of the unconscious and cohesive concepts existing on a conscious level. In reaching the level of consciousness, concepts are reshaped and differentiated from one another. Some are repressed if they disrupt the integrated whole, or if they contradict prevalent ones; others may be elaborated to emphasize and dramatize essentials of the work. Continuous *reality testing* examines the newly linked conceptual images and tests them against previous experiences. The frag-

1. Visual stimulation seems to be far more under the scrutiny of our objective discrimination than auditory impressions, making it more difficult to identify fully with visual art forms. However, if visual and auditory impressions are combined, we are more easily persuaded to become involved in the action. *Son et Lumiere* (sound and light) performances are a popular instrument used in many historical places to recreate the sentiment of the location. Simultaneous visual and auditory stimulation helps to elicit the brilliance of the past when presented in the historic setting of the Forum Romanum, in front of the pyramids, or in the Old Fort of New Delhi.

3.3. *Vassals paying homage are organized on a base line. Persepolis.*

mented concepts have become connected according to common interests and concerns, being linked into the total goal-directed system, the artistic creation.

The artist creates an object capable of absorbing and reflecting emotions (103). The successful work of art both serves the needs and fulfills the expectations of the outside world. Gombrich (53) relates Picasso's childhood experiences in Barcelona to the painting of the *Demoiselles d'Avignon*, which is considered the fundamental work of cubism. Picasso's personal history and early life experiences may have been motivating factors in his conception of the painting, representing the first phase of creativity. As the artist contemplates the way to proceed in his work, he fragments and de-differentiates his personal experience. However, without the creative ego rhythm, the essence of creative activity, these personal experiences would remain without social significance, not different from the meditations of the nonartist. It was the second phase of creativity, during which Picasso linked fragmented, isolated factors into new entities and transformed them according to his own concepts, that became an artistic landmark of cubism. The cohesive organization facilitated the acceptance of his creative imagery and integrated the highly personal content into a controlled structure. If Picasso had not exercised such great control, the painting would not have achieved any significant impact (103).

Obviously, personal experiences, no matter how vivid or strange, are not sufficient to produce a work of art. Even forceful and dramatic occurrences remain only personally significant without the artistic transformation of the second phase of creativity. The case of a twenty-year-old woman, an Australian aborigine from the bush country of the Northern Territory, seems to confirm this point. We visited the patient with the "Doctor's Flying Service," the nickname given to the medical services that are provided by the Australian government for aborigines living in isolated areas of the territory. The bush country's lack of roads and its vastness make the area inaccessible except by plane. As the government, respecting the rights of the population, wants to protect them from intruders, it forbids outsiders to enter the settlements. Anyone entering the area must be connected with governmental services or able to prove a legitimate research interest that may be of eventual value to the aborigine.

We joined the local psychiatrist on his regular flight to one of the mission hospitals. Our small plane took off in the dark of early morning; it was a five-seater, equipped with a stretcher to transport bedridden patients. After flying over predominantly uninhabited territory, we landed on a gravel airstrip built by the Royal Australian Air Force during World War II. We disembarked; after the plane had departed, a feeling of isolation crept over us, even though we knew that the plane would come back for us in seven or eight hours. A jeep drove us from the airstrip to the mission settlement. During the day, we interviewed several patients; one young married woman seemed to be of particular sociocultural interest. At the age of two, she had been promised by her family to a husband more than twenty years her senior, a common practice in this culture. (Some girls are even spoken for before they are born.) The age difference and lack of personal choice often leaves the marital partners feeling indifferent and personally uninvolved in their marriage. Frequently the marriage ends in open conflict and infidelity.

This young woman was brought to our attention because she had developed convulsive seizures several months prior to our visit. She suffered attacks of loss of consciousness due to *hysterical convulsions*. We were told that she seemed excited and overstimulated when the attacks occurred, and at other times she appeared moody and uncommunicative. As her history unfolded, we discovered that the attacks had started soon after a friend of the family, a sixty-year-old man, had suddenly died. She had been very attached to him, though apparently without sexual involvement. He had been attentive to the young woman; he teased her in a pleasant way and gave her small presents. His sudden death had stunned her; she became withdrawn and depressed, and her behavior pattern seemed to fluctuate with the phases of the moon. As the moon waxed, she would become more and more animated and increasingly talkative, but also emotionally detached and inattentive to those around her. When the moon was at its brightest, she would go into a trance; at that time, she had repeated convulsions. Between convulsions, she appeared ecstatic, unaware of people around her, and preoccupied with her fantasies. As the moon waned, her seizures decreased, and her excitement subsided, until, with the new moon, her mood reached its deepest depression. This behavior pattern repeated itself with·each lunar cycle.

During the interview, we learned that she fantasized that the dead man rose with the moon, as its "companion." According to local Melanesian folklore, women have intercourse with the moon at the time of their menstruation, and men stay away from them at such times (122a). Convulsions, often considered symbolic of orgasm, occurred in the patient with the waxing moon, when her illusory lover reached the height of his travel through the sky. The convulsions—and her exaltation—subsided with the waning moon; she became more depressed as her lover's image receded.

The patient's conflicts and her symptoms seem far more dramatic than Picasso's memories of his childhood in the Calle d'Avignon in Barcelona. Yet, while Picasso was capable of creating a significant masterwork, our aborigine patient expressed conflicts that had only personal significance and were not shared by her own social group. Her conflicts reached almost conscious levels, but they were poorly defined, and she was unable to integrate them into cohesive behavior patterns or into other forms of expression. Her unresolved conflicts found expression in the psychologically primitive mechanism of convulsions, while those of the well-integrated artist are transformed into cohesive works of art.

Ego psychology assumes that the personality sets up boundaries that separate the individual from his environment and delineate well-defined, clear-cut entities within the environment (38). These boundaries also isolate the individual's psychological substructures, differentiate those of which he is consciously aware from those less conscious structures that deal with conscience-controlled attitudes and standards that constitute the more aggressive and drive-dominated aspects of his personality.

During a psychotic process, the boundaries disintegrate, and reality concepts become threatening while emotional energy is withdrawn. Simultaneously, the personality disintegration of the psychotic leads to profound changes within himself. Established sequences of thought and conceptual links become interrupted and fragmented, resembling the first phase of creativity. In the psychotic, however, the poorly differentiated conceptual fragments remain vague and inarticulate (35). Because the psychotic is unable to repress the ideational segments which are contradictory to the overall goal-directed system, conflicting and opposing ideation persists, contributing to a lack of cohesiveness. The defective personality lacks the ability to shape the fragments into cohesive structures as they surface into consciousness. Effective scanning, as described in the case of the artist, is not possible; concepts are inadequately tested against past experiences, and they are

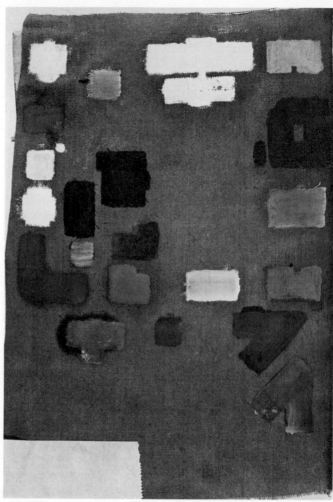

3.4. *"This much is left": the graphic expression of a schizophrenic young woman who is awakening from her disease.*

3.5. *Geometric designs were drawn by an American schizophrenic whose personality disintegration was highly advanced.*

linked only according to superficial similarities. A psychotic's distorted concepts, though often highly charged with emotion when formulated, may have no meaning at a later date. A young schizophrenic woman recognized the fleeting significance of her graphic expressions. She had produced several graphics at the height of her illness. A week later, when she had improved, she was asked about the meaning of her work (illustration 3.4). She appeared perplexed, stating that she could remember drawing them but that they had no further meaning for her—like a bad dream that had passed.

The psychotic's withdrawal of emotional energy from his surroundings changes his total outlook: his concepts of objects in the environment become less meaningful; his formerly clear-cut and decisive feelings become indecisive and ambivalent; unable to make choices he becomes helplessly perplexed: thoughts of equal significance intrude upon and compete with one another until he becomes unable to establish an adequate sequence for them. His structural space is also filled with competing simultaneous concepts. Thus, the hierarchic order of thought is disrupted; significant concepts become insignificant. The fear of empty space, or "horror vacui," may cause the patient to compensate by filling space with a clutter of insignificant details. In other attempts at restitution, patients may fill the space of their graphics with impersonal geometric figures (illustration 3.5) or ornamental designs (illustration 3.6), avoiding objects that might have personal, emotional significance. As the illness advances and more emotional energy is withdrawn, the patient's environmental space becomes empty and lifeless; at times it is perceived as dead, and the patient feels he does not exist. By such a reduction in affect, the patient's graphics are rendered flat, empty, and lifeless; images with poorly delineated designs appear. As his mental concepts become insignificant, the patient's drawings become shallow, shadowlike (illustration 7.1). He feels surrounded by emptiness and is disturbed by the ghostly appearance of figures (illustration 7.6). One of our patients felt overwhelmed by a multitude of fragmented thoughts that she could not put into sequence. She complained, "I can't say what I want to say . . . there is too much." But although verbal language was inadequate to the task of expressing the multiplicity of thoughts that forced themselves upon her, she was able to express them in her paintings. This multiplicity is seen in one of her landscapes, in which she painted three suns. Another patient was disturbed over "too many images pouring into my mind . . . I can't put it in words . . . they are not connected . . . fragmented . . . too many . . . it is as if somebody sat behind me on a wall and watched me . . . as if somebody else does my thinking and speaks instead of me. . . ."

Many psychotic patients find graphic expression a medium through which they can communicate their inner needs. One highly regressed patient who was hardly able to talk produced stereotyped drawings every day, accompanied by an empty smile (illustration 3.7). His drawings were an attempt to establish a meaningful relationship with others, as were the drawings of the dancer Nijinsky. Nijinsky, who had become schizophrenic, wrote in his diary about feelings of emotional isolation and made hundreds of geometrical pencil drawings in an attempt to make himself understood (illustration 3.8 [111]). He showed the drawings to his friends to impress his feelings upon them, but they failed to realize his distress. Since he thought of others as "only capable of thinking" and not of feeling, he felt utterly rejected. He had come to realize that his disintegrated thought processes had set him apart from the integrated individuals around him.

As pointed out earlier in this chapter, artistic creativity, in contrast to the graphics created by the disintegrated personality, has societal significance, and attempts to fulfill needs that may not be met otherwise. Art may be performed as part of a magic ritual in dark caves by an unknown prehistoric painter, it may be the expression of social protest by a contemporary writer, or it may offer solutions to the underlying conflicts and needs of the individual. The creative artist shares with the schizophrenic only the initial phase of fragmentation and de-differentiation of concepts. Only an integrated personality can successfully reintegrate the fragmented concepts. In order for the creative ego rhythm to mold the de-differentiated, inarticulate and fragmented structures into cohesive concepts, the ego must be flexible and capable of forming new imaginative links (35). As these links connect, they shape cohesive images that are satisfying and meaningful to the artist and his audience.

In creative art—as opposed to most popular art—the links of the artistic presentation are not always fully connected. They are sufficient to suggest solutions, but their partial omission gives the observer opportunities to complete the concept and create his own closed structure. He feels satisfied and his anxiety is relieved by being allowed to play an active part in solving the conflicts proposed by the artist.

Creativity, both artistic and nonartistic, can overcome the traditional limitations of reality and formulate imaginative and original ideas. In science, a creative

3.7. *These rigid figures, isolated in space, were drawn by an American schizophrenic who was hardly able to talk.*

leap may uncover revolutionary concepts which are later woven into a complete system by detailed experiment and observation that fills in the links that the original insight skipped. Magic, on the other hand, never supplies the omitted links; its pseudosolutions must be accepted on blind faith by the believers, who are supported in their belief by group support and slogans. But the psychotic, regardless of cultural background, stands *alone*.

Having lost the capacity for adequate verbal communication, the psychotic begins to paint. Superficially, his graphics may resemble primitive art, children's drawings, and even some contemporary art. But these comparisons are deceptive, as the psychotic's defective forces of restitution prevent him from including the cohesive imagery found in other types of art. The psychotic lacks the flexi-bility to scan de-differentiated fragments and shape them into cohesive concepts; inarticulated structures (35) reach conscious levels and often reflect the rigid primitive personality of the patient; isolated, unconnected, and distorted figures remain in the drawings (illustration 3.7).

In patients whose personalities are only moderately disintegrated, however, creativity may not be very much affected. It is often difficult to distinguish the productions of such artists from those of the Mannerists (109), who oppose traditional forms with elongated figures and distorted elaborations and condensations. It may be no more difficult to make a clear distinction between psychotic and nonpsychotic art than to make a definitive clinical diagnosis of schizophrenia (see Chapter 4). The personal histories of mentally ill artists indicate that their anguish and suffering were intense; some even took their own lives. But from a psychiatric viewpoint their personality disintegration was comparatively mild. The most celebrated case is that of Vincent van Gogh. The exact nature of his illness has not been established (diagnoses range from schizophrenia to confusional states due to epilepsy). He suffered greatly and was painfully aware of his aberrant mental state. When one compares his early art works with the paintings which follow his psychotic episodes, a definite change can be observed. The brush strokes change from relatively fine to bold, coarse strokes in his later paintings. Where his early paintings adhere strictly to classical three-dimensional perspective, the later work shows a vertical projection—objects in space are no longer seen in true perspective, but instead seem elevated (illustration 7.17). The paintings of Norwegian expressionist Edvard Munch, who was hospitalized for an undefined psychotic state, show masklike faces, often devoid of facial features. In his painting *Despair* (illustration 7.25), one side of the street is crowded with people, leaving the other side deserted. It underlines the painter's emotional isolation from those around him. Many of his other paintings depict the lonely figure and the people with blank faces. *The Shriek* (illustration 7.26) shows a lonely "sexless creature" lost in the vastness of space (70). Similar themes—empty space, isolated figures, masklike or blank faces—appear in the productions of psychotic patients (color plate 2), but these works lack the appeal and cohesiveness that the artist who is only mildly psychotic is able to preserve. We must assume that the severely regressed artist is incapable of retaining his capacity to produce works of art. His personality disintegration prevents him from shaping fragmented, inarticulate structures into integrated, cohesive entities that have artistic appeal. Creativity and psychotic expression retain their distinct and separate characters.

4.5. (left). *A New Guinean mask.*

4.6. (right). The Virgin of the Annunciation, *Simone Martini, around 1340. Musée Royal des Beaux-Arts, Antwerp.*

4

Crosscultural Diagnosis in Psychiatry

We had turned off the highway[1] onto a dirt road, slippery from the morning rain that falls daily in the New Guinea Highlands. Our medium-sized black car looked like an imposing limousine to the local population as we drove through their villages. Passenger vehicles, still an unusual sight in this region, attracted considerable attention. Our driver was not especially pleased to be driving on an isolated, narrow road through an area that had been rife with cannibalism within the past fifteen years. In his black suit and white shirt and tie he seemed stiff and aloof. His concern was not totally unfounded, though, for even today a driver who unwittingly hits a pedestrian is repaid with tribal vengeance (see Chapter 5).

We had left the hospital at Goroka that morning to bring a patient to his home village. The patient, a man of twenty-one (Case A567), had been away from the village for a year while hospitalized in the psychiatric section of the Goroka Hospital. He seemed pleased at the prospect of visiting his home, and expected a warm welcome from his family and the villagers. At the same time, he wanted to share in the prestige of the strangers who accompanied him. He insisted on carrying our camera bag around his shoulders, which was not an unwelcome relief. Two indigenous male nurses speaking the local dialect accom-

1. The road connects the northern coast of New Guinea with the Western Highlands. It is the only extended highway in the country, partly paved and partly dirt road (illustration 4.1). As it winds over a few hundred miles, it connects villages and towns, making them accessible to the outside world. The trucks travelling on the road bring trade to areas formerly unknown and inaccessible. The trade is important to the growth of the area. With their loose money, which appears as a small fortune to the mountain people, the truck drivers are able to buy the attentions and favors of some of the Highland women. The opening of this road improved economic conditions, but it brought with it an increase in the venereal disease rate.

4.1. *New Guinea's only extended highway can hardly be seen amid the jagged mountains of the highlands.*

panied us, not only as translators, but as mediators in case of possible misunderstandings in an area where *payback* was still practiced. The nurses were helpful as interpreters, but the villagers' open friendliness in receiving us made any protection superfluous. The only dangers we encountered were in driving on the slippery, winding mud road—more like a footpath—that led to the village. It took considerable skill to maneuver the car so that it would not slide off the embankments. These difficulties were somewhat mitigated by the lack of traffic: we did not meet another vehicle between the highway and the village, only an occasional villager who gaped at us in surprise.

We reached the patient's village, which was located ten miles off the highway, without difficulty. It is part of a cluster of huts built on a mountain ridge (illustration 4.2). Ten to twenty huts surround a small center square that has a single access path, making it easier to defend the village against attackers. As soon as we entered the village, we were surrounded by curious villagers who had come out of their huts; these were soon joined by others from the surrounding fields. The lack of any form of communication with the outside world had kept us from notifying them about our intended visit. Telephones and wireless do not exist in small New Guinea villages, and there is no postal service.

The men of the village all wore shorts. Some went bare chested, while others wore Western shirts. Only the head man wore a hat, a headcovering being a sign of distinction (illustration 4.3). One of the women leaned proudly on a shovel whose scoop was made of shiny steel (illustration 5.7).[2]

As we wandered around, we noticed that none of the huts bore decorations except one that had the impression of a hand on its walls (illustration 8.11). The design had impressed me before (illustrations 8.9, 8.10). The owner of the hut was unable to tell us when the hand had been painted. He gave an embarrassed smile when asked about its origin and meaning; it was not reluctance on his part, but honest ignorance—the meaning of such symbols frequently becomes lost and forgotten.

Before long the head man of the village appeared. He seemed quite nonchalant, as if receiving visitors from the outside world were an everyday affair (illustration 4.3). When we explained our intention to interview the patient's family,

2. The introduction of steel tools in place of stone implements, lead to significant societal changes. The efficiency of the steel tools enabled the farmer to work faster and gave him the opportunity to tackle new tasks that were not possible with the stone tools.

he sent for the patient's two brothers. Without hesitation they told us about the circumstances leading to the patient's hospitalization. They treated us with the utmost courtesy in an attempt to convince us of the validity of their arguments, making it obvious that they did not want their brother to return, as they considered him troublesome—a cause of embarrassment to the family and a danger to the entire village. The patient had been hospitalized after causing considerable dissension between the people of his village and their neighbors. "Voices" had told him that his village planned an attack on the neighboring village, and he considered it his mission to maintain peace. He saw himself as a "big man,"[3] capable of negotiating peace between the villages. He went to the neighboring village, warned them of the attack, and offered his assistance. Instead of attempting to negotiate, however, they attacked the patient's village that same night in a pre-emptive raid. Only after a few villagers on both sides were injured by arrows and spears did they realize that the bloodshed had been unnecessary. Both sides then turned against the culprit. In the past, the villagers would have taken vengeance on the patient, but here they recognized that he must have been "long long" (mentally sick) to have taken such action, and that he was a victim of his own delusions. It was considered senseless and completely foreign to local custom to forewarn a potential enemy of an intended raid.

To stress the peculiar character of the patient's behavior, his brothers reassured us that a raid had never been planned, that they had had the patient hospitalized to protect themselves from a recurrence of this disaster, and that they did not want him to return. The patient, who had been full of hope before his visit, now appeared visibly dejected. In the car returning to the hospital he was preoccupied. After returning to the hospital, he became disturbed and excited, talking rapidly and incoherently in his local dialect. He demanded in a loud voice to talk to the head nurse, seeming to need personal care after having been disappointed in his expectations.

When we later interviewed the patient, we were assisted by a young European nurse in charge of the psychiatric service. She had considerable compassion for her patients, and spoke their language, Nuiginin, rather well. The patient still

4.2. *The patient's village in the Eastern Highlands.*

3. As will be discussed in Chapter 5, "big men" are the successful community leaders, persuasive in their oratory. The village council may appoint them to negotiate differences with neighboring villages; however, negotiating on their own initiative is outside the cultural norm.

appeared considerably disturbed by the experiences of the day. He rationalized the rejection by his family and fellow villagers, stating that he had actually not wanted to return to his home village since the food in the hospital was much better. So excited was he that his speech became very rapid, preventing the nurse from translating all but a few short sentences. He had become extremely tense as the day's experiences developed. Utterly rejected, he had defended himself in the village with his family by withdrawing from an unacceptable, painful reality. The subsequent regression resulted in a marked increase of his personality disintegration and in increased difficulty in expressing himself verbally. Like disintegrated patients of any culture, he formed neologisms, often combining several disparate syllables, with the result that his sentences could hardly be understood. The nurse attempted to translate his statements literally, but as his

4.3. *The head man greets visitors.*

4.4. *Marie Antoinette built an artificial farmhouse in a symbolic return to nature.*

verbalizations became untranslatable, she felt increasingly helpless and became visibly tired. To translate the schizophrenic's language literally was beyond her capacity—it would have been beyond almost anyone's. Neologisms, newly formed sentence structures, and the vague and overlapping concepts of the schizophrenic (18, 72) render a patient's speech difficult to understand in his own language, and far more so when his speech must be translated from Nuiginin pidgin into English. At best, the interpreter can only summarize the patient's statements, only occasionally being able to translate an entire sentence. Whereas the complaints and disturbances of the neurotic, the moderately disintegrated psychotic, and the physically ill patient can be translated by a competent interpreter, the difficulties of translating the statements of the schizophrenic or disintegrated personality are almost *pathognomonic* and can be considered a diagnostic aid in recognizing personality disintegration.

In all but the most sophisticated societies, the initial detection of mental illness is made not by the patient (in contrast with physical illness) but by his societal group (153). His strange behavior, differing from his own past actions and from the established social and cultural norms of his own group, becomes disturbing and unacceptable. Disapproval and non-acceptance separates his conduct from "normal" behavior as being pathological within his own culture (2).

Attitudes prevalent in the patient's cultural group influence his conduct only if he is capable of making a fairly adequate social adjustment. The type and content of the symptoms of the same mental illness vary in different cultures and are subject to local systems. Visual hallucinations, a common symptom of schizophrenia in the West forty to fifty years ago, hardly ever to occur any longer in that group; auditory hallucinations and *catatonic stupor* have also decreased among today's Western patients. Delusions of being of royal blood—the illegitimate son of the King of England, for instance—were common only so long as royalty was held in high esteem. When Western man became fascinated with the power of machines during the industrial age of the late nineteenth and early twentieth centuries, delusions related to "influencing machines" were frequent. Today's concern with international superpowers, or the fear of being programmed by computers, may be reflected in a psychotic's delusional system. In the societies of Africa or New Guinea, beliefs in sorcery or possession by spirit beings may be interwoven with psychotic delusions, causing cultural variants in behavior between Western and non-Western patients (76, 85, 149 b). One must be able to distinguish pathological thought from traditional beliefs, necessitating thorough familiarity with the sociocultural patterns of the local societal group. The old belief that all savages are content (97) and that consequently, insanity among primitive people must be rare has long been disproven. Yet the romantic image of primitive village life as healthier, nomadic life as freer than life in Western cultures, still makes itself felt, even in scientific reports. The return to nature was a flight from Rousseau's urbanized France of the eighteenth century and an outgrowth of the dissatisfaction of the prerevolutionary aristocrat who sought peace and tranquility in the artificial farmhouses of Trianon (illustration 4.4) which had nothing to do with the hard daily life in the villages. The tribal economy, supposedly supplying a stable subsistence to the people of the tribe, actually supplies them with poverty. In crisis situations, strong kinship relations often fail to render the needed mutual support. An individual's anxieties are frequently exacerbated by inflexible taboos and the belief in fearful spirits that are capable of causing physical and mental disease (68). Societal pressures may actually play a significant part in leading to the stresses that contribute to mental illness (32b). Traditional village life is no protection against mental illness. It may, however, alter the symptomatology associated with Western illness, and may induce specific culture-bound illnesses—the Eskimo suffering from arctic hysteria, the Japanese farmer developing *fox possession,* and the Malaysian running amok.

Stresses of many kinds—distrust, cruelty, biological and genetic deviations—exist in the inner cities and suburbs of the West, just as they exist in the jungles of Africa and the highlands of New Guinea. The threat of being victimized by sorcery (Case 506) or the possible feeling of shame after killing one's wife (Case 511) may trigger psychotic reactions in susceptible personalities in New Guinea. In Western societies, financial reverses or severe feelings of rejection may precipitate equivalent reactions. The nature of the threats to one's existence and one's basic value system may be different in various cultures, but they are equally disturbing to the functions of the individual.

New Guineans' increasing contact with and admiration of the West is beginning to narrow the distinctions between the two societies. As customs change, the traditional patterns which remain are affected by these contacts with the West. In New Guinea, the bridal price customarily paid by the groom and his family has been affected by Western inflation. When one of the patients from the Gulf area married some forty years ago, he paid a bridal price of fifty Australian dollars, a tribal mask (illustration 4.5)[4], and two pigs. When his son married a few years ago, the cost of a wife had increased substantially. The patient's share alone was two hundred Australian dollars, which is only part of the total amount since other family members must contribute. Recently, the price has skyrocketed to several thousands of dollars. Shells, formerly of significant exchange value, are seldom used. The traditional matchmakers, the fathers of the bride and groom, may no longer select the couple to be married; a young man often chooses his wife according to his own inclination. But as in the past, the groom will live in his wife's village until the bride price is paid in full, at which time he is allowed to return to his home village. While the newly married couple live in the wife's village, they are under the control of her family.

Cultural change in recent years threatens existing institutions and beliefs. The impact of Western standards on the New Guinea Stone Age culture forces limits on many traditions. Cannibalism, tribal wars, and payback are outlawed.

4. An Italian Madonna (illustration 4.6) painted around 1340 shows a remarkably similar structure; the face of both art products lean in the same direction; the raffia ornaments surrounding the New Guinean mask resembles the halo of the Madonna.

The ritual killing of pigs replaces the sacrifice of human captives. The new ceremonials, however, do not sufficiently support the established societal structure (95), and are held partly responsible for the social disorganization which has developed. In more elastic cultures (149 a), such as the Bantu tribes of East Africa, a greater degree of adaptation to foreign concepts results in reduced fears and anxieties. While sociocultural changes may not bring about major conflicts in an accepting and tolerant environment, they can precipitate pathological reactions in predisposed individuals and can contribute to psychiatric disturbances (Case 510). If a patient becomes unable to relate to the society in which he functions, he becomes socially and culturally isolated; he withdraws from reality, becoming increasingly susceptible to a disintegration of his personality. Traditional beliefs in magic and related concepts may be absorbed by the regressing personality and incorporated into his delusional system. If the patient's beliefs lie outside those accepted traditionally, the psychotic disintegration is accelerated (Case 506).

Life in an isolated village is often filled with apprehension and fear of the unknown; new experiences, and even daily routine, may become highly charged with emotion, arousing insecurities and self-doubt. The strain becomes greater during societal and personal crises, and the individual seeks comfort in simple and quick explanations and solutions. Unable or unwilling to tolerate delays, he feels indebted to anyone who promises to provide quick and easy answers, even if these are only pseudosolutions. In the absence of customary means of dealing with stress, such ready answers take on the appearance of miracles, and the persons who provide them become miracle makers. Although they do have answers and conviction, the miracle makers often exhibit moderate personality disintegration. They appeal to their followers to abandon the concepts that have failed. Just as the parents of a critically sick child may turn to a healer as a last resort, so groups of people, sometimes entire nations, disillusioned and distraught over economic and political failures, may become ready to abandon their established methods and follow a pied piper into a world of magic. The determined leader's magic force entrances the community. Promising to surmount unconquerable barriers, he captures the fantasies of his entire social group. The disorganized personalities of the cult leader, the healer, and the sorcerer[5] omit deductive links in their concept formation and develop distorted views of reality. These men stress and enlarge certain points while de-emphasizing others in order to soothe the distressed and disenchanted, who desire to regain their dignity.[6] The followers are willing to sacrifice part of objective reality and accept substitutes, although their personalities are not sufficiently disintegrated to depart entirely from established customs. Thus, a people who are overcome with frustration and unfulfilled needs will turn to demagogic leaders who can offer them comfort through witchcraft, astrology, and other cults.

The way an individual with marginal adaptability interacts with his social structure determines whether he will hold a place of respect or be rejected. If the spiritual needs of the group are able to accommodate the pathological magic of one the members, stress may be avoided and the group may react with a mixture of qualified respect, possibly blended with apprehension and fear. In his own village the sorcerer is treated as an outcast; he is a strange man with bloodshot eyes who separates himself from others (78, 147 a). But although he is feared, he must be endured because of his unusual powers. Inevitably, though, his inability to adapt to reality leads to failure; unfulfilled, indefensible promises

5. Compare with Case A510 in Chapter 8.

6. Similar mechanisms are discussed in other chapters; but in order not to interrupt the continuity of the argument, some aspects are elaborated in several places.

become exposed; the system of magic, based on pathological fantasies, inevitably collapses. In New Guinea, many cargo cult leaders who played upon the people's desire for riches, have proven to be psychotic (24b, 89). When such a leader's system of salvation failed, when people realized that the millennium had not arrived and that the leader's reasoning was pathological, they quickly ousted him (see Case 510).

Mental illness undoubtedly existed among nonliterate societies long before the arrival of the white man, but it is difficult to know the extent of it. Today, it is almost equally difficult to determine with what frequency such illnesses occur in isolated cultures. The number of hospital admissions is not a good indicator, since so many variables control the admissions of patients to hospitals: distance from the hospital, fear of hospitals (particular those operated by culturally alien personnel), and negative attitudes toward mental illness. A community is often reluctant to send one of its members to a distant place about which they have little knowledge. As long as a patient's behavior does not disrupt or threaten life in the village, the family and the community will tolerate it. But when the behavior drastically disrupts village life, the people change their attitude (Case A546). It is not rare for a village to employ its own peculiar methods for dealing with a disturbed patient who has become a threat. Commonly, villagers organize special hunting trips from which the psychotic is intended never to return (24c). Only recently have villages begun to send their disturbed and violent male patients to a hospital (as women are easier to control, most remain in their villages).[7] Language difficulties, the reluctance to discuss mental illness when it involves spirit possession, feelings of inferiority in relating to the doctor, or simply a concern that mental illness will reflect on the prestige of a family make the collection of data a difficult matter. But for our purpose, knowing the exact frequency with which mental illness occurs may be less important than knowing that it affects a comparatively large number of people.

Considerable difficulties may be involved in the diagnosis of mental illness—schizophrenia, in particular—among indigenous people. Schizophrenia has never been considered a single disease entity. In coining the term, Eugen Bleuler (18) spoke of a group of diseases which he called schizophrenias. The divergency in making this diagnosis is shown by the difference in the number of cases diagnosed in two related cultures such as Great Britain and the United States. The diagnosis of schizophrenia is made ten times as frequently in this country as in Great Britain, while manic-depressive psychosis is diagnosed ten times as often in Great Britain as here (153).

It is not only the patient's behavior, but also the personality and sociocultural bias of the examiner that contributes to making the diagnosis. If a culture has prevalent tendencies toward mysticism, magical thinking will not seem unusual, while cultures predisposed toward changes of mood may tolerate affective disorders more easily than magical thinking. Another factor to consider is the dependency of pathological behavior on the environment in which it develops; different sociocultural attitudes may precipitate illness in some individuals while giving sufficient support to others to neutralize their pathological tendencies and prevent the manifestation of illness (153, 16). Sociocultural standards vary most significantly between Western and non-Western countries, but considerable variation exists even within areas of the same country, increasing the difficulty of making a uniform diagnosis.

7. The considerably higher male population in the hospital, most of them admitted for violent acts, may distort greatly the demography of mental illness.

Finally, the application of different diagnostic methods by different examiners to the same patient has led some schools of psychiatry to abandon labelling any specific mental disorders. .These schools are concerned primarily with the patient's success or failure to adapt and adjust to his environment (99, 153). Although we do not entirely share that extreme point of view, we realize how difficult it is to apply diagnostic standards to nonwestern cultures. The inability to function due to mental conditions is nonspecific and may be caused by a variety of psychiatric conditions: a patient may suffer from *organic brain syndrome,* from affective disorders, from severe neuroses, or a host of other problems. Abnormal behavior is not polar; it lies along a continuum between health and illness, on which it is difficult to mark off the various degrees of illness. Culture-bound magical concepts, sorcery, or the fear of being poisoned may be pathological in one culture and nonpathological in another. Even more complex conditions develop when culture-bound symptoms are interwoven with a delusional system. Members of the same community may be of assistance in classifying a patient's behavior as acceptable (autonormal) or as illness (auto-pathologic) in that specific society (2). While some behavior patterns would be considered highly pathological in any society, others have to be evaluated for their meaning. A belief in sorcery and ghosts may not be unusual unless it develops in an individual who had never placed any trust in apparitions and if the beliefs are accompanied by a personality change, in which case they may be of pathological significance. Thus, an intimate knowledge of the beliefs and institutions of a specific society is necessary to evaluate the behavior of a patient. An intuitive diagnosis may be of value, but it must be accepted with reservation.

As discussed previously, mental illness among nonurbanized groups arouses attention by the patient's "peculiar" behavior rather than by any treatment needs. His unusual conduct may alert others, but the symptoms are far from diagnostic, often being influenced by local cultural attitudes. Catatonic stupor, which resembles a state of trance, is less common in the West than in Asian countries, where Hinduism and Buddhism encourage social and emotional withdrawal; paranoid symptoms are less organized and systematized in African, Indian, and South Pacific areas than in Western countries. In previous years, when travel was limited for most people, and before the mass media brought the outside world into the home, the people of any given country were less experienced outside their own sociocultural setting; they had little opportunity or necessity to test their established ideas against new experiences. They were less critical, and their concept formation was less discriminative. This tendency spilled over into the pathological behavior of psychiatric patients. As long as the patients were capable of maintaining any reality contacts, they could test their symptoms against prevailing societal attitudes and values. This allowed their fantasies and delusional ideas to be more florid than those of today. Schizophrenics had visual hallucinations of an order that has rarely been observed among such patients for many years. Even the nonpsychotic hysterical patient's symptoms have shown profound changes; convulsions, once considered a classical manifestation of the illness, are hardly ever observed any more.

In New Guinea patients are hospitalized when their behavior becomes so disturbing that it interferes with the customary life of the village. Aggressive behavior resulting in attacks upon the village, erratic spirit possession, and unacceptable reactions to sorcery (Case 506) are among the aberrations which disturb the indigenous population. Such culture-bound symptoms, interwoven with traditional beliefs, form a continuum that may be difficult to distinguish from nonpathological states (149 b). Most of these symptoms relate to the content of mental disease, not to the structure of the disease itself. A diagnosis based on content alone—delusions, hallucinations, or pathological excitement—may indicate that a mental illness exists, but it does not identify a specific illness. It is important, therefore, to base the diagnosis not on symptoms, which are likely to vary with culture, but on the structure of the illness itself. What is characteristic of mental illness in all cultures is the disintegration of the personality. It is not necessarily pathological when a patient from the Gulf District thinks that a sorcerer was responsible for his wife being killed by a crocodile (see Case 506); such opinions are culturally acceptable. It is his disorganized thoughts, reflected in his speech, his *affect,* and the inappropriateness of his behavior, that reveal the pathology of his personality functioning.

Lambo (76) draws distinct lines between the symptoms of schizophrenia among rural (nonliterates) Nigerians and Westernized, urban patients. In rural patients, the disease appears as an amorphous reaction in which few symptoms are clearly developed. Hallucinations and bizarre magicomystical delusions are ill defined; vague feelings of unreality are combined with marked mood disturbances. Poorly described fears and apprehensions and, at times, a frenzied fury, result from beliefs of "bewitchment." Apparently, symptoms of personality disintegration are more pronounced in this nonliterate group than among their urbanized countrymen, even in the beginning of the psychosis. Patients of the nonliterate group seem to show less personality strength and fewer inhibitions, leading to more intense and obvious confusion of their thought processes. Among urbanized, educated, and Westernized Nigerians, on the other hand, schizophrenic psychosis shows manifestations similar to those found in European and American patients. The culturally influenced contrast in symptoms between rural and urban Nigerians is paralleled by the changes observed in the symptoms of Western psychiatric patients during the past fifty to one hundred years. Yet, as previously discussed, cultural influences play a significant role in the symptom formation of a psychosis only so long as the patient remains fairly well integrated. As the Westernized Nigerian schizophrenic regresses and his personality disintegrates, his delusions increasingly resemble those of the nonliterate patient. The culturally determined symptoms that separated the rural, nonliterate patient from the literate, urban Nigerian are replaced by culture-free symptoms, which can be observed in both the bush people and the severely regressed Westernized patient. Hallucinations and delusions become less prominent; thoughts become vaguer, more highly disorganized, and fragmented; severe incoherence makes verbal communication almost impossible; and pronounced emotional detachment prevents nearly all relationships.

Diagnosing mental disorders on the basis of their content has resulted in confusion over diagnostic labels (140, 25). The value of these labels is reduced even more by periodic changes in the way they are used, and by the utilization of subtyping of mental illness (101). As the content of a psychosis is a result of the interplay between the inner structure of a patient's personality and the impact of his environment, a diagnosis based on content alone is almost meaningless in crosscultural psychiatry. The case of a Guatemalan witch doctor (see Chapter 9) shows how the existing cultural climate may enable it to integrate pathological thought processes and magical thinking into the prevailing local attitudes.

Content analysis appears insufficient in distinguishing between nonpathological and pathological magical thinking. Transcultural psychiatry needs controlled comparative studies to define pathological behavior within a specific

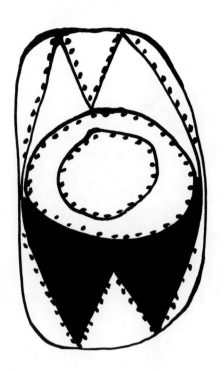

cultural group. Many techniques that are usually considered objective cannot be applied in diverse cultural settings (32a). Questionnaires do not easily lend themselves to crosscultural application; not only must they be translated into another language, but many concepts are culture specific and have no meaning in the value system of a different culture. If cultures react differently to the use of clothing, the taking of food, and other aspects of daily life, they are even more at odds over questions of abstract morality: loyalty, ethics, and guilt. Many concepts that have significance for a New Guinea Highlander are meaningless to a Westerner, and it is unlikely that many Western concepts have significance to a New Guinean. Simple words such as checkbook, bookcase and electricity have no meaning in the more primitive culture, even when the terms are translatable. Similar problems develop when we attempt to translate terms indigenous to another society into our own language. Faced with this problem, researchers have found benefit in unstructured procedures such as the Rorschach technique for personality evaluation; their comparatively unspecific designs do not force a foreign value system on the individual (16).

Art plays a far more intimate role in the lives of many primitive people than in the West. Sculptures and bark paintings are abundant in New Guinea (illustration 4.7), conveying an ever present spiritual power that protects the possessor. The presence of such works has long been a source of support and security to early man and his descendants. The psychotic patient whose personality disintegration results in a loss of linear thinking returns to graphic forms of communication and revives traditional styles, however distorted. Pictorial imagery conveys the relatively inarticulated intrapsychic structure of the disintegrated personality more adequately than words. It assumes an even greater importance in crosscultural studies, with their profound linguistic limitations. Graphics overcome both the difficulties of translating schizophrenic language and the difficulties faced by the disintegrated personality when he tries to formulate his thoughts. Experience has shown that schizophrenic imagery is not arbitrary; it includes concepts which, though disintegrated, are nonetheless understandable to others who are receptive to the patient's thought disturbances (illustration 4.8).

4.7. *Kokave mask, Papuan Gulf, New Guinea. Used by permission of the Papua New Guinea Public Museum and Art Gallery.*

4.8. *Bark paintings of the Hewa people, Western Highlands, New Guinea. Courtesy of J. A. Abramson, York University, Toronto, Canada.*

51

52

5

New Guinea
and Its People

Portuguese sailors were the first Europeans to land on the shores of New
Guinea, in 1511 (84); others followed, but the contacts were of short duration.
These landings must have aroused curiosity, but they could have had only superficial significance to the natives. Their cultural level had not changed when various
European nations explored the islands three hundred years later. It was only after
1874 that Europeans: Portuguese, Spanish, Dutch, French, and English, settled on
the offshore islands of eastern New Guinea. They found a Stone Age civilization
whose only inhabitants seemed to be "blacks with frizzled hair." The new settlers
gave these people the name Papuans, from *papuwah,* a Malayan word for frizzle-
haired (127). The Dutch, who landed in 1822, found that New Guinean culture
was still in the Neolithic Age. The use of metal was virtually unknown (with the
exception of the use of bronze in the Lake Sentani area), and tools were made of
stone. Tribal wars, headhunting and cannibalism were rampant (illustration 5.1).

English missionaries were placed in charge of the original settlement.[1] Their
principal task was to convert the non-Christians and make them abandon the killing of humans. This proved to be a tall order. The first installed resident, the
Reverend W. G. Lawes, duly began sending off a stream of reports to the head-
quarters of the London Missionary Society. He acted as go-between and interpreter
during the annexation ceremonies performed for the British Crown by Commo-
dore Erskine in November, 1884. Lawes claimed that his principal aim in life was
the translation of the Scriptures into the native language, and he left a valuable
record on the languages and life of the people. His colleague and successor, the
Reverend James Chalmers had a very active career in which he assisted with the
early administration of the settlement, but he was ultimately killed and eaten by

1. The formerly Dutch colony of western New Guinea (West Irian) has remained isolated even today; it is
only the eastern part that is the subject of our study.

the Goaribari Island people. The presence of these two gentlemen had stimulated the interest of England and Germany in New Guinea, leading to the proclamation of the Protectorate of British New Guinea in 1884, and the annexation of the north and northeast of the mainland and surrounding islands by Germany shortly afterwards.

British New Guinea was transferred to the newly established Commonwealth of Australia as Papua in 1902, and German New Guinea, then known as Kaiser-wilhelmsland, was captured from Germany by an Australian expeditionary force in 1914 and became a mandate under the League of Nations after World War I, and a United Nations trust territory in the middle 1940's. The two divisions, the Australian Territory of Papua and the United Nations Trust Territory of New Guinea, were then governed as one in an administrative union provided for in the United Nations Trusteeship Agreement in 1946, until the new combination achieved independence as Papua New Guinea in 1974. The result was a political artifact, but there is great hope that the inevitable secessionist movements now arising will resolve into some form of federal system congenial to the majority.

The standard cliché for most new arrivals from overseas during the first eighty years of European penetration was that nothing of any great importance really happened in New Guinea. And for those whose roots lay elsewhere, this may have been so. But for the islanders, it was a period which saw the development of a set of attitudes and values—the product of intercultural contact—which has offered at least a partial explanation for the racial situation and the political movements of more recent times. By 1960 the newly emerging nation was at last undergoing change at a rate that was more rapid than that predicted by the officials. A system of local government councils based mainly on the cultural-linguistic unit was arising, and the hitherto unacceptable idea of indigenous entrepreneurship was now welcome. The general trend of population movement into towns accelerated, and the urban scene began to show the breakdown of traditional systems of law and order. Offenses against property skyrocketed. A great influx of overseas

5.1. *A headhunting raid in New Guinea, from* Pioneering in New Guinea *by James Chalmers, 1896.*

capital by government and private enterprise had a highly visible influence on the life patterns and behavior of all groups living in the country. And in the last few years, preparation for self-government and independence, and independence itself, have increased the confidence of many people, so that traditional patterns of response have achieved a new significance in the context of building a nation, and a distinctive Melanesian style of government is emerging. Thus in the course of a very short modern history, Papuans and New Guineans have been successively referred to, in increasing order of respect, as kanakas, natives, indigenes, and nationals. As a new social reality presents itself on the island, some of the people cope better than others.

New Guinea is a large island, second only to Greenland in size. It is divided into two fully independent parts: the Indonesian Province of West Irian, and the eastern Papua New Guinea mainland. The latter, plus hundreds of smaller islands, makes up what is now the new nation of Papua New Guinea. The shape of New Guinea has been likened to that of a huge prehistoric bird; the west end bears the name Vogelkop (head of a bird, so called by its former Dutch rulers). The western portion was transferred by Holland to Indonesia in 1962. Our study covers areas in the eastern half of the island, which was an Australian territory, but acquired independence in 1974. Although the country is one of the most forbidding and unprepossessing parts of the tropics, it is attractive in a number of areas, particularly the Highlands, which have a rugged beauty. The vegetation is luxuriant, with the larger part of the mainland covered by dense forests. The lowland coasts are often bordered by salt marshes. The interior is noted for its impressive range of mountains, over 1500 miles long and rising to a height of 15,000 feet (illustration 5.2) in the peak of Mount Wilhelm in the eastern half. The chain is actually a continuation of the Himalayas, and it extends from one end of the island to the other. Many of the offshore islands are also mountainous. With the exception of Port Moresby, which is dry for eight months of the year, the country has a heavy rainfall, the Gulf District of Papua probably being the wettest area in the world. Excessive rains promote erosion and consequent reduction of soil fertility in some areas.

5.2. *A mountain range in the Eastern Highlands.*

5.3. *Mountain rivers.*

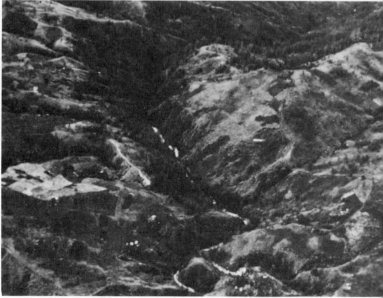

Many rivers cut through the mountains, forming picturesque waterfalls; coastal swamps (illustration 5.3) and rain forest form a dramatic landscape. The topography is full of contrasts. Flying over New Guinea, one is reminded of the local saying that God created the island on a Saturday night. He was running out of time and threw the mountains, the volcanoes, the swamps and the jungles together in a great hurry. The ruggedness of the land makes many areas inaccessible. Roads are difficult to build and usually extend only twenty to thirty miles beyond the larger towns. The only exception is a highway being built from the coast near Lae to the Western Highlands; a large section is dirt road and is impassable during the rainy season (illustration 4.1). Severe earthquakes occur from time to time, and in some areas the sub-earthquake, *guria,* is a daily event. There exist more than a dozen volcanoes, which occasionally burst into violent activity. Mount Lamington in southeast Papua erupted in 1951 resulting in a great loss of life.

The extreme geographic isolation of the country created the static Stone Age culture that existed at the time of the first European penetration during the middle of the nineteenth century. People of many areas had been unaware that any human life existed beyond a fifteen-to-twenty-mile radius from their home villages (40 a). Contacts with the outside world gradually changed the social and cultural patterns of the coastal areas and the offshore islands—the Solomons, New Britain, etc. But the Highlands, in the center of the country, remained isolated and were generally thought to be unpopulated and uninhabitable until forty years ago. The area was first explored by a few gold prospectors during the early 1930's; they did not receive a friendly reception. The Highlands stayed relatively undisturbed until after World War II. Only then was it discovered that a larger concentration of people lived in that area than anywhere else on the island. But even today, the population is largely isolated from the modern coastal cities, and travel in most areas is still restricted to footpaths, or to the waterways in dugout canoes.

The difficulties created by its geographic isolation are aggravated by the diversity of languages spoken in New Guinea; the country has from one-sixth to one-quarter of the world's languages. Seven hundred different languages—not just dialects—are spoken on an island which has a population of somewhat over two million people. Some languages are related to one another, but others differ as much as English and Japanese (40 a).[2] Some are spoken by people of a single village, while in other areas, such as the Highlands, up to 60,000 indigenes may speak various dialects of a single language. The various languages are associated with different cultures, and correspond to distinct patterns of customs and social behavior. At least four linguae francae—Neomelanesian Pidgin, Police Motu, Bahasia Indonesian, and English itself—help to bridge the language barrier.

Pidgin is a fascinating language. Contrary to popular belief, it is essentially a creation of the people themselves and not superimposed by the aliens from overseas. It is structurally a native language and has spread among the people without intervention on the part of the Europeans. Rural patients who come to Port Moresby for treatment soon acquire a knowledge of pidgin in the hospital when speaking among themselves, as they cannot understand the language of Melane-

2. In some areas, particularly the Sepik areas, neighboring clans have completely different languages; one may have a simple structure and syntax, employing two genders, while others may use twelve such categories. It may be of interest to the psychiatrist that each has its own term for the obligatory nonconformist, the person exhibiting psychotic manifestations—*Dabanepaia* in Mumeng, *jirodusari* in Popondetta, *mango* to the Bakovi speaking people of Kimbe, *gongo* among the Gijura, *babo* among the Wana speaking people, *awa'awa* in Marshall Lagoon, and many others.

sians from other areas. The rapid spread and common use of this language make it almost certainly the national language of the future, irrespective of the wishes of the government.

A single village or the combination of a few villages form a clan, the basic social unit. The lineage of the clans may vary in different regions, but each of them shows considerable independence (40 a). They are essentially ministates. Neighbors, when not at war, support each other by the exchange of important decorations, essential for the performance of vital ceremonials. In case of tribal warfare, some may also form alliances and send their warriors to increase another clan's strength.

The economy of the country was based principally on subsistence farming. The villagers planted yams, taro, and palm trees to meet their food requirements. What an individual did not use himself, he shared with others in the village. His farm tools were simple, mainly an axe, traditionally made of stone. Its replacement by steel in recent years greatly increased its efficiency. Pigs were highly valued; they were raised not only for food but also for their importance in ceremonial feasts. Highland women allowed piglets to nurse from their breasts, sharing the milk with their own children. Fishing, in the coastal areas, and hunting wild pigs and *cassowary* added to the staple food of sweet potatoes and taro. In recent years, tobacco and a few bags of coffee have been grown for profit. Each person performed the work necessary for his subsistence: the growing of food, the making of tools, weapons, etc. He built his own house using available material. The only specialist was the artist, who was always male. He carved masks, sacred instruments, and slit gongs. For the most part, the cultural-linguistic groups were egalitarian and stateless in character, in contrast to the larger pyramid social structure prevalent in some parts of Africa. Most groups were *acephalous,* there being very little authority. Being a successful farmer brought respect and prestige; neglecting one's garden was considered strange. Such neglect brought social disapproval and was recognized by the villagers as a sign of personality change and possibly an indication that one had become "long long."

The population of the villages consisted of fifty to a few hundred people. In the Sepik area they built their huts along the rivers; in the Highlands, they laid them out on mountain ridges, a single access road leading into the village. This plan offered natural defense lines in case of attack (illustration 5.4). Twenty to fifty small, round houses built for the women and children of the village flanked the road. The men lived in separate houses, oval in shape and segregated from the women's houses.

The New Guinean was highly individualistic; each man's opinion counted. Group decisions were not made by the majority but by consensus. Agreements were brought about by skillful and persuasive orators who manipulated and coerced the members of their clan. Men who were capable of such powerful persuasion became influential leaders; they were the *big men.* Their position within the group was highly important and respected, but it was not hereditary. Clans were not ruled by hereditary chiefs, nor was there an established hierarchy. However, some families had become influential by virtue of their wealth.

It may seem strange that in a society where warfare, cannibalism and headhunting had been of overriding importance, the warrior was not necessarily the most appreciated man. He may receive recognition after a successful raid, and in the past he was given the best pieces of a victim's flesh, but he was considered too volatile and unreliable to conduct the daily affairs of the clan. It was the "big man" who played the most significant role and won the acceptance of the group.

5.4. *The Highlanders laid their villages out along mountain ridges, with only a single access route to defend in case of attack.*

He disputed with the enemy and negotiated alliances with neighboring villages, arranging for the exchange and loan of decorations necessary for ceremonial festivities (40 b). He was the master of the ritual. His shrewdness and skill enabled him to acquire more land and thereby grow more food and raise more pigs. As he shared his wealth by sponsoring more feasts, his influence as a big man increased. He carried the exchange tallies, in the form of short bamboo sticks, hanging from his chest (illustration 5.5); each stick marked a feast in which he had donated pigs to entertain his own and neighboring villages.

Traditionally, a strict separation between men and women has been maintained in all aspects of life, both in daily activities and religious rituals. Specific tasks were assigned to men, others to women. The men planted yams and taro, while women gathered them. But only men collected the yam tubers used for rituals of the phallus (40 b) and competed in growing the largest yams (some reach a size of twelve feet).

The status of women was inferior to that of men. They were assigned menial tasks and played no role in the affairs of state. In many cases, they were placed in the same category as pigs—subject to exchange like any other commodity. They took care of the children and had specific duties, such as making sago (an edible starch). When they travelled, they sat down in the canoes; men stood up while paddling in order to be more visible (illustration 5.6). Today women are still excluded from the men's houses and from many religious activities by strict taboos; violations can be punished by death. Nor are they allowed to view the sacred objects: important plaques, masks or *bull roarers* that are kept in sacred houses. These objects, possessing magic powers, are hidden by the men and taken out only for religious ceremonies or war parties, with the intent to frighten an enemy. Upon hearing the sound of the bull roarer, women and children must hide.

Boys remain with the women until they reach adolescence. At that time, they move into the House Tamberan, the spiritual house of men, where they undergo the long process of initiation. An essential part of the initiation ceremonies is not only to separate the boys from the women but also to make them aware that women, and particularly sexual contacts with them, are dangerous (40 b). As the boys take leave of the women, joining the men in their ceremonial houses, they are forced to run through double lines of women who beat them. This ceremony, designed to impress the initiates with the cruelty and spiteful behavior of women, marks the end of their childhood. They now face the long, painful road of initiation into the secret and magic world of men.

The fear of women may be partly related to the local myths of creation. Originally, the earth and the sky were connected, but later they were separated. The earth-mother freed humanity from the man-eating sky-father; she controlled the earth and directed her descendents, a pair of twins, to trick the sky people and to kill the giant sky-father, who threatened the inhabitants of the earth. As if controlled by the threat symbolically expressed by this myth, New Guinean men want to keep themselves free from the power that woman obtained by deceit and trickery and from the fear of being eventually defeated by woman. The men attempted to protect themselves by placing women under strict taboos. In recent years, the rigid separation and exclusion of women from important clan activities has diminished but has not disappeared. When we visited a patient's village in the Highlands near Goroka (Case A567), only men discussed the possible return of the patient to his native village, a very important matter to the community. The women kept a respectful distance in spite of their obvious curiousity (illustrations

5.5. *The importance of this "big man" is reflected in the band of exchange tallies he wears around his neck. Each of these bamboo sticks represents a feast he has sponsored.*

5.7, 5.8) about the unusual visitors arriving from the outside world in an automobile.

5.6. Men had a higher social standing than women in New Guinea. Here, the man stands while paddling in order to be more visible.

Geographic isolation and the difficulties of establishing adequate communication due to language differences have contributed greatly to the distrust between neighboring clans. Disputes were often settled by war, headhunting, and cannibalism. The Australian government has almost succeeded in eliminating cannibalism; it is still practiced occasionally, however. A recent news item reported that courts acquitted seven men of cannibalism, since such rituals were considered "part of the cultural pattern" (108). Similar acts may have occurred since that time.[3]

Cannibalism served ritualistic needs rather than being a source of food. It was not, as often asserted, a means of adding protein to the diet. The irregular feasting on small amounts of human flesh could not possibly have served any nutritional needs; it was of ceremonial use only. Specific parts of the victim were distributed according to the social importance of the participants in the feast. In some parts of the country the nose was the most valued, and the little finger was the least prestigious piece of meat (95).

Prior to the imposition of governmental controls, cannibalism was nearly universal in New Guinea. It was used to avenge a personal wrong or an act which brought shame, and it served to increase one's power by incorporating the *Imunu*, the life force of the victim's soul, into the eater. It also fulfilled, in part, ceremonial functions dealing with creation myths and fertility rites (95). As previously discussed, in one of the creation myths, a set of twins, descendents of the earth-mother, killed the giant man-eating sky-father. They dismembered him, and parts of his body were buried. Crops of taro and yams grew from those parts. The details of the story of creation may vary in different parts of the island, but the

5.7. In a village near Goroka, the women keep their distance as men discuss important affairs.

3. A tribal war in which six people were killed by arrows and spears was reported in the Papua New Guinea *Post Courier* (November 3, 1975). The fight broke out over a pair of lovers violating intertribal taboos (see appendix).

basic elements are characteristic of the Melanid culture (129 a). The rituals associated with the killing and dismembering of the sky-father are based upon the mythology of creation. The planting of human flesh being responsible for the success of vital crops made cannibalism and headhunting a symbolic necessity.

Cannibalism occurs infrequently now. "Payback," however, is still a fairly frequent practice. Tribal wars continue, although the newspapers prefer to describe them as riots or simply as fights. According to recent reports, two local subclans fought each other following a card game in the Chimbu District (114). Four hundred people were involved in the fight, which lasted for several days in spite of attempts by the local police to break it up. One man was killed and several hospitalized from arrow wounds. Sixty warriors were arrested. Once started and set in motion, tribal wars are difficult to stop. They are apt to be self-perpetuating, for any wrongdoing or attack requires payback in the form of another raid by the victimized group. If anyone is killed, the victim's ghost is believed to harrass his clan until his death is avenged.

The spiritual world of New Guinea has always been populated with cult heroes, ancestral spirits, and ghosts. These abstract beings are thought to exist in concrete shapes; they are imagined to be real even if they are not visible (77). They show human behavior but they are endowed with supernatural powers. The fundamental spirits are the cult heroes, who are thought to have created the world. They are not worshiped as deities, as are the creators in Western and some Eastern religions. The myths of creation are merely explanatory and do not concern themselves with moral laws. Nor do these myths include moral obligations as in most other religions. The cults serve the social and economic welfare of the community (77); they do not deal with good and evil, concepts that are foreign to traditional New Guinea. The cult heroes are removed from the people. Their actions are determined by their own struggles and their own needs, and they show little concern for the living. In turn, few rituals are performed in their behalf in most regions of New Guinea. Only in a few areas, such as the Gulf of Papua, are the cult heroes more intimately involved with the lives of the people. Here, they are believed to have behaved in a human fashion but on a greater and more glamorous scale. They feasted, joked, seduced, deceived, raped, and murdered just as the people did (147 a), not unlike the Greek gods on Mount Olympus.

The ancestral spirits, in contrast to the cult heroes, were born from the human body. Even though they may have died months before, they continue to be part of the life of the community and they maintain their interest in it. They stay in their native localities and live in trees or behind rocks. They mediate in the clan's behalf (77 a), offer protection in raids, and take part in initiating the young into the secret societies. The ancestral forces are powerful and potentially dangerous (40 b); they have to be courted for their support, and only the most elaborate ceremonies satisfy them. If they are not properly respected or if they consider themselves neglected by inferior and inappropriate ceremonials, they may show their displeasure by bringing ill-fortune and death to their descendents. Rituals are performed to please them and to entice them to bring good crops, fertility, and general prosperity. The large feasts take years to prepare so that enough food, mainly pigs, can be accumulated to feed hundreds or even thousands of participants. The people are elaborately adorned for the ceremony. If the clan lacks the necessary sacred objects, even if they are only a few feathers of the right color, the big men negotiate an exchange with a neighboring clan to satisfy the ritualistic demands.

New Guinean ceremonies are performed to gain material advantages and to secure safe contacts with the spiritual world. This is best accomplished by ceremonial feasts and by the famous *Sing Sings,* all of which requires considerable equipment. The ceremonies necessitate the cooperation of many communities and force neighboring villages to enter into alliances. The exchange of plumes, shells, wigs, and other significant objects makes it possible to stage impressive Sing Sings, not only to show the proper respect for the ancestral spirits, but also to impress and intimidate neighboring villages with the clan's power (141). The exchange systems require close cooperation between clans and result in increased contacts where otherwise sociocultural isolation would have been the rule (40 a). The competency of the clans and the skills of their big men are challenged when alliances are shifted, necessitating new negotiations among neighboring clans. All this contributes to group interaction.

Death, particularly sudden death, is puzzling and produces fear and apprehension. It is frequently attributed either to punishment by enraged ancestors or to sorcery, and the surviving members of the family are obliged to find the cause. If ancestral spirits have been angered, they must be appeased by attentive and elaborate rituals. If sorcery was involved, the death must be avenged. Death due to sorcery would bring shame if left unavenged, and the spirit of the recently deceased would punish the ones who failed in their duties. The spirit's retribution would befall the entire clan.

We witnessed the people's reaction to the death of a young woman in a car accident. In travelling in the Highlands, we had been repeatedly warned about the precautions to be taken if we should be involved in an accident. Just a few months prior, the driver of the local health officer's jeep had killed a child who unexpectedly ran across the road in front of the vehicle. The accident was apparently unavoidable. As the indigenous health officer and driver stopped to offer any possible aid, the family of the child and their neighbors quickly assembled. The gathering crowd stoned them to death to avenge the child's death, a traditional form of payback.

Being forwarned, I came to the scene of an accident in the same area. A small pickup truck had failed to maneuver a curve and had overturned in a ditch. The driver of the truck was not injured, but a young woman rider was pinned under the truck. The uninjured driver ran away in fear of payback which could lead to his being killed on the spot. We were the first on the scene and no other people seemed to be nearby, but in a few minutes, twenty to thirty people appeared. The driver of our car, a local man, organized a group to free the woman. After several attempts, they lifted the truck, and brought her from the ditch to the roadside. There was excited talk and considerable, somewhat aimless, activity. Being an American doctor, I was expected to save the injured woman. When I tried to tell them she had died, everyone seemed stunned. Silence replaced the excited talk; fear showed on their faces. Since the woman had died suddenly, they feared her ghost would avenge her death on them. No one dared to touch her now, and the people started to drift away; the body was left lying on the ground. We had no choice but to put the dead woman in the back seat of our car and take her to the hospital, eight miles away.

Death is feared, yet it is often denied, being considered merely a transition from one state of life to another. In some areas of New Guinea, the dead lives as a ghost but behaves as the living do. Ghosts grow older, and some show recognizable signs of age (77). Their hair becomes gray, their arms and legs lose agility. Some clans perform rituals during which the young dancers leap through the air to limber up the stiffened legs of the aging spirits whom they represent (51).

Ghosts of the recently deceased continue to be concerned with the welfare of their families. Male ghosts are supposedly as protective of their families and as benevolent as living males. Female ghosts, even more than living women, are dangerous to their descendents; they attack their families and bring illness. And like living women, female ghosts are considered greedy. The sacrifice of a pig may appease them (77). The ghost's personality resembles that of the deceased; those who were weak during their lifetime are less feared, since they supposedly continue to be weak as ghosts. During the days of headhunting and human sacrifices, the chosen victims were usually the very young, the weak and the sick, as their ghosts were considered less powerful and their vengeance was less feared.

Cultural change in New Guinea is slow; Forge (40 b) attributes this to the lack of an established hierarchy. The absence of a hereditary leader may have produced an egalitarian society which was reluctant to change its structure for fear of losing its tradition. Furthermore, the geographic, cultural, and linguistic isolation prevented contacts even among neighboring clans. Rigid taboos reinforced the static Neolithic culture.

The colonization of the coastal areas and the smaller islands by Europeans forced rapid changes, often traumatic ones, upon the lives of the people. Local groups resisted when European planters attempted to round up young and healthy men for work on their plantations. The natives' spears, bows and arrows, and stone axes were no match for the rifles and modern weapons of the Europeans. They were easily subdued (127). Through their contacts, however conflict-ridden and disturbing, they overcame their isolation more rapidly than did people of other regions.

At one time, the exchange systems and the war parties were the integrating forces in the loosely organized New Guinea society (147 c). Even considering the language difficulties and the lack of contacts and social interchange, the small communities were basically united. Major raids required the cooperation of neighboring clans. Alliances had to be negotiated; defenses had to be built; subordination to competent leaders was necessary even in this rankless society. The different clans organized a cohesive social unit otherwise lacking in their daily life. Maher (95) believes that giving up cannibalism and tribal wars contributed to the weakening of the village's importance as a social unit and to the individual's feel-

5.9. *Natives reenact the ceremony that traditionally accompanied a cannibalistic feast. Cannibalism has been suppressed throughout the country.*

5.10. *A "cannibal" during a Sing Sing.*

ing that he no longer belonged to a people. When the clansmen felt surrounded by an unknown, threatening world, they had depended on a regeneration of their courage and spiritual strength through the ritual consumption of the Imunu, the life force that they could obtain only from the life of another human being. Forced to abandon this practice, the cannibal was deprived of the source of his strength. The collective protection against outside dangers that traditional rituals, cannibalism,[4] and tribal warfare had offered him ceased to exist. He could no longer depend on the cohesive action of the clan. The outward appearance of their strength such as they displayed in the impressive men's houses, became superfluous and the buildings fell into disrepair. Men did what they would never have done—they moved into the huts with their wives. Their traditional values had disintegrated without being replaced by any of the wordly advantages of the

4. Local villagers reenact cannabalistic rituals for the tourist (illustrations 5.9, 5.10); but old engravings give a more accurate picture of the original action.

European. Thrown from their Stone Age culture into the twentieth century, they could not find adequate replacements for their beliefs. There were no traditional answers and no adequate substitutes for the collective solutions which had been successful in the past. They turned to sorcery to find protection against the supernatural, evil forces which they believed were weakening them, and sorcery became a major force in the life of the individual, who could no longer find security in community action (78).

Sorcery attempts to restore the relationship between the individual and his society by calling on the supernatural to supply easy solutions to the perplexities of life and death, guilt and innocence, right and wrong (23). Witchcraft had existed to a limited degree prior to the European penetration, but its use has greatly increased since then (see appendix). Its practice increased particularly among warlike groups that had not shown any interest in it in the past. They embraced it because they could not find any other substitute for the protection that headhunting and cannibalism had given them (78).

The governments of Germany, England, and Australia, occupying many parts of New Guinea, attempted to force Westernization on the areas under their control. The coastal areas and the offshore islands, unable to resist, had to submit to the foreign ideologies. Governmental policies attempted to encourage, and often to impose, the adoption of Western standards. The traditional practices of cannibalism and headhunting were outlawed; villages that continued to participate in raiding parties were burned. Villagers living in small communities of sixty to eighty people were encouraged to merge into larger villages. Whether this advice was in itself good or bad, it meant the end of their ancient traditions. Unable to assert themselves effectively, many natives were forced to serve in labor camps; they were forced to assume an inferior, humiliating role. Although the villagers appeared apathetic (95), considerable underlying resentment built up. They felt that they had been deprived of dignity. Many were angered because of unfulfilled promises, and because they were not allowed to share in the wealth of the Europeans as tradition said they should have been. The Melanesians had always shared their crops and divided their goods with those who helped them. They felt entitled to a part of the wealth that they had helped to produce. Had they not diligently worked in the offices, on the plantations, and in the homes of the white man? Why were they not allowed to enter the front door? The new rules were puzzling, and the white man's unfairness created strong antagonism and eventually hostile attitudes against the Europeans.

Missionaries attempted to bring Christianity to New Guinea. Some of the concepts of Christianity were readily accepted, but the Melanesians never abandoned their beliefs in ancestor cults, spirit-beings and ghosts. The crucifixion of Christ was viewed as a sacrifice similar to those that the indigenes had practiced for a long time and seemed not very different from their own rituals. They had always brought offerings to their ancestral spirits in the hope of returning prosperity. The sacrifice of Christ impressed them as more successful and efficient in bringing greater power and greater wealth. When they accepted Christ, He was given the name of local deities (77); He became a cult hero. But being disillusioned over not being able to share in the wealth of those who had brought them Christ, they grew dissatisfied, but not with their belief in Christ. It was not that the new cult hero had failed to bring the expected fortunes. No; they believed, in keeping with local customs, that the priests were withholding knowledge of the effective rituals from the people. They accused the missionaries of having torn out the first page of the Bible where the rituals were described for obtaining the riches that were promised to them.

The New Guineans felt betrayed and they were angry (127). They had been persuaded or forced to give up their own rituals of cannibalism and headhunting in the expectation of accepting the obviously more effective rituals of the white man, which were supposed to bring them material wealth. When Christianity failed to provide this wealth to them, as it had to the white man, the natives felt that the whites had stolen the wealth (cargo) that was due to them. Feeling they had been deceived, they created their own rituals in the form of cargo cults, which have sprung up periodically in the coastal areas of New Guinea and its neighboring islands over the last sixty years. Lawrence (77) considers the movement a form of rudimentary nationalism which incorporates European goals. The cults appear particularly in periods of prolonged frustration, when the traditional social structure has disintegrated, and the national self-image is severely damaged. The Melanesians attempt to revive their ancestral beliefs without fully denouncing Christianity; they use the familiar tools of magic, but they accept the vocabulary of Christianity. When resentments and dissatisfaction grow, a self-appointed leader begins to preach salvation and the coming of the Millennium; he pledges that ancestors will arrive by ship, plane, or helicopter, returning the cargo that rightfully belongs to the people. He promises an abundance of food, cars, tools, building materials, even transistor radios—all the goods for which they envy the white man. Airstrips and docks are built to prepare for the arrival; crops and pigs, the customary food supplies, are destroyed as being unnecessary. The cargo cult leader stirs up the local population against the Europeans by accusing the Westerners of having taken possession of the cargo sent by the ancestors of the Melanesians before it could reach New Guinea (77). Some of the cultists commit human sacrifices (see Case 510) to imitate the crucifixion of Christ (24 b). Even-

5.11. *The impact of the modern West on a Stone Age culture creates strange contrasts. Here, a warrior uses a basketball for a mask.*

5.12. *A warrior in traditional costume posed for this picture as he was about to board a plane.*

tually, as the promises do not materialize, the individual movement disintegrates, but it does not prevent another movement from developing at a later time. The cults are repeated again and again as a weapon against continuing dissatisfaction and low self-esteem. In spite of its inevitable failure, the movement seems to restore some of the people's dignity and self-respect.

The attitude toward Europeans varies considerably among the various areas of New Guinea, depending upon the kind of treatment that the local population has received. The people on some of the islands—the Solomons, New Britain, etc.— were conquered by force during the period of colonization in the nineteenth century; their traditional societal and cultural beliefs were suppressed. The white man forced his standards upon a local population which developed a growing resentment and hostility against their masters. In those parts of the country, nationalism expanded and traditional magical beliefs returned—without, however, doing away with a desire for the white man's wealth and way of life.

Governmental policies have changed since the early days of colonization. More tolerance has been shown in the Highlands, which were contacted more recently, around the second world war. Western standards were not forced upon the local population; instead, the Highlander was encouraged to develop his own resources. He was taught to raise cash crops of coffee, copra, and cocoa; health services were substantially enlarged and sound education was encouraged. The missionaries respected the traditional local customs. Only violent acts of destruction, cannibalism, headhunting, and tribal warfare were outlawed; polygamy was discouraged. Self-administration and local political councils were sponsored and supported by the Australian government; the individual's dignity was protected. As a result, the Highlanders show far less hostility toward Europeans than do the people of the coastal areas.

The shift in attitudes is illustrated in one of the cargo cults that developed during the 1960's. During World War II, the local population had had friendly contacts with the American G.I.'s, as they had had with the Australian soldiers. The soldiers were often generous, sharing their food when the New Guineans were hungry and giving them small gifts. When a cargo cult developed in New Ireland (1964), the people remembered their American friends, and they collected funds to buy "President Johnson of the United States of America" to be their cult leader (127).

The sudden impact of the twentieth century on a Stone Age civilization creates strange contrasts. A Highlander near Goroka, when reenacting a *sing sing,* uses a basketball for a mask (illustration 5.11). We saw a Mount Hagener in his traditional warrior makeup (illustration 5.12) carrying a vinyl suitcase as he boarded a plane for Port Moresby. Such changes and inconsistencies are unavoidable in a period of profound transition; they reflect the perplexity and confusion of the individual in New Guinea. Those changes must be understood when considering the psychopathology of the psychotic. The beliefs in magic and spirit-beings that have remained greatly color the content of the psychosis. But it is the basic structuring of reality and the organization of thinking that distinguishes the individual using the magic of his culture from the disintegrated psychotic using magic as a pathological manifestation. That disintegrative process is similar in everyone, regardless of cultural background.

6

Societal
Significance
of Tribal Art

We needed to do some soul searching to find the proper title for this chapter, being undecided about whether to use the term tribal art, primitive art or some other terminology. The dilemma is not just ours. A few years ago, twelve anthropologists were asked about their preference in naming the art of people from isolated cultures with limited Western contacts (27), from areas in Africa, Melanesia, and parts of South America, where people have preserved their traditional ways of life. The authors participating in the survey found considerable objections to the categories used by other researchers, implying that they had strong opinions about the use of terms which they were not already accustomed to using themselves. One suggestion was to use geographic terms, such as Benin, Sepik, or Egyptian art (48), which would be of definite value as long as the investigations were limited to single areas, but such self-limiting terms are difficult to apply in crosscultural research. It becomes necessary to find satisfactory generic terms to deal properly with art forms from vastly divergent societies and from various regions which may use significantly different styles but which nevertheless belong to groups showing common characteristics. Terms such as tribal or primitive art have been dismissed as being unscientific or prejudicial, and terms such as "preliterate" or "precivilized" (as opposed to "civilized" Western art) imply similar value judgments. Once a scientific term has been introduced into everyday speech, it is almost impossible to free it of value judgments. When technical terms are adopted into the language, they may take on a broader meaning than was originally intended.[1]

1. Terminology in other professional fields suffers from the same lack of accuracy. In psychiatry, the term

The term "tribal" originally had a limited definition: it referred to a society ruled by a single leader whose role was often inherited. Some anthropologists have broadened the term to include organizations that are led not by one man, but by an oligarchy—by a council or group of respected big men. But in spite of its not being entirely correct in describing a given social organization, the term "tribal," in connection with art, conveys the idea of a style distinct from Western and most Asiatic art. This term, however, does not deal with the essential character of the art objects in themselves; rather it describes a social organization which venerates a single autocratic figure. Moreover, similarly structured art objects can be found in both acephalous and tribal groups. The funerary figures of the Bakota tribe in Africa, created in a strictly tribal society, have common characteristics derived from condensing or elaborating parts of the human body, similar to the Hohao plaques of New Guinea. The plaques are created by an acephalous group, yet both art works fall into a large category of nonwestern or non-Asiatic art, for which we attempt to find an appropriate term.

Objections to terms other than "tribal" are frequently based on the idea that they reflect a social bias against a society and its art. Unfortunately, the term "primitive" became incorporated into daily use and has become a target of social discrimination, implying an inferior status. The term primitive, however, means nothing more than the first or earliest of its kind (112), actually suggesting original creativity. It has only been since the days of colonial powers that the term implies a disparaging value judgment. We can probably accept the term "primeval," as it is less commonly used, with far less hesitation than "primitive," although the definitions are closely related. Our use here of the term primitive refers to a lack of technological knowledge and implies only that Stone Age tools were used rather than steel tools. Despite many objections and reservations, most anthropologists still prefer the term "primitive" to others (27).

Whatever term is chosen, the art of primitive people is an important spiritual instrument in a society that lacks a recorded history. The only other knowledge of the clan's past is the verbal account given by its elders that has been transmitted from generation to generation. The information is incomplete and dramatizes events of uncertain authenticity, but it heightens the heroic deeds of the clan's ancestry essential to its self-image.[2]

Art, having its roots in the sociocultural beliefs of the community, is highly traditional and stylized (90). The ceremonial carvings bring the ancestral spirits into the presence of the worshipper, and put him into a continuum with his ancestors. As they are being honored and respected with proper ceremonials and with feasts, the ancestral spirits are expected in return to favor the hunter or the warrior for his efforts and devotion. The artifacts, not just representing his ancestors, but *being* them, stand behind the warrior in battle, instilling courage with the ominous noises of their bullroarers, to frighten the approaching enemy. In the West, before the days of mechanized warfare, the battle flag served a

6.1. *New Guineans act out the legend of the mudmen.*

"hysteria" is such an example; the term referred originally to *hysteros* or *uterus* since it was thought that the illness could only affect women. This assumption is completely wrong. Men can be afflicted with this condition just as women; in spite of its inaccuracy, the term has remained in wide use and is accepted in the international professional nomenclature.

2. One story tells of the Asoro people of the New Guinea Eastern Highlands in a victorious battle against a numerically superior enemy. According to legend, as the attacked clan were fleeing from certain defeat, they fell into a lake. As they came out of the muddy waters, their bodies and faces were completely covered with mud (illustration 6.1). Their ghostly appearance frightened their enemies, who vanished in all directions, saving them from destruction. The event is often reenacted, preserving an image of courage and cunning in withstanding the onslaught of a superior force. But their account would be far less impressive if it were given without their mud masks (illustration 6.2).

similar purpose; it symbolized King and Country. Thus do the plaque and the mask of the indigene make the spirit-being an actual participant whose support is needed to defeat the enemy or to be successful in other endeavors.

In some societies, the carving men, painters, and artists form a closely knit community (48). Their creative powers bring them respect and recognition. They are not feared as the sorcerer is feared, as they do not use their skills for evil but in the interest of the community. The Polynesian artist-priest intones the Chant of Creation as he chisels a shapeless piece of wood into a spirit-being. His chant functions as a combination prayerbook and instruction manual, directing him both in the use of tools and in the molding of the divine figure. The basic design of the sculpture is strictly controlled by tradition, as is the behavior of the artist-priest. Nothing is to interfere with his creative powers, which are kept from being dissipated into other forms of creation—strict sexual taboos channel the artist's creative energies into his work and are intended to strengthen his creative potency (90). The intense efforts make his work an act of procreation which reaffirms its creator as a priestly figure.

The divine aspects of creativity may be more directly stressed in Polynesian society than in other groups, but most primitive art adheres to rules regarding color and design.[3] The artist may not know the origins of the many taboos that he must obey, but he respects the rules imposed by his society. He cannot deviate from the established order, since any unaccustomed design or color brings strong disapproval (98). The traditional designs were bequeathed by ancestors; their significance was kept secret and passed from the older men to the young, from father to son as in New Guinea (110c) or from the sister's brother to the nephew, as in Africa (104).

Some of the sculptural patterns are of common knowledge to Melanesians and have no specific significance for the group; they do not require secrecy. But the more powerful symbols, capable of controlling the fortunes of the clan, are only gradually revealed, depending on the rank of the initiate. Only men are allowed to know the carvings; women are prevented from seeing them. As the carvings possess spiritual might, the elders must be certain that their meanings will not be revealed to an enemy. Often, the elder men do not share the most secret and particularly powerful knowledge with the young warriors until they feel close to death. And even then, a young man must prove himself worthy of the secrets by undergoing severe, invariably painful, and often humiliating trials (95). He must have convinced others that no potential enemy could force the secret knowledge concerning the meaning of the indentations, niches, and colors of carvings and plaques from him, for they affect the existence of the entire tribe, and are sources of its strength (110a). When the young man is accepted as an artist and ready to produce important spirit figures himself, he works in utter secrecy on the involved and intricate patterns, his work often lasting several years. And when the elders give him the instructions for his work, they speak in a nearly inaudible voice to prevent outsiders from hearing them and gaining power over

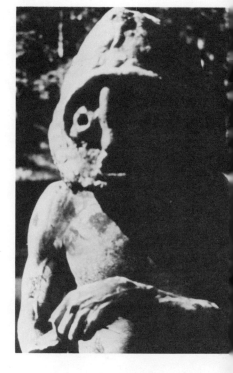

6.2. *A performer in a mudman mask, Asoro Valley, Eastern Highlands.*

---

3. The quality of primitive art varies greatly; minor utensils, particularly for daily use, are often carved by the villager and are without artistic distinction. But important pieces, as a ceremonial paddle, are of distinguished quality and of elaborate design; they are made by the experienced *carving men*, while paddles for daily use may be decorated by their undistinguished owners (48). The divine spirit-beings reside in the art objects, which are formed from memory; models are never used. Some features and parts of the body are exaggerated according to their spiritual significance; some are omitted; invisible parts may be made visible. The living are hardly ever portrayed since any mistakes in a sculpture or painting, intentional or not, would bring harm to the model. A few societies dealing in black magic may occasionally reproduce human figures that are to be destroyed in effigy. Even though naturalistic Western art work appears to be meaningless and somewhat calculated to the primitive artist, he admires the technique (90).

the clan by knowing the intricacies of the artistic details of a sacred art piece, or by capturing the core of the rituals regulating and controlling the spiritual life of the clan. After the plaques and carvings of ancestral figures are finished, they are kept in the dark recesses of the men's houses and removed only for ceremonials. A change of images, of the traditional patterns, is thought to offend the ancestors. The clansmen believe that their ancestors no longer recognize themselves in the changed designs (79a). Any images altered in design or color would be considered a lack of deference, and the violator, even the entire clan, would be punished by the spirits, who would refuse all support in an unknown, hostile world. Untraditional forms and colors, being unrelated to the past, are thought to interfere with the established continuum of time and space, isolating the people and suspending them in emptiness. But as traditional values have deteriorated or been abandoned, the elders of the clan consider the younger generation unworthy of the ancestral secrets; they have kept them to themselves, and consequently the secrets have been lost (110c).

As long as the fear of the power invested in spirit-beings continued, acquiring knowledge of magic designs beyond one's rank, even accidentally, was severely punished. We interviewed a psychiatric patient in a mission station in the Northeastern Arnhem country of Australia. He was a young man in his twenties who had worked in a curio shop in Darwin where he packaged and shipped bark paintings to tourists. He saw many designs that should have been secret to someone at his stage of initiation. In the past, he would have been severely punished for seeing them, but living away from his customary environment, he had become less concerned with the restrictions that had existed in the bush. After working in the shop for two years, he returned home to the bush country. Soon after his return, he became increasingly depressed and developed delusions that not only he, but also his entire family, would be killed for his cultural transgression.[4] He believed that he was condemned for having handled objects of great significance to the spiritual existence of his tribe at a time that was premature for him according to his state of initiation. It did not matter that the bark paintings were curios and that he had not seen them in the proper spiritual setting of his tribe. He was still convinced that he had violated the spiritual tenets regulating his existence.

The belief in spirit-beings and magic is indicated in the paintings of ceremonials and dances by the stoneage hunters who lived near the caves of Lascaux and Altamira. With no other recorded evidence of the existence of these early hunters, the paintings on the rock walls of their caves and cliffs come almost alive as they give a realistic account of the toils of these people, of their hunts, and of the animals that provided them with food. They depict man as he existed during many generations of prehistory. But the drama of life unfolds in even greater detail on the rock walls of South Africa. The "Art on the Rocks" (83) not only depicts hunting scenes, but shows other aspects of man's life as well—the clothes that he wore and the costumes camouflaging him as he went off to hunt. There are also scenes of war, the weapons of stone, and the spears; the warriors on each side are distinctly different in physical appearance, seeming to dramatize an invasion by foreign people. The scenes record the battle and its conclusion (83). Different generations appear independently on the walls, bearing witness to the history of human development. When little other information is available, paintings alone fill the gaps.

4. We were told by his mother's brother who, as in many clans and tribes, was responsible for the patient's spiritual life, that the patient would have been severely punished in earlier years, but that such taboos had been abolished in recent years.

There is no evidence of a written paleolithic language. It is possible that primeval man had not yet developed the ability to bridge the space between the images that he saw. He remained isolated, missing the continuous flow between concepts necessary for the development of verbal or written language. To develop a language, he would have needed the ability to abstract the symbols of written language (words) and organize them into a linear order. One could assume that primitive man was not able to establish a hierarchic order of thought, and felt stymied because he wanted to express equally significant experiences that took place simultaneously. He could not put the events in his life into sequential order. Early man's inability to count beyond three or four (which was just "many") offers evidence of his difficulties in forming sequential, linear concepts (21). Man did not reach such a high degree of sophistication until the time of the first high civilization of Egypt or Mesopotamia (50). The early hieroglyphics of the Egyptian, the Sumerian, and the Mayan people were still closer to pictorial imagery than to written language symbols; they were a form of artistic expression that allowed the simultaneous representation of a multitude of concepts.

From prehistory until just recently, most visual creation—art—has been concerned with spiritual or religious matters; it develops in parallel with a society's level of cultural development, which is what shapes the style characteristics of a period. The apparent sophistication of the primeval cave paintings, and the lack of written chronicles, encourages the impression that the art of that time was more advanced than the verbal language. But these graphics, unrelated and free-floating in space, do not form complete scenes; they remain single images. The weak light flickering in the darkness of the cave must have evoked staccato-like pictures, deceptive in their appearance, suggesting motion (50). The mystical atmosphere, the dim light of the oil lamps flickering and throwing long shadows on the cave walls, made the uncompleted pictures appear to be completed entities. The effect was enhanced by the cave man's needs for fulfillment of his goals and were less related to realistic goals. The very limited knowledge possessed by primeval man must have added to his dependency on forces beyond him. As knowledge was undeveloped, the belief in magic power thrived. The unconnected images in the caves correspond to the isolated guttural sounds of prelanguage (118).

The inability to order time and space separated early man from later civilizations. Early man concerned himself only with what was going on around him at any given moment, as he was not aware of a sequential order of events; a distinct separation of the present from the past and the future had yet to be formed. Nor had he established his identity properly, possessing only the vaguest concepts of his position within the temporal and spatial framework. Not having mastered the force of gravity, he sought refuge in natural shelters. He was unprepared to leave his caves, and unable to build the simplest dwellings that would protect him from the forces of nature and of men.

As the primordial hordes became organized into more integrated social systems, group members became increasingly dependent on mutual understanding. They established systems of communication, integrating events within a framework that stabilized a sequential succession. This led to early language forms and more organized visual concepts (56). Man began to establish a hierarchy of space and time; he became aware that things happen in succession, and arranged his thoughts in a linear sequence (4a), substituting it for the multidirectional dimensions of the paleolithic period (50).

Having become aware of the spatial order around him, man was now capable of assembling the first rising structures, and he left his caves and rock shelters. He was forced to respond to the gravitational field of the earth, and it made his behavior subject to its invisible force, requiring him to adapt. When he built his first huts, he had to erect them around a vertical axis, resting on a horizontal base that gave substance and support. The vertical and horizontal directions became the first orientation in space (Table 2). At the turning point of prehistory (which occurred in different cultures at different periods of history but on corresponding sociocultural levels), neolithic people and their early successors were no longer roaming the lands as nomads. As they settled and planned to till the earth, they became aware of their dependence on the elements of nature, but they could not harness the rain, the wind, and the sun. If they were able to foretell the climatic variations of the seasons, however, they could successfully plan to work their fields. Some peoples developed astronomical skills to observe the stars and the seasonal changes of the sun. And some of these skills survive the peoples who developed them, only as legends, or as artifacts.

In the plains near Salisbury rises Stonehenge, an architectural and astronomical wonder. The technical skill required to move those huge blocks of stone is still puzzling today. It has not been established who its builders were, possibly the Wessex people, but carbon dating establishes that the megalithic monument was built between 1900 and 1500 B.C. (60). It was erected by almost superhuman efforts; stones weighing up to five tons were transported over distances greater than 135 miles, by water on barges, and on land by sledges, until they reached the building site.

The phrase "Contact with eternity" is inscribed on the peaks of the pyramids at Gizeh (50). That aspiration motivated the ancient Egyptians to undergo immense sacrifices and labors to erect their amazing edifices. The pyramids give witness to the newly discovered concepts of up and down, here and there, of the vertical and horizontal directions—in spiritual terms, of heaven and earth. They signified, and eventually deified, the separation from the almost timeless and spaceless chaos of primeval man. The timeless and infinite chaos of prehistory was now ordered into a universe in which the forces of nature could function according to stabilizing laws.

Both primitive art and that of the first high civilizations (50) of Egypt and Mesopotamia fulfilled a far more distinct societal function than their Western counterparts. The power of the privileged royalty or of the chiefs in autocratic systems was supported by a committed priesthood. The priests made art their servant, often being its exclusive sponsor. Art was used to reinforce strong controls over the people; it strengthened and protected the spiritual image of the god-king and established his roots not only by the glories of his own successes but also by those of his forefathers. Art, aided by pictorial writing (the hieroglyphics), also secured man's position within the continuum of history. No longer did art conjure up spiritual ancestors out of a vague past. Now the walls of temples and tombs reported fairly accurately the deeds and the military expeditions of the Pharaohs. Their history was permanently recorded. Man overcame his isolation during prehistory by creating visible spiritual companions in his art. His creations oriented him in his environment and guided him in his relation to other men.

In primitive societies, the artist is called upon to support existing attitudes, often not being allowed to make conceptual or stylistic changes. When twenty black Africans were asked to copy drawings of trees and birds, they were unable to produce realistic copies, but transformed them into geometric forms (48), a prevalent art form in their tribes. Social structure seems to control artistic designs, and artistic style is a kind of shorthand summary of its society (129b). Berndt (10b) connected the patterns in the art of northern Australian aborigines to their way of life. Clans living in the open space of the bush country, where the individual is more self-reliant, where he depends on his own abilities to fight and on his own prowess, prefer artistic designs in which individual figures stand isolated with blank spaces between them. In regions where people are socially interdependent and the individual's interests are subordinated to those of the group, figures are painted on a background of crosshatchings that cover the barkpainting with designs, typically leaving few open spaces. Berndt's highly explicit viewpoint relates the geometric designs of spiraling or concentric patterns to the wanderings of the aborigines of central Australia, contrasting them with the tight designs of New Guinean art, which he attributes to the steadfast village life of the islanders.

Primitive art apparently cannot be removed from its cultural setting without losing its reason for existence; it is of social significance only as long as it represents the values of the community in which it was created. Its form and content can be understood as characteristic of their setting; its function and design is rooted in its culture (129b). Verbal language, regardless of its symbolic strength, is considerably more limited in expressing needs beyond conscious levels and is unable to reach deeply buried complexes (130).

Works of primitive art are originally created as part of a cult practice for specific purposes that are spiritual in nature. The motifs and forms rigidly maintain their formal and traditionally regulated images as long as they serve a sacred end. As the artifacts become increasingly familiar to subsequent generations, however, they are no longer venerated. And eventually, as the designs are used to decorate household articles and utensils, the rigidly preserved patterns can be modified and changed. At that point, they no longer need to be hidden from outsiders, and they move from the dark recesses of the men's houses; they become accessible to everyone. The designs, once sacred, now embellish meat hooks, bowls, and mortars. The uncontaminated sacred designs allow glimpses into a culture that is rapidly passing, and they contribute considerably to our knowledge (129b). As long as the culture was not greatly influenced by foreign contancts, the designs retained their original significance for the people. For example, the Hohao plaques of New Guinea played a significant role for the villagers of the Gulf area before their contacts with the Europeans. Mythological, stylized figures appear in these plaques, their arms and legs raised in a protective gesture (110 a). The navel symbolizes the center of the clan, and the indentations bordering the plaque indicate clouds (illustration 6.3). The totality and balance of the combined parts made them powerful instruments for evoking magic forces that could battle enemies (7). The ancestral figures of the Sepik area, rarely equaled in their vitality by any other Pacific people, portray cult heroes linking the individual to a long passed *dream time.* Their cult heroes and ancestral spirits became alive in the art object, even if these spirits were abstracted into idealized geometrical designs (57).

As the Western powers penetrated into the islands of the South Pacific and Africa, the sudden impact of foreign values on the tribal societies disrupted the nonwestern civilizations, leaving their established societal values in complete disarray. Old concepts of life were shattered, creating doubts in established beliefs. Ritualistic ceremonies that had been of utmost significance in the past lost most of their meaning (95). The individual, and the community in which he lived, were puzzled by the change. Past rules regulating existence, anchored in a rigid framework, seemed to fail completely under the influx of the seemingly far more effective Western systems. The people were overwhelmed by Western technological efficiency, which they soon came to desire, feeling deprived of all the amazing possessions of the invaders. Their achievements seemed unbelievable to the New Guineans; the new masters could push a button, talk into a black box, and summon treasures to come flying in on an iron bird (77). The values that had been significant to the natives in the past and that had maintained their self-esteem were ignored or regarded with condescension. Their self-esteem suffered and they became ready victims to the missionaries' promises that partaking in the suffering of Christ would reward believers with the wealth of Western man (24b, 24c). Traditional values disintegrated and were abandoned, as was the art through which the ancient beliefs found expression. Much valuable art was destroyed because it was considered heathenish by the followers of zealous missionaries. When the art of the Hohaos was revived in 1966, it had lost its cultural importance; the designs were no longer the traditional ones (illustration 6.4), and ceased to have any significance for the people (7). The sacred patterns had degenerated to mere decorations; only the basic structure and shape of the artworks had been preserved. The modern imitations became more ornate than the originals: the introduction of European tools and commercial colors in place of the original clay gave them a slick appearance that appealed to the tourist trade. This cheapened the quality and character of the products (48), and they could not regain their cultural importance (129b). As the people's traditional life was destroyed, the plaques lacked the spiritual creativity that had motivated their making; they became empty imitations of the originals.

Western counterparts to this process are not unusual; new art forms, not steeped in tradition, cause a conservative audience to fear loss of contact with the heritage of the past. They feel secure only if their beliefs can remain rooted in the past; being separated from it by new thoughts or any new art forms produces feelings of isolation that they find difficult to tolerate. New art forms are often considered revolutionary, propaganda tools of a foreign ideology aimed at the destruction of traditional values and, consequently, of the entire social structure. In western art, the creative process elaborates, differentiates, and polishes the fragmented links of cultural influence as they emerge and reach conscious levels in the work of art. Frequently, depending on the historical environment, they are subordinated to social demands. The banal art of the French Rococo (illustration 6.5) emphasized sheer decorative form, its superficiality pretending to solve any conflicts of its period, spelling out its solution in a manner that was "too readable" (53).

During other periods, creative works of art offer a query and stimulate the audience to find its own solution. Primitive art, being far less explicit than Rococo, offers incomplete images, distorting and stressing essentials rather than embodying smooth, elaborate details. During the creative process of primitive art, the undifferentiated, fragmented images are combined according to rigid, ritualistic demands prevailing in a specific society. The links which emerge to unite these images are less clearly defined and less differentiated than in Western art. Their incomplete and distorted forms do not imitate nature, but have a highly charged, symbolic character. The forms are disturbing or reassuring rather than purely decorative. Frequently, the size of an important part of the body is overstated, or desirable characteristics of diverse origin are combined to express the magic force of a mask or an ancestral figure. The mask of the African Poro society has telescopic all-seeing eyes, the mouth of a monkey to indicate cunning, tusks,

6.3. *Traditional Hohao Plaque; used by permission of Philip H. Lewis, curator of the Field Museum of Natural History, Chicago.*

6.5. *This detail of* Allegory *by Jean-Honore Fragonard is an example of the banal art of French Rococo.*

and upright horns that imply strength (illustration 6.6). The tribal initiate experiences no difficulties in accepting this conglomerate spiritual figure, which may impress the outsider as being disproportioned or even bizarre.

To state that art appears in all cultures is a truism, but it may challenge us to find the meaning of the role of art in man's sociocultural history. Why has art existed at all times and in all cultures since prehistory? As a way of expressing man's needs and ambitions? To record his triumphs and failures? In order to determine the sociocultural significance of art, we have to find its common basis and its universal elements; but to understand its specific value, we must turn to areas where art has survived comparatively untouched by outside influences, and where it exists as an integral part of its culture (29).

6.4. *A revival of Hohao designs.*

Understanding the nonverbal language of art requires not only sensitivity to its underlying universality but also to the specific, often highly regional, elements which restrict its comprehensibility. Ritual art may instill fear and ecstasy in an initiate, but it has no spiritual meaning to another social group. The non-Westerner may admire European art as technically highly developed but consider it "too easy" (detached from the expression of conflicts), and avoiding the essentials of the spiritual world (53). The Westerner may consider tribal art exotic, foreign, and disturbing to his established concepts. Their own sociocultural systems, being less isolated, rapidly absorb their neighbors' styles: art originating in one area may soon spread, lose part of its character, and be modified by the different cultures which absorb it. Gothic architecture, originating in France during the twelfth century, was soon found with minor variations in Germany, Italy, and England.

Tribal art, functioning mostly on a nonliterate level, has reflected both the fears and the strengths arising from traditional beliefs. The marginal existence, and the unrelenting pressures of threatening diseases, hunger, and neighbors who are not to be trusted, all contribute to an environment that can be controlled only by appealing to magic powers. Supernatural imagery gives the people access to the spiritual world, and helps them to control an otherwise intolerable environment. The hunting charm of the Korewori River protected hunter and warrior alike from defeat or the embarrassment of an unsuccessful hunting expedition (color plate 1). If the spirit residing in the carving did not deliver the desired results, the charm was thrown away and replaced by another. Faith in the magic was not destroyed. The fault lay with the carving, which did not please the spirit.

6.6. *A mask of the secret African Poro Society is a composite of the powerful attributes of different animals.*

6.7, 6.8. *Although these two carvings may seem similar to a Western observer, the Bambara mask of Mali, Africa (left) and the Bakuba cup of the Congo (right) are as different as the languages of the artists who carved them.*

The need for magical control of an almost ungovernable, unfriendly world may differ in the way it is expressed from area to area, but it is a universal element in the mind of man. His impotence in dealing with the space around him, whether it is the jungles of the tropics, the vastness of arctic ice, or the overpopulated metropolis, causes him to seek means for its control. This need exists universally among men. Culture-bound beliefs mold only its specifics.[5] These specifics are often the result of careful training rather than of spontaneous expression.

Paintings by aborigine children who have yet to be indoctrinated with cultural beliefs show great similarities to the paintings of children in various other cultures, including that of Europe. The content of their drawings is influenced by environmental experiences only to a very limited degree. Older children, up to the age of thirteen, draw excellent naturalistic trees and animals (102). At the age of

5. In Western societies, where verbal language has replaced much of the action directed behavior of earlier societal structures, verbal appeals to the divine power have almost excluded the nonverbal expressions of the "savages."

thirteen, children are removed from the tribal camp site to an area where they will undergo rigorous training in the traditional ritual customs. When they return to the village, their drawings will have completely changed. Prior to initiation, the children draw a man as Western children would draw him; but after initiation, a young man or an adult will produce stylized figures (79a) in the specific tradition of this region. Apparently, the structure of art has many similar, basic characteristics which appear universally, until strong cultural influences lead to specific culture-bound traditional patterns which have spiritual meaning within the cultural setting of a certain group. We can recognize that the primitive art styles of Africa and Oceania show similarities (110a), but specific differences exist between African and New Guinean art. We take language differences for granted, but laymen are often puzzled when they attempt to contrast the distinctive qualities of a Senufo mask of the Sudan and a Bambara mask of Mali (illustrations 6.7, 6.8). The artistic styles, however, are no more different than the languages spoken by the carvers of the masks. The difficulties that a Westerner has in understanding why two varieties of primitive art are different may be partly due to the fact that we are more attuned to verbal than to nonverbal forms of communication. Art is created for a specific audience, and deals with its specific needs.

The artist's sculptures, or his bark paintings, rely not only on their own visual impact but also on their symbolism and the ceremonies that may surround them. When taken from the dwellings and the spirit houses into the open for use in ceremonies, other nonverbal expressions (such as body movements and dance steps) are added to reinforce the message that the art works are to convey. Drums, horns, and flutes may complete the ceremonial drama. Words are hardly ever spoken, except for guttural sounds; shrill cries add excitement to the scene. Verbalization plays a secondary role in ritualistic primitive art. The world of the aborigine, the indigene, and even the ancient Greek, was created by action. In the beginning, it was not the *word* that created the Judeo-Christian world of Western civilization,[6] but the action, the primal battle between the sky father (Uranus) and the earth mother (Gaea) which led to the separation of unending space, of the spiritual and sacred from the earthly and temporal. Primitive art bridges the gap between the sky and the earth (13), as did the world of Greek mythology, when gods still wandered the earth.

Perhaps the most dramatic use of art as "protection" may be seen in the matter of death. The cessation of life is difficult to comprehend and to accept. Death without lingering illness is almost incomprehensible to a primitive society, and the spirit of the suddenly deceased creates particular fears and contradictory feelings. Funerary rituals attempt to break the ties with the deceased (124), resulting in elaborate taboos in separating the living from the dead. Eating, which has always played an important role in ceremonial life, particularly in feasts and in cannibalism, becomes regulated in order to control further contacts with the dead. In the Arnhem country, unrelated clan members spoon-feed the surviving family for twenty-eight days to protect them from the evils of the spiritual world which their mother or father has entered (19). In spite of the taboos, breaking contact with the deceased spirit is never fully achieved (see Case Histories 506, 511). Images of the ancestral spirits are carved to summon them, to placate them, and to obtain their good will (illustration 6.9).

When we see how closely art seems to be connected to life and death, we can comprehend that the melodramatic popular belief that the true artist must suffer so that he can create is not entirely without foundation. The sufferings of the artist originate in a conflict between his emotional need to create and the socially imposed discipline of his art form (31). The strong affect involved in primitive art requires a more rigid discipline, more specific rules, and more controls than exist in Western or Asian art. This discipline results in greater distortions, condensations, elaborations, and in less naturalistic representations. The distorted forms and unrealistic colors are strictly prescribed by culturally established rules. The distortions of the human body reflect the nightmare vision of the African or New Guinean world (31). Art in primitive societies enables the members to harness their fears without fully repressing them. The primitive artist creates according to the demands of his societal group; he remains anonymous, while the post-medieval Western artist interprets individualistically what he believes society should be. His identity is known, and he is either rewarded or scorned. The primitive artist conforms to the strict rules of his group, while the Western artist frequently attempts to be a moral force and to reform his society (illustration 6.10).

Art often concerns itself with social issues, whether it depicts the magic ritual of the prehistoric hunter, the escapism of the allegoric allusion to pastoral life in French Rococo, or the social protest of a twentieth-century artist. It may be considered a harmless safety valve (31) as long as the social setting in which it

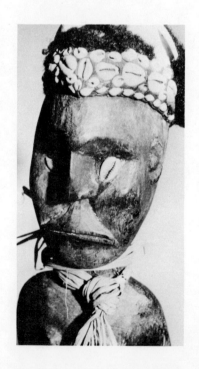

6.9. *An ancestral statue from the Sepik River, New Guinea.*

6. "In the beginning was the Word and the Word was with God and the Word was God...." (John 1:1).

is produced remains stable. It allowed the minnesinger and troubadour to express his love for the noble beloved; channeling his affection through song and poetry not only protected him from the anger of the feudal lord but it also brought him acceptance and shelter under the same roof with the chaste lady. The political satire of Beaumarchais in France's prerevolutionary days, and Brecht's plays during the German Weimar republic, were tolerated by their opponents until the social crisis which they anticipated erupted. At that point, revolutionary thought, which had expressed the unacceptable in the guise of art, was recognized as dangerous to its society and was ruthlessly repressed.

The appeal of art lies in its ability to take a repressed conflict (regardless of social acceptability) beyond the period of the artist and his cultural barriers (31). The artist's success lies in his ability to convey significant feelings even when they shatter social taboos, to make the controversial acceptable through the artistic use of form and technique. In contrast, the mere craftsman or technician shrewdly recognizes the popular appeal of his work, but remains relatively uninvolved and detached from it. His technique plays on the superficial emotionality of his audience, disguising little of their conflicts, expressing acceptable conflicts by obvious means, and completing the answer for the conflict which he has staged.

In today's art, the skilled technician is likely to deal with the feelings of isolation and loneliness in the contemporary world by manipulating spatial-temporal relationships, perhaps emphasizing a vast emptiness and the senseless ticking away of time with melting watches: spelling out the details of the conflict. Such melodramatic techniques suggest lack of emotional involvement of the adept virtuoso. The motivation of the technician would be incomprehensible to the tribal artist, who creates images of intense spiritual significance, even if he creates traditional designs transmitted from his ancestors. He must be involved and must involve his audience. His creation pierces the outer shell of the tribesman's defenses and stirs his inner conflicts by magic powers, appealing to the fears within him. Significant art, regardless of its period, challenges the eternally unfulfilled part of us which is seeking gratification, but stops short of its complete fulfillment. It remains tantalizing, almost reaching a climactic solution which is never spelled out completely. The ultimate gratification remains the responsibility of the viewer.

6.10. Guernica *by Pablo Picasso is on extended loan to the Museum of Modern Art, New York, and is used with permission.*

7.19. Crows in the Wheatfields *is among Van Gogh's final works. Used by permission of the Stedelijk Museum of Amsterdam.*

7.2. *A patient at an early stage of personality disintegration dramatizes the fragmentation of his world.*

7

Schizophrenic Expression and Western Art

"Seldom or never have I had a patient who did not go back to neolithic art forms to revel in evocations of Dionysian orgies."
—C. G. Jung

Jung (71b), comparing Picasso's art to the graphic expressions of psychotic patients, seems to be considerably involved in the patients' distortions and the seemingly "grotesque unconcern for the beholder;" as an analyst steeped in traditional Western art, he saw these characteristics as symptoms of madness. His essay, written in 1932, relates the creativity of Picasso and James Joyce to the style of the schizophrenic. Jung's remarks received considerable unfavorable criticism, and he later clarified his statement. He had meant that while there appeared to be similarities between schizophrenic and contemporary art, he considered Picasso's paintings to be analogous to those of his patients. The loose application of psychiatric diagnostic terms to artistic creativity has confused the definition of art. Many authors have insisted on relating creativity to mental aberrations; however, we believe that creativity and mental illness are two entirely different facets of human functioning. We agree with Jung's metaphor that the "descent to the Mothers"[1] delves into processes remote from consciousness. It enables the total man to merge fragmented elements into new, original creations.

1. Jung refers to Goethe's *Faust* (Second Part, Act III) descending to the World of the Mothers where Helena reigns. Having caused the Trojan War, she is aware of her destructive beauty. She cannot rest in eternity and it makes her deny that beauty and happiness can exist together. She invites the entering Faust to be close to her, but as she embraces him her physical embodiment evaporates—only her gown and veil remain. The scene symbolizes the universal conflict arising from the desire for fulfillment; satisfaction does not last beyond the

The fragmentation of thoughts is in fact neither pathological nor artistic in itself; it may be the first stage either of personality disintegration or of creativity (35). It is the subsequent capacity to link the fragmented concepts into integrated entities, meaningful to their sociocultural setting, which produces art. The pathological aspect is seen when poorly articulated structures lacking societal appeal and serving only the individual's needs escape to conscious levels. We have to accept a clear-cut distinction between the creative process, however radical and even bizarre it may be, and the emergence of inarticulate, incohesive pathological structures. Only then can we consider the creative to be distinct from the psychotic.

Jung emphasized that the psychotic's descent to the levels of the unconscious is neither aimless nor purely destructive. The descent follows "the journey through the psychic history of mankind which has as its object the restoration of the whole man;" it is an aim that the psychotic tries to achieve by the process of restitution but which he never achieves sufficiently as long as he remains mentally ill.

The unsuccessful attempts to establish an equilibrium between disintegration and integration create a world that is in constant flux. It is a terrifying experience to the schizophrenic as he feels his personality disintegrating (130). His expressions lend insight into the disturbed structure of his world; it is a world of vast wastelands, of distorted shapes, of extreme isolation and loneliness, of time that is almost standing still; a world in which no boundaries exist and from which there is no escape, in which superpowers rule, knowing every secret thought. But at the same time the patient's thoughts become equally and frightfully powerful, leaving him with a fearful responsibility that his thoughts and actions are of cosmic magnitude.

The schizophrenic's conscience, being self punitive and self destructive, establishes rigid and arbitrary rules (22). As the New Guinean or African feared the wrath of his ancestors if he should fail to show them proper respect, the schizophrenic of any culture (see Cases 506, 510) needs to defend himself against the threats that he projects as coming from others, but which actually arise within his own personality.

Patients may be painfully aware of their incomplete and futile attempts at reintegration. A twenty-year-old schizophrenic woman, feeling frustrated in her striving for integration, was highly disturbed by her feelings of being "amoeba-like . . . jelly-like without substance, floating through space" (Case 133). During the treatment sessions, she sat immobile with a look of dejection, fearful of physical disintegration if she should speak or move, behavior similar to the ritual requiring the Mikado to remain immobile while sitting in his throne room to prevent his movements from destroying the equilibrium of the world. Her actions and behavior became dominated by her inability to differentiate between herself and her environment. She feared the omnipotence of her thoughts, yet she felt helplessly controlled by the thoughts of others. She panicked as she believed that the forces of gravity had dissolved and that spatial boundaries would disintegrate; she felt defenseless as she feared losing her identity by being without substance. She painted an almost endless number of oils, stereotyped in structure. They were silhouettes standing on a baseline, isolated in space without interweaving back-

moment of triumph. Only before the goal is reached do hope and desire remain, lending the impetus to seek ways to achieve. Faust, symbolizing man in a constant search, is condemned when he wants time to stand still (14c). In his continuous pursuit, he delves into the depths of unconsciousness, attempting to create new forms. Jung's metaphor coincides with the stated view of creativity as a linking of unstructured fragments emerging from the unconscious into new original concepts (see Chapter 3).

ground, similar to the spatial conceptions of the primitive (Illustration 7.1). The movement and the composition of each painting indicate that the patient was sophisticated enough artistically to be able to paint more integrated pictures. Not varying from the same basic structure reflects the patient's feelings of isolation and unrelatedness to her environment, leading ultimately to the loss of identity.

The case histories of schizophrenic patients show a continuous inner struggle to abolish an aribtrary control system (22), reflecting the patient's own overpowering conscience that his life experiences have imposed on him. The inconsistencies and the severe rejections of his formative years may have produced feelings of inadequacy, dependency, and unrealistic obligations to others. These early experiences perpetuate beliefs of being unable to rely on one's inner resources. The individual feels controlled by the smothering, overprotective or excessively punitive parental authority. The strict reign of parental figures forces him to absorb their attitudes and make them part of himself; it enables him to anticipate possible disapproval or avoid being made to feel guilty. But in protecting himself, he identifies with the fearful or overprotective parental authority. The early controls of his overly demanding conscience make him believe that independent action or self-assertion is forbidden and will be met with severe censure. They prevent him from separating himself from the image of demanding authority figures and from forming independent concepts. These personality features may remain dormant until adolescence or adulthood. Later, emotionally disturbing experiences (often only minor events) may activate an overwhelming concern with alien, outside influences and controls. The rigid demands made on the patient early in life surface, causing intolerable anxiety to intrude upon him from every direction. In attempting to find relief from the all-pervasive threats, he focuses on specific, often arbitrary sources of danger. He makes a defective adjustment by forming delusions of being controlled by external forces occurring in a limited area, instead of diffuse feelings of panic penetrating all his functions.

7.1. *Early in the course of her disease, a schizophrenic woman (USA) painted these moderately elongated, shadowy figures.*

One of our patients, an eighteen-year-old college student, became increasingly frightened of being controlled by a powerful outside force, believing it to be the voice of the President of the United States. Every evening, "the voice" threatened that he would be drawn and quartered because he had betrayed his country. It accused him of treason by thinking of treason. The President had computerized the patient's thoughts and was able to read his mind. He heard the President accuse him of having caused floods and crop failures whenever he masturbated. His hallucinations caused him to panic—every day at sundown he expected to be killed. There was no trial to be held and there was no escape from his fate. The fact that he was still alive in the morning did not relieve his fears, but only made him more convinced that the voice was cruel in prolonging his torture.

The patient's childhood had been filled with emotional insecurities and threats. His father's business travels had caused him to be away from home during most of the boy's formative years. The boy became very attached to, and yet fearful of his mother, who was inconsistent in her relationship to him. She was at times affectionate, but was at other times a very strict disciplinarian, producing in him feelings of guilt and obligation. She used religion to make her son afraid of a God who saw and knew every wrongdoing; he would be punished for the slightest disobedience and suffer eternally by being sent to Hell. He developed a highly confused image of his mother as someone to be loved but also feared, an inconsistent image not providing the stability for adequate emotional growth. This lack of constancy (22) prevented the patient from forming a clearly defined concept of the important dominant parental figure. His feelings toward his mother oscillated between love and fear, and in absorbing her attitudes toward him, he developed a poorly defined self-image, inconstant and vacillating between being omnipotent in his ability to make rains and cause floods, and being helplessly tortured by an all-powerfuld and cruel authority.

The content of the patient's delusions is culture-bound, triggered by the immediate political events of the country, specifically the Watergate affair. His pathological personality structure, his disproportionately powerful, punitive conscience, and his disintegrated *ego boundaries* caused a reaction characterized by magical thinking. It differs from the magical thinking of tribal societies in that his beliefs are not shared by others, and express only personal, solipsistic needs. For him, reality is highly subjective and exists within his delusional system, in spite of any opposing objective evidence.

Early Disturbances in Spatial Concepts

While the patient just discussed submitted to the demands of his overwhelming pathological conscience, even to the point where he expected to be tortured to death, another patient (Case 115) attempted to defend himself against his feelings of rejection and the subsequent isolation by fantasies of destroying the world, which he considered an "insolvable mess." This second patient was a young man of superior intelligence; he had been admitted to one of the country's most prestigious universities at the age of seventeen. His family background revealed many emotional insecurities. The father, financially very successful, had always been emotionally aloof and distant in his personal relationships; it impressed the patient as rejection. Comparatively late in life, the father had married a beautiful woman twenty years younger than he. The young boy was deeply attached to his mother, who alternated from overwhelming the child with attention to suddenly turning her interest to someone else, "dropping the little boy." The patient believed that his mother considered him a toy that she would "drop when she became tired of it or pick up at her fancy." Dependent on his mother's attention, he waited passively for signs of being wanted, but was fearful that making demands for her attention would result in disapproval and rejection. He became a timid child, not daring to assert himself. He realized at an early age that only his intellectual achievements brought him persistent recognition, and this resulted in continuous needs to prove himself—"I like thinking better than anything." He spent most of his time alone, reading far beyond his age level. Vivid fantasies began to preoccupy him during his adolescence. He imagined being an inventor controlling the world with masterful designs, or rescuing a beautiful woman being held prisoner by a clever opponent whom he successfully defeated. His fantasies, thinly veiled disguises of his own desires and life experiences, protected him from dealing with a painful reality.

At the age of twenty, he was drafted into military service. He bitterly resented the control exercised by his superior officers. He did not express any open hostility and carried out orders punctiliously, but he withdrew more and more from the unpleasant environment. His behavior became bizarre: he mixed pieces of military uniform with his civilian clothes; he made unfounded reports of suspicious behavior of military personnel to his superior officers. Eventually, his mental illness was recognized, and he was hospitalized. When interviewed, he said that he was being observed by an elaborate foreign spy network that wanted to kidnap him because he had invented a system for controlling the actions of the entire population. This concretion of his disintegrating ego boundaries made it increasingly difficult to differentiate his thoughts from environmental influences. The patient's ideational processes were fairly well integrated; in spite of a tendency toward lengthy circumstantiality, it was possible to follow his thought without difficulty. His affective response, however, appeared to be more severely disturbed. In spite of the intensity of his delusions of wanting to destroy the world, he expressed them in a detached, monotonous voice, exhibiting little emotional concern. The contrast between the highly disturbed content and the flat tone was striking, a significant characteristic of the schizophrenic.

The patient's world was fragmenting. As in the previous case, and as is characteristic of the schizophrenic, the boundaries of his personality, like the objects in his environment, seemed to disintegrate (Case 115). He had fantasies of "mixing a thousand Cadillac engines into the brains of all the people in (his home town) and throwing them from the face of the earth . . . they (the engines) start running at terrific speed . . . flying upward into the sky . . . spinning and spinning."

He began to paint spontaneously, his graphics reflecting his delusional preoccupations. The first watercolor shows a globe in space, split apart by two bolts of lightning. As he talks about his watercolor, his voice is calm and detached, in marked contrast to the disturbed content. He verbalizes his feelings of frightful isolation by stating, "Are we not all a group of people together on a small planet surrounded by the mystery of vast interstellar space? (illustration 7.2) Are we not all brothers; But, oh God, how we act towards one another! The barbarism, the cruelty, the hate, the smallness . . . the small hate. Is there any hope at all? . . . [He concludes] to tear apart with my bare hands. . . . I would like to destroy this whole god damn little world."

The next watercolor consists of a flag with horizontal stripes (illustration 7.3). The design is similar to that of the American flag; however, the number of stripes is increased and the colors are yellow and black. On the left side, in place of the fifty stars, is a human figure suggesting a woman whose contours appear to be melting away. The patient's comments reveal his anger and helplessness over

7.3. *The same patient expresses his conflicts in his drawing of a woman melting away. A modified American flag forms the background.*

7.4. *A male figure dramatizes feelings of rejection by holding back the heart that is leaving his body. Early schizophrenic disintegration, U.S.A.*

feeling rejected: "Jesus, the sight of a pretty woman is revolting. At times, I would like to kick her to death. . . . Closeness, warmth, understanding, a common cause, God, I hate them. . . . Destroy it all violently. . . . Beauty [apparently a reference to his beautiful young mother], at times, I hate them all . . . they deserve nothing, they are nothing . . . they are worse than an empty nothing in space. . . . To destroy this whole rotten, filthy world, or, second best, isolate myself with a group like me, or at least not to be swine. . . ."

The patient's watercolors reveal his intense conflicts, his destructive fantasies, and his feelings of isolation. His father's aloofness may have motivated the young, attractive mother to seek emotional satisfaction elsewhere. The clinical history states that the mother's relationships to her son were inconsistent: at times, overaffectionate; at other times, distant and cool. He felt as if he were her toy, her attention to him being completely subject to her whims. He seems to view the inconsistency of the mother's behavior as an "unbearable, revolting situation" while "we could have built a beautiful world." He was utterly frustrated at having been suddenly deserted by his mother. He expressed, both verbally and by his graphics, a marked ambivalence toward women. Although he spoke in affectionate terms of beautiful women, of their "soft hair" and of the closeness and warmth which he felt toward them, he experienced them as dangerous and revolting. In his watercolor, he annihilated the world by painting the earth breaking apart, being struck by lightning, and he destroyed the woman of his second painting by melting her away.

The patient's graphics allow a degree of insight into his inner conflicts, but their cohesive and fairly well-integrated structures would lead us to expect that his personality structure is not severely fragmented. The disintegration of the conceptual borders, the globe breaking up under the bolt of lightning, and the melting girl's figure, give evidence that the patient's ego boundaries are threatening to disintegrate.

As schizophrenic illness advances, reality appears increasingly empty; patients become concerned with this change, and are acutely disturbed over having become unreal, depersonalized automatons in a flat and empty world. The schizophrenic fears the loss of his individuality; he feels faceless, unable to communicate, isolated among the masses. He struggles to make himself heard, desiring to speak a language understandable to everyone (148). He is perplexed and frightened by being alone, he feels exposed in a "country opposed to reality, where reigned an implacable light . . . leaving no place for shadow . . . an immense space without boundary . . . stretching emptiness. . . . I am lost in it . . . isolated." These comments were written by a schizophrenic girl. Graphics produced by a patient at this stage (Case 83) convey the anonymity of a partially faceless woman (color plate 2), or a desertlike landscape extending behind her, with figures becoming mere shadows (illustration 7.1).

The confusion and distress often experienced by the schizophrenic in a state of early disintegration is apparent in this patient's crayon drawing (illustration 7.4). He had recently been admitted to a psychiatric hospital. He appeared emotionally detached, unable to organize his vague thoughts; he expressed love for a girl living in his neighborhood but whom he had never met. At times he was enraged at himself for not being able to formulate the many simultaneous thoughts emerging into consciousness. This crayon drawing expresses his frustra-

7.5. *Severe fragmentation reflects a more advanced stage of personality disintegration. A dagger is barely recognizable among the fragments.*

7.6. *A ghostly apparition was drawn by a woman at an early stage of personality disintegration.*

tion. Such suffering appears in *The Shriek* by Edvard Munch (illustration 7.26), in which a sexless creature cries out silently at the fears of isolation. Our patient's drawing is no less eloquent in showing his feelings, but in his despair his thoughts disintegrate and become disorganized. The character in the drawing attempts to hold back the heart that is leaving his body; the girl's eyes are leaving their sockets; apparently she is indifferent to his feelings of love. The drawing seems to be overdramatized, which may be due to the need of schizophrenics to substitute concrete ideas for their failing abstractive abilities.

Advanced personality disintegration caused considerable confusion in a patient who had withdrawn psychic energy from reality contacts (Case 125). His world had become increasingly devoid of content, objects became less structured, details were lost. The distances between objects seemed to increase, and the effect of great vistas in his landscapes was emphasized by their emptiness (color plate 4). Individual figures appeared lost in the immense space around them; they were structured—drawn in their barest outlines or as silhouettes. As he talked about "resurrection," he painted a highly disturbed watercolor (color plate 3). At the bottom is a graveyard with tombstones; on the left, a hangman's noose; a white, ghostly figure floats from the graveyard into a dark sky which is filled by a threatening, luring face. The gigantic black face lacks familiar features. Its wavering contour, its staring eyes, and its white tusks make it more fearsome. It has also risen—as though sucked up by a tornado—from the graveyard. Below it, a long green snake is painted on a yellow background; its disproportionately small wing and two small legs in the center give it an unreal appearance. Farther below is what seems to be a black whale with a large open mouth showing its fangs; two orange circles indicate its eyes. At the other end of the watercolor is a red sun partly covered by black clouds. By naming the painting *Resurrection* the patient attempts to dramatize the anguish of his disintegrating, dying world and his attempts at restitution. He is concerned over his disintegrating future, which he anticipates with even greater fear than his present disturbed state. The floating and wavering images and their disproportionate size give an overall impression of confusion, in contrast to the earlier watercolor, which is more tightly organized.

Later, the patient's disintegration becomes more severe. The images in his paintings are more fragmented and hardly recognizable except for a few threatening objects (illustration 7.5). An isolated, curved dagger appears in the center; lurking eyes, an animal's face, a snake winding its way, a flattened figure on the bottom, again reflect the patient's fears. His concepts of the world have become more disintegrated.

The patient's illness had developed four to five months prior to his hospitalization. He had become increasingly withdrawn, expressing concern over his health. He began to read medical books and, later on, psychology textbooks, as he attempted to find a solution to the frightening changes taking place in his world. He felt he could not trust people, since they acted strangely around him. At times, he refused to eat, believing the food to be poisoned. Unable to explain his condition, he turned to the supernatural and to mysticism. When hospitalized, he showed mild thought disturbances, and his statements appeared mildly vague, circumstantial, and evasive.

Spectral figures drawn by another patient (illustration 7.6) illustrate the lifeless vacuum by which she felt surrounded. While depth seems defensively emphasized during the early stages of personality disintegration, other patients reflect the early signs of spatial distortion in their artwork by elongating their

7.7. *A regressed schizophrenic created this severely elongated figure. Courtesy of Leo Navratil. M.D., Priv. Dozent, Austria.*

7.8. *El Greco used elongation for artistic effect. His sinuous heavenly figures contrast with the normally proportioned mortals at the* Burial of Count Orgaz. *San Tomé, Toledo.*

concepts (illustration 7.7). On the same level of personality disintegration, the basic overall structure may still be fairly well integrated and organized but the figures tend to be shadowlike, silhouettes instead of full-bodied figures; they lack interaction with others, and are often displayed on a barren background (illustration 7.1). The contemporary art works of Giorgio de Chirico and Salvador Dali emphasize depth perception to the point of distortion. El Greco used elongation to stress the spirituality of his divine group, contrasting them with the naturalistically proportioned earthly attendants of Count Orgaz (illustration 7.8). The withdrawal of psychic energy by the early schizophrenic is often not yet severe enough to lead to pronounced distortions which would differentiate his graphics from those of the nonpsychotic. However, the difficulties in recognizing the pathology of a borderline schizophrenic patient are equally great to the clinician.

Subjective Space

As the psychotic disintegrates further, his contacts with reality become more and more reduced; familiar established object relationships become lost; his ability to evaluate the reality around him in relation to his inner self has been impaired. As he withdraws from his environment, he develops difficulties in differentiating his experiences, and in organizing them according to realistic values. The loosened concepts are unstable, being controlled by emotionally charged experiences that are not adequately tested against stable, well integrated concepts. Their specific characteristics are not properly defined and perceived; they are no longer placed in space according to their meaning or hierarchical order; the appropriate spatial distances between them are disregarded. Three-dimensional perspective, the ability to shade objects so as to give them a plastic dimension of depth, is lost. Figures appear flat, and often shadows are lacking (14b).[2] Simultaneously occur-

2. In Western fairy tales, in the mythology of the East, the loss of one's shadow is equated with the loss of the soul (80), often lost in bargaining with the Devil.

7.9. *A patient mixes planes in his painting to give a simultaneous but divergent view of the assembled objects.*

7.10. *Hospitalized after committing a number of criminal assaults, this patient draws transparent figures, and fills the empty spaces between them with sexual and religious writings. Courtesy of the Camarillo Hospital.*

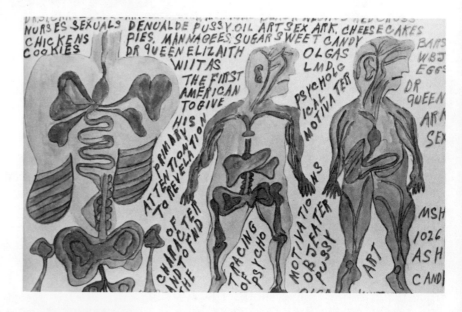

7.11. *Writings and ornamentation fill the empty spaces in this drawing of a transparent house, an example of the patient's fear of empty space, or "horror vacui."*

ring experiences and thoughts cannot be arranged in proper sequence. As conflicting and contradictory elements coexist, at the same time interfering with the formation of coordinated, integrated concepts of reality, accustomed relationships are dissolved and an invasion of extraneous concepts takes place (38). External (objective) and inner (subjective) reality become fused; reality can no longer be adequately differentiated from internal thought processes.

The loosened conceptual boundaries affecting a patient's view of himself and his world appear in the watercolor by a young American schizophrenic patient (Case 128, illustration 7.9). The customary relationships of the objects to each other are changed; they are seen from divergent viewpoints simultaneously, contrary to conventional Western art. A piano is seen from the top, a fence in side view, and a transparent head in profile, showing a sparse few hairs on the top. The artist exposes the brain, the eye, and the bone structure, including the vertebrae. Such an exceptional view cannot be attributed to amateurish attempts by an inexperienced painter. Rather, it reflects the patient's view of his reality at that given moment.

The structuring of space by mixing various perspective planes seems to express emotionally conflictive material (14b). The transparent head is, according to the patient, "a jaw bone and the teeth with a few cavities . . . it adds a feeling of emaciation and a feeling of the destruction of the body, giving the impression of blowing the top. . . . I first drew the piano . . . the man (invisible) on the piano is Dad. . . . It indicates synchronous harmony but with a wall of unhappiness between us with the light-sound passing through the knot hole (in the fence). . . ." The purple fence in the center of the watercolor is painted in slanting side view to emphasize the separation between the patient and his father, the unsatisfactory relationship borne out by the clinical history. The patient emphasizes that the moon is surrounded by a red ring—"The moon will turn to blood. . . ." According to folklore, an eclipse turns the moon to blood, significant as a bad omen (80). The patient had often expressed concern about his father's indifference, which caused him to feel insignificant. His poor self-image was intensified by the ambivalent, unpredictable behavior of his mother. Unable to establish secure relationships, he withdrew from reality. He sought security by joining various religious groups. At first, he became a Christian Scientist, but found no solution to his personal conflicts; then he converted to Catholicism, also without lasting satisfaction. In an effort to shut out his irritating surroundings, he spent hours cloistered in his room, reading the New Testament. He neglected his personal appearance; his face was unshaven and his clothes were unkempt. He seemed unresponsive to others, often staring into space. His detached behavior was interrupted by sudden, inprovoked outbursts. His thoughts appeared disconnected, his affect was flat when not broken by his outbursts.

This patient had become unable to handle the underlying emotional conflicts that weakened his personality structure, or to deal with his concept of an external reality that he could no longer tolerate. As he was not able to find adequate solutions to his conflicts, he withdrew into himself, and the world around him disintegrated. Cohesive spatial relations dissolved: objects were no longer linked according to their objective appearances, but their relative positions were determined by their emotional significance. The patient became aware of the disintegration of his personality, and he spoke of the destruction of the body. As the boundaries of his concepts fell away, their inner structure became exposed, making the objects transparent and distorting their perspective. He painted them according to what he saw as their characteristic essentials; he presented the fence

7.12. *Vertical projection: a patient divides the space in his drawing into several layers.*

and the piano from viewpoints that made them most easily recognizable, the fence from a side view and the piano from a top view. The objects are not integrated into a cohesive whole, but appear in their separateness; their proportions are inaccurate. The mixing of perspective planes does not happen by chance, but reflects a specific level of spatial disintegration to which the personality regresses (Table 2).

Another patient, a black man in his mid-forties, had spent most of his adult life in mental hospitals or in penal institutions, where he had been commited on several occasions for criminal assaults (Case 138). He was diagnosed as a schizophrenic, and his prognosis was considered poor. Clinical symptoms revealed his preoccupation with violent sexual attacks on women. Severe identity problems caused him to have fantasies of being white. His affect was *labile*, his thought processes and emotional instability reflected his disintegrating control over his personality functioning. His loosened concepts lacked adequate boundaries, reducing the inherent limits and differentiation of concepts. They still remained separate, individual concepts, but the intrinsic limitations of external reality were removed, and objects became transparent to him.

He painted numerous stereotyped watercolors of white men and women—their bodies were often rudimentary, the facial features incomplete, the eyes and mouth forming empty ovals; the arms were often not painted. The spaces between the figures were filled with disconnected writing, mostly of sexual content mixed with religious statements. Most significantly, all of the figures were transparent: the outline of each figure was proportionate in size and shape, but the lungs, the intestines, the spinal column, the pelvic bone and the bones of the leg appeared; they were distorted, but identifiable (illustration 7.10). Similarly, transparent bodies exposing the vital organs of animals appear in Australian rock paintings (Chapter 6).

The crayon drawing of another schizophrenic patient (Case XG) demonstrates that dissolved reality boundaries affect various aspects of space. The drawing is completely filled, leaving no empty spaces (horror vacui). The basic structure, a

92

7.13. *The "Bride of Jesus" and the bridge to "The Tree of Life" are organized on a baseline by a patient at an advanced stage of schizophrenic regression.*

large house, is transparent (illustration 7.11). The outline of the exterior of the house is maintained; it shows gray walls and a blue front door with a pink gable; the windows and the roof are shown simultaneously with some of the furniture in the interior. The disintegrated conceptual boundaries permit the observer to see through the wall. In addition to this transparency, the furnishings within the house are placed on top of each other, in vertical projection (Table 2).

Vertical projection seems related to the progressive disintegration of the schizophrenic personality, resulting in further loosening of spatial organization. As the transparencies had disregarded the surface boundaries of objects, enabling the viewer to see through the walls, the loosened integrative frame places them in sequence on top of each other (14a). The altered structure leads to a stratification of space as it appears in the next watercolor (illustration 7.12). The patient expresses the stratification in a concrete manner through a spiritual message: "The supremely Divine: Confucius or Buddha, the Past Master of Everything [is placed] in Heaven," in the upper part of the watercolor. The three figures, vague in their outline, appear elongated. Heaven is separated from the lower third by "dividing the space between Heaven and everything below Heaven." The lower part seems to deal with earthly functions; the exploding center is a "sewer," according to the patient; outhouses on the right are drawn in three-dimensional perspective; human figures appear on the lower right and left. The patient, preoccupied with distorted spiritual values as are many schizophrenic patients, paints elongated, upward-striving figures of vague shapes, while the earthly figures are more realistically proportioned and are arranged in a three-dimensional order. The patient's drawing appears to portray a transition from fairly realistic features to the upward striving, spiritual, and less structured upper part of the drawing. The vertical projection appearing in the patient's graphics reminds one of the stratification of spatial structure seen in East Indian paintings (120) and it is also characteristic of the school of mannerism (El Greco's *Entombment of Count Orgaz* or the paintings of Michelangelo's later period, such as the *Last Judgment* in the Sistine Chapel), symbolizing the separation of heaven and earth.

The conceptual aspects of the drawing correspond to the level of the patient's personality disintegration. He had always been a reserved, somewhat withdrawn person with relatively few friends, but he was able to make an adequate adjustment until he entered the military. He complained that others there ridiculed him by mimicking him and insinuating that he was a homosexual. Whe he was examined at the mental hospital, his affect seemed inappropriate, indifferent, and apathetic; his thoughts were disconnected and vague and wandered aimlessly from subject to subject. He was evasive when questioned about his suspicions. In spite of his apparently considerable feelings of insecurity, he presented himself as condescending and arrogant. He was depressed, and he attempted suicide by hanging himself by the belt of his robe; he was revived, but only with considerable difficulty. His psychiatric condition was diagnosed as schizophrenia, *paranoid* type.

As a patient's psychotic disorganization becomes more marked, the spatial structure of his graphics regresses to objects resting on a baseline, the most primitive state of conceptual organization (14a). The objects are built on a single horizontal line which usually runs through the lower third of the paper and extends across its entire width. A highly regressed schizophrenic patient (Case 51) painted a blue band representing a river in the center of a watercolor (illustration 7.13). She added a rigidly drawn female figure dressed in yellow. The figure, whom she identified as the "bride of Jesus," stood motionless, with an expressionless, masklike face. The patient connected the figure, by a semicircle penciled in a thin line, with the tree on the other side of the river. This was the "tree of life." The spatial structure of this watercolor is characterized by the positioning of all objects on a single line, the baseline (50). At the time of this painting, the patient had been psychotic for more than five years; she was *regressed*, hallucinated, and indifferent, showing little variation in her emotional expressions. Fearing reality, she lived a life of fantasy, believing herself to be the bride of Jesus who stands on one side of the crystal-clear water and is united with the divine tree of life by the bridge. The daughter of a Baptist minister, she was familiar with the New Testament; she was attracted to the Book of Revelation, where, in the twenty-first chapter (9), one of the seven angels refers to the "Bride, the wife of the Lamb," the Lamb symbolizing Christ (69). The patient's thought processes, like those of many schizophrenics, are reduced to concrete interpretations; in her delusions of being Jesus's bride, she finds the satisfaction and acceptance of which she is otherwise deprived. The patient's fantasy life exhibits thought patterns characteristic of severe schizophrenic personality disintegration. The space in her drawings corresponds to the earliest level of organization.

The only stage beyond such early spatial organization appears in the form of inarticulate structures of concept formation (35). As psychic energy is further withdrawn from the integrative capacities of the personality, the conceptual process becomes highly inadequate. Only fragmented, ill-defnied structures reach conscious levels (Chapter 3). Their forms are poorly controlled, unshaped, coarse, and lacking in nuance; they are vague and poorly delineated; if they appear with other fragmented concepts, the new fragments seem unrelated and out of place (Table 3, illustrations 7.14 and 7.38).

Eventually, advanced schizophrenic withdrawal makes reality contacts highly tenuous; the painted objects disintegrate beyond distortions, elongations and transparencies, to a stage where the borders of concepts dissolve and the concepts become completely fragmented. The patient's clinical behavior shows a profound indifference to the environment; he will hardly respond verbally, and appears

7.14. *A Western schizophrenic draws inarticulate structures.*

severely withdrawn and uninterested in his own appearance. In extreme cases, he ceases to take care of even the simplest tasks; he has to be spoon-fed and needs assistance in every aspect of his daily life. At this stage, the regressed schizophrenic can no longer separate himself from his environment, and he becomes immersed in it, a state described as *oceanic feeling*. He conceives of the space around him as limitless, without borders; his spatial concepts are incohesive. His fragmentary graphics consist of short pencil or brush strokes, without any attempt at organization (illustration 7.15). No order, no single direction, dominates—a state parallel to the designs of prehistoric cave dwellers which Giedion described as "multidirectional space."

Table 3
Levels of Disintegration

Patient's Clinical Condition	Spatial Structure of Drawings
Beginning withdrawal of object relationships	Emptying space, shadowy figures; Elongations and distortions
Disintegration of the boundaries existing be-	Perseveration. Spatial relations destroyed
Inadequate balance between external reality and the self	Impoverished and condensed design; Mixing of planes; "X-ray" pictures (transparencies); Vertical projection
More advanced disintegration	"Horror vacui"; Fragmentation of concepts
Appearance of universal concepts	Inarticulated structures
Severe repression of relations to external reality	Baseline with vertical direction; Geometric designs; Abstract mandala-like designs
Feelings of undifferentiated oneness between the self and external reality	Multidirectional space, "scribblings"

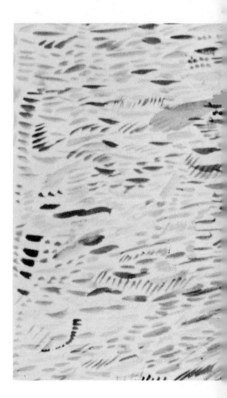

7.15. *Unorganized brush strokes reflect a "multi-directional" spatial structure.*

Because the graphic expressions of mental patients, particularly schizophrenics, have been compared with both primitive and contemporary art (109), structural changes in the works of recognized artists who have become psychotic may be of significance. The artist suffering from a disintegrating mental disease may create patterns of spatial disorganization like those of patients who lack artistic skill and creativity.[3] In order to evaluate the disintegration of an artist's work, we must consider his style as it appears when he seems free of clinical symptoms, and relate the disintegration seen in his graphic designs to the level of personality disintegration after he has become mentally ill.

The success and appeal of an art work depends on the balance between "aesthetic activity and regressive pleasure" (53). If the aesthetic activity (75) becomes overpowering and mere empty technique, it loses its creative function. Gombrich compares the significance of Botticelli's *Birth of Venus* with *The Birth of Venus* by A. W. Bouguerau, painted in 1879 (illustration 7.16). The central theme has remained basically unchanged, but the nineteenth-century painting is slick, forcing the painter's concepts on the viewer without eliciting his creative

3. By raising this issue, we do not want to inject the problems of artistic value; in our opinion, this is entirely independent from the issue of spatial organization. Twentieth-century artists Picasso and Braque have produced "non-objective" art works as Bosch and Breughel created surrealistic paintings. Such art works may show a spatial structure, willfully conceived, not dissimilar to that by psychotic patients. They use regressive patterns to express underlying social issues, but the designs remain cohesive in spite of their intentionally regressive forms (illustration 3.2).

thoughts. If, however, the balance tilts too far toward the other pole, toward regression, art loses its societal appeal and no longer strikes a responsive chord in the viewer. The psychotic's productions, lying on the other end of the spectrum, express regressive conflicts and needs without the necessary artistic integration. He uses graphic forms of communication but they are not works of art. The creative artist must successfully integrate the private meanings of his inner needs with the visual and spiritual needs of his audience. Only when he reaches a successful balance between regression and aesthetic attitude can he create a work of art.

Just as we are concerned with the interpretation of reality by schizophrenic patients as experienced and reflected in their graphics, we are also concerned with the effect of psychotic disintegration on recognized artists who become mentally ill. For purposes of comparison, we studied only those painters who have been hospitalized themselves. Since psychiatric treatment facilities were almost nonexistent prior to the last century, we shall limit our cases to the late nineteenth and the first half of the twentieth century. We shall select painters whose psychiatric illnesses have been medically diagonsed. In order not to invade anyone's privacy, we shall restrict our search to artists whose personal comments have been published in the form of letters (143) and memoirs (65, 135).

In spite of the valuable contributions of these writings, we are fully aware of the difficulty of making a psychiatric evaluation without having had direct contact with the individual to be evaluated. Van Gogh's letters or de Chirico's memoirs may contribute considerable insight into their concerns over financial problems or interpersonal relations, but they permit only a glimpse into their feelings and thoughts. The written reports are subject to the informant's needs; they may disguise his stress, his feelings of mistreatment, his conflicts, or his fears and apprehensions. Van Gogh consistently understates his mental illness but channels his despair and anguish into his financial problems. In a letter dated January 1, 1889, he apologizes to his brother Theo for the inconvenience he caused him in summoning him to Arles after cutting off his ear. A letter written a week after Theo's visit de-emphasizes Vincent's emotional stress: "My dear boy, I am so terribly distressed over your journey . . . for after all no harm has come to me, and there was no reason why you should be so upset" (143, letter 566). A few days later, he writes to Theo that he has completely recovered (letter 569a). In contrast, de Chirico's memoirs are filled with open resentments and complaints of physical suffering. His interpretations of the behavior of others, his feeling of persecution by other artists and intellectuals, indicate a highly subjective reaction that is seemingly based on his delusions. Additional information obtained from de Chirico's contemporaries reinforces the impression of existing psychiatric difficulties. But any interpretation of his mental condition by others has to remain subjective, depending on his contemporaries' feelings about the artist. Available data on the artists of past centuries are insufficient to allow even the most remote guesswork as to the nature of their illnesses.[4] El Greco's life, for instance, has been a source of considerable dispute; in spite of the lack of any clinical evidence, his elongated figures have been explained as being due to bad vision, astigmatism, epilepsy, and schizophrenia. It is, however, possible to obtain more reliable information about the mental illnesses of more recent artists.

4. A rare exception are studies about Franz Xavier Messerschmidt (1736-1784) who was, however, a minor artist (75). Attempts at a medical interpretation of his art had only resulted in incomplete distortions, not based on any form of pathology. They seem to be an attempt to stress the spiritual significance of his paintings.

7.16. The Birth of Venus *by A. W. Bougereau, French, nineteenth century. Musée de Luxembour, Paris.*

Adequate hospital records were not kept until fifty to seventy-five years ago, but the fact that a patient was hospitalized may justify the assumption that a psychiatric illness may have been present. Eventually, some artists improved and made a marginal adjustment that fostered a partial reintegration of their personalities. No longer severely disorganized, their loosened personality control allowed them to find new, original art forms still sufficiently integrated and cohesive to be of some meaning to the viewer. Without at least a partial reintegration of their personalities, their art would have become disorganized to the extent of being almost meaningless, as is apparent in one of Van Gogh's last paintings (F816, July 1890).[5] Other artists developed rigid defenses against the threatening disintegration that became stifling to any creative productivity. Nijinsky (111) the famous Russian dancer, drew rigid stereotypes through which he desired to communicate his feelings, but became highly frustrated by his failures when he felt that no one was aware of his emotional isolation. Other artists who had suffered emotional and mental disturbances attempted to defend themselves against the threat of disintegration by a rigid adherence to what they had accomplished in the past. They dared not seek new ways of self-expression. Their fears became so stifling that they were unable to produce any further original works, and began to copy their own paintings from earlier, more successful periods (135).

The creativity of Van Gogh, Munch, and de Chirico was not severely reduced until their illnesses had produced a severe disintegration of their personalities. They may have suffered extreme anguish and discomfort, such symptoms being very painful to the individual. It is only after the illness becomes highly advanced that the subjective discomfort is replaced by apparent indifference and apathy, resulting in artistic unproductivity.

Van Gogh's suicide, despite its extreme destructiveness, indicates a residual ability to exercise coordinated, coherent action. His last letters, expressing despair

5. The *F* numbers refer to the catalogue of Van Gogh's paintings by J. B. de la Faille.

and uselessness, are fairly coherent and lack any sign of marked disintegration. A severely regressed patient would not be capable of carrying out the integrated efforts which a successful suicide requires. At the beginning of a disintegrating psychosis, in schizophrenia or in an *organic psychosis,* suicide is not uncommon; it is usually related to the emotional panic caused by the patient's awareness that his personality is beginning to disintegrate—the fear of "going insane." Anxieties, apprehensions, and depressive feelings are most disturbing to a patient before he is severely disintegrated.

The changes in the artist's style may of course be due to his growth, but this growth must still be correlated with his emotional state. Any creativity has personal motivations; without these, the original incentive to create would be lacking, and contrived craftsmanship would replace artistic creativity. The artist's growth means not merely acquiring new technical skills, but also changing emotionally and growing as an individual. These factors frequently contribute to stylistic changes. However, pathological disorders may also cause stylistic changes. We are often hampered by insufficient data from gaining insight into an artist's inner conflicts.

Van Gogh's detailed correspondence over several years offers a rare exception because it supplies considerable information about the artist's concerns and his many insecurities. The lack of clinical case material makes an adequate psychiatric diagnosis difficult, particularly as the diagnostic criteria in psychiatry have drastically changed in the last eighty to one hundred years, as they have in every other field of medicine.

The information available about Van Gogh's early life indicates that he was affable and well-liked until he reached adulthood. After having been separated from his family, and disturbed over a disappointing love affair, a marked personality change took place. He withdrew from social contacts; his behavior became bizarre (107). In the letters to his brother Theo, he attempted to conceal his conflicts, and wrote little about his emotional upheavals. Vincent's psychiatric illness produced acute anguish, yet his personality disorganization was not severe. The many comments, articles and books on Van Gogh deal with the diagnosis and with his subjective symptoms, but are less concerned with the intensity of his illness. Van Gogh's works do not show severe disintegration. Only the highly disintegrated individual produces nothing but splotches that are disorganized and completely lacking in direction (Table 2). Van Gogh's personality disorganization, as indicated by his letters and by his behavior, confirm the impression conveyed by his paintings, that it was of moderate intensity from a psychiatrist's viewpoint. This is not to deny his severe subjective feelings of distress. He may have been quarrelsome, withdrawn, and bizarre in his dress and behavior, but he remained fairly adequately integrated in his total functioning. Nagera (107), in his psychiatric study of Van Gogh, says that the artist made an adjustment bordering on the psychotic. He continued to function on the same level until his condition declined further in December, 1888.

The spatial structure of Van Gogh's earlier paintings is three-dimensional, and the perspective is naturalistic. Only during the fall of 1888 does his handling of space change substantially. In his *Night Cafe* (illustration 7.17, September, 1888) and his *Bedroom* (F482, October, 1888) space is less naturalistically painted. The horizon is raised, making the floor appear to be pulled upward. Objects are seen from a vantage point higher than the traditional angle, and they appear in vertical projection. His adjustment problems, dating from his London years of 1873 to 1876 (107), fluctuated within moderate limits without affecting the structure of his paintings. It seems that only as his mental illness intensified in the autumn of 1888 did spatial distortions such as vertical projection become more evident. He projects his preoccupation with self-destruction by describing the *Night Cafe* as a place where one can "ruin oneself, go mad or commit a crime" (letter 534).

Patients whose graphics exhibit a level of perspective akin to that of Van Gogh's later work are still not severely disintegrated; in many cases, such as Case 101 (illustration 7.12), the patient has been ill for only a short time (this patient had been hospitalized for two months at the time the watercolor was painted). There are other patients, however, using the same spatial organization of vertical projection, whose personality disintegration is more advanced; the loosening of their personality boundaries is more severe and the projection of the objects painted is more pronounced and bizarre. The principal subjects of a crayon drawing (illustration 7.11)—the house and its individual parts—are not only two-dimensional, but the furnishings inside the house are placed on top of each other, disregarding any cohesive relationships. The degree of disintegration in this particular drawing, the arbitrary arrangement of the objects in space, goes considerably beyond the vertical projection of the previous one (101). It seems obvious, then, that the level of disintegration leading to vertical projection can be of vastly different intensity in different psychiatric patients. A patient can continue to function on a borderline level, not requiring hospitalization, or he may be fairly severely disturbed and disorganized in his thinking and actions (illustration 7.1).

Van Gogh's life became more disturbing, his conflicts often insufferable. His condition fluctuated from relative comfort to extreme distress when he felt that life had lost its purpose. His continuous emotional disturbances and mental suffering caused him to be hospitalized six times between December, 1888 and July, 1890, when he committed suicide. His art during that period shows similar extreme contrasts. His worsening personality disorganization made him feel increasingly confused, and he felt stymied in his efforts to paint. He replied to his brother's correspondence more sparingly, giving less and less information about his feelings and incapacities. His artistic work fluctuated considerably during that period, alternating from concise, sharply delineated, almost compulsively drawn designs, such as the watercolor of sailboats (F1429), to coarse pen and ink drawings (F1430 a, b, and c). One could attribute the variations in his style to the

7.17. *Some vertical projection is apparent in Van Gogh's* Night Cafe. *By permission of the Yale University Art Gallery, New Haven, CT.*

use of different media. But even in a single medium—his pen and ink drawings—there is considerable fluctuation from coarse (F1430a) to highly controlled designs (F1432). The oil paintings of his earlier period show even more marked variations, from well controlled brush strokes to the broad applications of the brush of his later works. *Potato Eaters* (F78, September, 1885), painted during his early career, is a classic example of his attention to fine detail and conventional spatial structure. In contrast, the oil canvases painted during the last month of his life, in July, 1890, appear disorganized, indicating reduced control, and the brush strokes are broad and coarse. As he felt rejected, he felt emotionally drained. His last letters (650, 652) show a mood of utter uselessness. The coming disaster is reflected in the disturbed spatial structure of his paintings. *Trees, Roots and Branches* (illustration 7.18) appears far more disorganized than any of his other works and sets off an eerie response in the spectator, as does his last, better-known painting, *Crows in the Wheatfields* (illustration 7.19). The same scene (F778), which he probably painted a few days earlier, is still cohesive and integrated, in remarkable contrast to his supposedly last painting, reflecting the wide variations of his feelings. His final work conveys his desperation. It seems as if the fields are in turmoil, the clouds driven by whirlwinds, frightening the crows into disordered flight. The coarse brush strokes of these oils lack control; the perspective has disintegrated—the roads go in different directions; the lack of integrative control becomes most obvious from the fact that the painter has painted two suns.

Van Gogh's art had a great effect on other artists for at least the next thirty years. Edvard Munch and Giorgio de Chirico were greatly influenced by his handling of space, which struck a responsive chord in their disturbed personalities. The spatial distance in their paintings is even more striking than in Van Gogh's, reflecting their threatening sense of isolation from the empty world around them. Munch's paintings show the same severe, almost fateful sense of isolation of the Nordic artist seen in Strindberg's plays and Ingmar Bergman's films. While de Chirico's work is no less menacing, its quality mirrors the lurking dangers that one associates with the Italian "bravo" (a hired assassin). The stagelike buildings extending almost endlessly into the distance create an atmosphere of apprehension; each step into the chimerical scenery seems to intensify the unseen danger. The emotional stress is acutely portrayed by combining the effect of distance simulating depth, with the unreal, mystical, two-dimensional buildings and illusory mannequins.

Both Munch and de Chirico were hospitalized for several months during their psychiatric illnesses. The available descriptions of their clinical conditions are vague. Their art, augmented by their own comments, seems to be a more reliable explanation of their inner life than the clinical information.

Giorgio de Chirico's writings confirm that he viewed life as he painted it. He states repeatedly in his memoirs that his paintings reflect his inner feelings. He was born in Florence in 1888; his family moved from their native Italy to Thessaly, a coastal province in Greece, where his father was an engineer building railroads for the Greek government. The elder de Chirico, of aristocratic Italian ancestry, was a suspicious but a gentle man (135). The contacts between father and son were full of contradictions. Despite mutual deep affections, their relationship was distant and cold. The father's influence, if not his control, is evident in the almost compulsive repetition of the train motif in de Chirico's art work. The incongruous title *The Child's Brain* (illustration 7.20), applied to a detached, brawny male figure, must have emotional significance for the painter since there is nothing in the content of the picture to suggest the title. Does it reflect his relationship to his father, in whose hands he may have felt like the ghostly shadows and mannequins of his paintings? In contrast to the father's aloofness, the mother was openly controlling; she was possessive and overprotective, always maneuvering to stay with her two sons, whom she accompanied on all their travels.

We can surmise from his memoirs that de Chirico's life was emotionally traumatic from its beginning. The family was displaced from a city proud of its history and its artistic creativity, to a rugged underdeveloped Greek province.

The family's aristocratic background, which Giorgio often stresses, and the father's prestigious position isolated the small child from social contacts; "acceptable" playmates were rare. His childhood experiences made an indelible impression on him, influencing his attitudes toward life, creating life patterns that he maintained through adulthood. Later in his career, he likened the attacks of the former friends of his surrealistic period to the attacks of "street urchins" in Thessaly who ridiculed and fought him, knocking him down with stones; both had been jealous of his superior wealth and intelligence. The influence of an austere father caused the boy to become aloof and distant in his personal relationships. De Chirico felt embarrassed when, as his father was nearing death, the old man embraced him. Giorgio developed personality traits—insecurities and anxieties—which were intensified by his overprotective mother and which plagued him later in life.

Giorgio, the older of two brothers, had a long history of "nervous disorders and an almost extreme crisis of melancholy." He complained also of suffering from a long and "painful intestinal disease" caused by emotional factors (135),

7.18. *Van Gogh painted* Trees, Roots and Branches *when he was undergoing a period of severe mental disintegration. Collection, Stedelijk Museum of Amsterdam, used with permission.*

but he continued to function in spite of these difficulties. When he moved to Paris with his mother and brother, he found ready acceptance among painters of similar artistic inclinations. He became an inspiration to the surrealists. As he gained recognition in Paris prior to World War I, his condition improved. And, according to Mary Crosland, the editor of his memoirs, as he became a successful painter he seemed convinced that he was the center of the universe and that everyone else was subsidiary, stupid and hostile toward him. These memoirs show that he was convinced throughout his painting career that intellectuals, artists, and critics had conspired against him whenever they disagreed with him.

But when he was drafted into the Italian army in 1915, he became severely disturbed. In the army, being an "aristocrat," he felt insulted and outraged when simple sergeants addressed him with a degrading *tu* or *toi*. The dignity that had meant so much to him, as it had to his father, was destroyed. Feeling helpless under the control of the less educated and less qualified, he turned his anger against himself; he developed a "deep melancholia"; the pains from his recurrent gastrointestinal disorder intensified and became intolerable. He never fully recovered from his melancholia. The treatment he suffered at the hands of common soldiers, who were placed in a superior position simply by their military rank, reactivated his childhood traumas of being humiliated by the street urchins of Thessaly. He spent most of the war in army hospitals, having been found unfit for military service, and his emotional and mental disturbances continued after his discharge.

De Chirico's paintings show a remarkable consistency in the handling of space. Arched buildings of antiquity, marble equestrian statues, and empty city squares create haunting images. The shallow fronts of his imposing buildings, bathed in blinding light, remind one more of Potemkin's sham villages[6] than of substantial

7.21. Enigma of the Hour *by Giorgio de Chirico. Collection, Peter Watson, London.*

6. Potemkin (1739-1791) was a Russian statesman and favorite of Empress Catherine the Great. In an attempt to conceal the weakness of his administration, he supposedly erected facades of nonexistent villages to impress the visiting empress with his prosperous performance.

7.23. Troubador *by Giorgio de Chirico. Collection, Carlo Frua De Angeli, Milan.*

7.20. The Child's Brain *by Giorgio de Chirico. Collection, André Breton, Paris.*

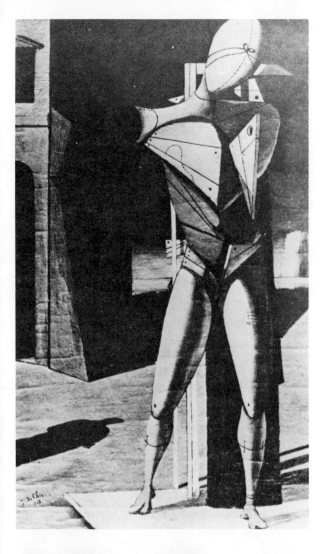

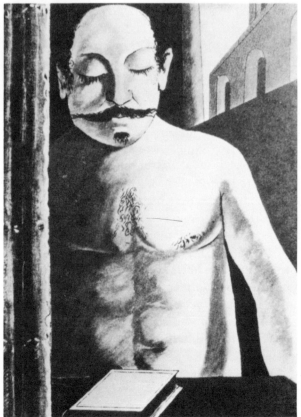

7.22. Nostalgia of the Infinite
*by Giorgio de Chirico. (1913–
14? Dated on painting 1911.)
Oil on canvas, 53¼ x 25½",
Collection, The Museum of
Modern Art, New York.*

three-dimensional buildings. They are specters of the past—denying life, they seem to make time stand still. De Chirico, aware of the ambiguity in his works (reflected in his attitude toward time and space), named his paintings *The Enigma of the Hour* (illustration 7.21) or *Nostalgia of the Infinite* (illustration 7.22). When human figures appear, it is usually in silhouette, their long shadows intensifying the feeling of being lost in the immensity of space. They are insignificant in their smallness, their shadows rather than their bodies catching the attention of the viewer. In almost all of the Italian piazzas de Chirico painted between 1911 and 1914, trains appear on the distant horizon; smoke billowing from the locomotive is the only sign of motion. Are they arriving or leaving? Are they delivering more of the ghostly shadows of men or are they departing, taking with them the only evidence of life? De Chirico's later work is peopled with mechanical mannequins (illustration 7.23), automatons, often without arms and with hollowed heads, underscoring his detachment from life. Art, in his opinion, requires a violent break with reality; thought must "detach itself from all logic and sense" (135). Space goes far beyond the limits of reality and life; it assumes a spectral and metaphysical appearance. Man does not live in space, but is a separate, lonely figure full of fears and anxieties. He seeks stability, even if unreal, in a living death which is as remote as a theatrical stage. People are puppets, toys mechanically guided and controlled.

The enigma of de Chirico's work may be partly answered in his painting *The Child's Brain*. This is an unusual title for a picture of a robust man who looks down with his eyes closed. Does the man refuse to see life around him? Is he a parent who governs without seeing the child or considering its needs, ruling according to the closed book before him? Is de Chirico referring to his father's influence, as the repeated use of trains would indicate? The same emotional climate found in de Chirico's paintings was expressed by a young schizophrenic girl (130). She viewed life as a "country, opposed to reality . . . an immense space, limitless . . . in this stretching emptiness, all is unchangeable, immobile, congealed . . . objects are trappings, placed here and there . . . I am lost in it . . . in absolute solitude, I am terrifyingly alone" (compare with illustration 7.6).

Even before entering military service, de Chirico had withdrawn to a world of isolation. The vast emptiness of his paintings vividly conveys the silence of a Mediterranean siesta that stretches beyond the limits of time and space. Quiet and privacy were very precious to the artist. He could not allow anyone to break into the isolation of his life. His isolation became the motivation for his creative inventiveness, a defense against the suffering and the "melancholic" turbulence which he felt and about which he wrote. His earliest memories were of being in a big room with a high ceiling, overwhelmed by its size and gloominess, his mother sitting in an armchair. Such feelings persisted throughout his life.

Eventually, strict adherence to the rigid system by which he had controlled his life and his art became impossible. His inventive creativity had once been a successful defense against his conflicts and the threatening disintegration of his personality; in his paintings he had discharged the anxieties that threatened to overwhelm him. When his pretense of superiority failed, however, his creative productivity ceased. After he was discharged from the military hospital, following demobilization in 1919, his fears and self-doubts became so overwhelming that he was no longer able to create original works. He copied his own paintings from earlier more successful periods or he restricted himself to an empty, neo-baroque style (135). When his former supporters and admirers, André Breton and others, attempted at first to dissuade him from this slavish and sterile reproduction of his past forms, he attacked the surrealist movement—of which he had once been a leader—in vitriolic outbursts. His friends did not understand that he had suffered severe emotional and mental disturbances, and that he had to defend himself against the threats of disintegration by a rigid adherence to what he had accomplished in the past, even to the point of self-imitation. He dared not seek new ways of self-expression. He abandoned his metaphysical surrealism and became a pseudoclassicist. Many surrealists and dadaists—Max Ernst, Tanguy and scores of others—for whom de Chirico had been a trailblazer, felt that he had betrayed them. He became a tragic figure: no one understood the helplessness that had forced him to revert to the traditional forms for which he originally had had only contempt.

His commitment turned from revolutionary art forms to techniques of painting. He hid behind a pedantic preoccupation with expanding on the method of lead oxide varnish and diluents for oil painting. Instead of the brilliant, powerful paintings of his metaphysical period, he produced canvases that his friends considered empty; they lamented his "collapse as an original creative artist" (135). His inability to create made him increasingly defensive. He took refuge in bizarre schemes: he purposely forged his own paintings, misdating them and later denying that they were his own (135). These deliberate attempts to create confusion about his earlier great artistry would seem to be a symptom of his illness. Feeling criticized when he became unable to produce reinforced his apparently paranoid system.

As long as the individual is only somewhat disintegrated, he can create, but only within a rigid, compulsive system. De Chirico's prewar work exemplifies his functioning within well-established, obsessive rules. His canvases are considered original, but the basic structural concepts do not vary from one painting to another and are rigidly maintained. The only change results from substituting his small silhouettes for mannequins. Artistic creativity ceases as the artist's personality disintegrates. When he attempts to defend himself against the disintegration, his productions show severe unproductive formalism, which is as evident in the productions of de Chirico as it is in the graphics of a New Guinean patient (see Case 110E).

Rigidly drawn designs of a spatial structure similar to de Chirico's but without the latter's artistry, were painted by a forty-three-year-old schizophrenic North American patient who had been hospitalized for nineteen years. In spite of the duration of his illness, he remained fairly well integrated; his speech was coherent as long as he restricted himself to short, superficial answers. When he tried to elaborate on a theme his sentences disintegrated and he became obviously confused. He displayed an air of superiority and aloofness characteristic of schizophrenic patients who attempt to protect themselves from rejections and emotional involvements which have proven to be traumatic in the past. His personality disintegration and subsequent isolation resulted in a painful feeling of separateness and in an awareness of a changing reality frightening in its vastness. At times, his bizarre, grandiose behavior broke through the restraints that he had (unconsciously) imposed on himself: "Hallelujah! I am one of the country's foremost spiritual figures, but I don't say that I am God." He needed no encouragement, stating that he was the "chosen messenger of God, a prophet."

The patient's watercolors are rigidly organized, composed of geometric forms integrated into sceneries. A dark blue sky with brilliant stars is a recurrent theme. The content varies from a precisely drawn room interior, which is geometrically arranged, to a moonlike wasteland filled with various unrelated objects (color plate 5). The masklike face (lower left corner) is next to a cross made of human bones with a bird perching on its tip; two hands top a bowl; further to the right are unidentifiable objects. Desertlike dunes fill the space to the horizon, on which stand several cones of various heights. The sky is dark green and filled with small stars; in the upper center appears the earth, which can be identified by its map of the American continent. The earth is surrounded by a Saturnlike ring. The relationship among the various depicted objects gives the impression of depth, but actually all the figures are two-dimensionally flat, with the exception of the bowl and a few unidentifiable rounded objects in the right lower foreground.

The four walls of a room in another watercolor (color plate 6) seem to over-emphasize space. The borders of the two side panels, the floor, and the roof seem to rush to the background; the seams of the four panels intersect on the horizon, giving the illusion of three-dimensional perspective. But the individual objects within the room are strictly flat and two-dimensional; starting with the volcano-shaped cone in the foreground, the pictures hanging on the side walls seem part of the wall; they do not stand out. The wall framing the background gives the effect of a proscenium. It is difficult to decide whether the two small human figures are standing or lying on what seems to be a platform. The backdrop has a repetitive dollar sign motif in addition to flat circles depicting stars. The patient's drawings seem to focus on spatial aspects of reality, but on closer scrutiny, the viewer retains merely an outline of individual objects that lack depth; they convey the artificiality of the painted flats of a stage set rather than a realistic three-dimensional effect.

Another schizophrenic patient produced several watercolors of similar design (illustrations 7.28–31). These give an unrealistic effect of depth by having surface lines converging into the background. In contrast to African and some twentieth-century Western art (such as Picasso), where the essentials are abstracted and combined to form new concepts, this patient's concepts are based on surface appearance, shielding him from close relationships and keeping others from penetrating his facade. The structural similarity to de Chirico's paintings of Italian city squares (illustration 7.24) is significant. The exaggerated depth emphasizes the

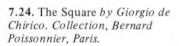

7.24. The Square *by Giorgio de Chirico. Collection, Bernard Poissonnier, Paris.*

isolation of the individual and conveys the aloofness of the schizophrenic patient, the same attitudes one senses in de Chirico's work. But unquestionably, the artistic abilities of de Chirico give his work much greater impact and convey meaning to others, while the schizophrenic is unable to elicit any significant response in his viewer.

Edvard Munch was another troubled artist whose psychiatric illness determined the style and structure of his art. His life was full of suffering, and he learned about the dangers of life early; he could not believe that even death offered peace. There was no escape for "eternal punishment awaited the children of sin in Hell ... Disease, insanity and death were the angels which attended my cradle" (65), and Munch could never free himself from their torture. His mother died of tuberculosis when young Edvard was five years old, followed by the death of his favorite sister several years later. His father practiced medicine in a slum area of Kristiania (later Oslo) after having been an army physician. With a generosity that created considerable financial hardships for his own family, he refused to accept fees from his poverty-striken patients. He was a shy, sensitive man with rigid religious standards who became even more reclusive and "melancholic" after his wife's death. His religiosity and fears bordered on insanity (65), and he was given to outbursts which resulted in severe punishments of his children. The bleak, puritanical home atmosphere was somewhat tempered by Edvard's aunt, who became the housekeeper and educator of the children after their mother's death. The aunt was a kind, gentle woman who recognized the young boy's artistic talents. She succeeded in persuading the reluctant father to permit his son to study art. Edvard's early paintings are naturalistic but darkly colored; the facial features and the hands exhibit signs of his later style. For example, the faces of his early oil *Family Evening,* painted when he was twenty-one years old, appear emptied of their features, a characteristic returning in many of his later paintings, particularly those painted prior to his psychotic episode in 1908.

The father's prayers that his son be saved from sinful attractions to women and alcohol made the young man all the more rebellious. He fell in love with a married woman when he was twenty years old, an alliance that caused him to suffer deeply. Of his numerous encounters with women, none were satisfying and all were painful, leaving him convinced that he should avoid marriage. His inability to find satisfaction in love influenced the content of many of his paintings. He painted women as vampires whom he thought had "nutcrackers in their thighs" (138). He saw a friend who had recently married as only "mush, ashen and toothless." He panicked when a girl whom he loved flew into hysterics, threatening suicide should he refuse to marry her, an experience that made him increasingly suspicious and ill-tempered. He had a number of barroom brawls in the following years. In 1905, he shot at a friend, barely missing him; he became frightened by his tendency to violence and left Norway. Continuing to be disturbed, he was hospitalized in Germany in 1907. In 1908, he entered a psychiatric hospital in Copenhagen, where he stayed for a year. He was a frightened man, depressed and plagued by delusions of persecution. His hospitalization was the culmination of a tortured life, filled with extreme apprehensions and fears. He was no longer capable of drowning them with excessive drinking or escaping from them by endless travels. While hospitalized, he wrote the poem "Alpha and Omega," articulating his love and fear of women that led inevitably to destruction.

Hospitalization seemed of some benefit to the artist. The macabre scenes of his earlier paintings, full of anguish and turbulence and preoccupied with sickness and death, receded; the new paintings were tranquil, decorative, and traditional. Facial

7.25. *The features of the faces in Edvard Munch's* Despair *are either barely indicated or totally absent.*

features—missing in his earlier work—appeared in the pictures that followed his psychiatric treatment. Yet his private life became more secluded. He isolated himself more than before, living alone, attended only by a housekeeper whom he kept locked out of his part of the house. Only rarely did he receive visitors, and he tolerated them only if they spoke little and listened to his discourse. As he talked, he avoided their eyes in order not to disturb his thoughts (138). His paintings became his children: rarely could he be persuaded to sell them, even at the high prices they brought in the galleries of Europe. He was convinced that his works and his creation protected him from the turbulence around him. When he was dissatisfied with a painting, he would whip it.[7] He felt that contacts with the world around him made him consume it. When Stenersen, one of his close friends, brought a stranger for a visit, Munch told him later that he had been forced to take the stranger literally into his mind and that only by reproducing the stranger on the canvas could he free himself.

Prior to the acute psychotic episode, Munch was constantly overwhelmed by fear of his environment and by his inability to handle personal relationships. The paintings of that period expressed the *Anxiety* (painted in 1894) that had terrified him, and he felt the *Shriek* (painted in 1893) that he could not utter. After his hospitalization, he used his paintings as a protective wall against external dangers. He assimilated the dangers; they became part of him, and he expunged them in his paintings. In what were apparently attempts to undo the threats that

7. Munch's treating his paintings as children might seem bizarre, but in other countries, as among the Ibos of southern Nigeria, the wood carving of the Alosi, nature spirits, are considered not representations of the spirits but the artists' children (144). Sacred spears of intricate design, Kakars, of the Sepik River people (New Guinea) are not considered to be carvings but actual relatives of the people; they are regarded as extremely sacred and are worshipped as family members (136).

he had felt, he reworked some of his old paintings. The dark colors of the oil painting *Despair,* originally painted in 1892 (illustration 7.25), convey the threat, the isolation, and the remoteness of the featureless face in the foreground. He reworked the painting in 1915 (seven years after his psychiatric hospitalization). In the reworked version, the colors are far less ominous; the man in *Despair* appears rejected but no longer annihilated into faceless obscurity by the destructive power of his feelings; he has achieved a personal identity. The isolation remains, but it has a human quality, and even in his despair, man no longer seems condemned to hopeless nothingness. Whereas de Chirico copied and misdated some of his paintings to mislead his critics and to throw his adversaries off his track, Munch reworked his paintings to undo the fears and apprehensions of his early years. Both artists used *denial* or *undoing,* as unconscious defenses against underlying anxieties.

Munch's paintings, more than the work of most other artists, record his feelings, his anxieties, his despair, and his isolation. These are best expressed in *The Shriek* (illustration 7.26), a motif that recurs, and from which he could not free himself until his hospitalization. In this dramatization of the artist's suffering (65), the figure shouts in helpless anguish, but no one hears him. He covers his ears with his hands to shut out intrusions, but without apparent success. As in many of Munch's works, the spatial structure reflects the painter's view of reality; the perspective of the painting is exaggerated, the face is almost blank, deprived of its features. Munch manipulated and distorted reality to satisfy the needs within him, but his personal imagery expresses the universal aspects that fulfill unsatisfied wants in the viewer. His art, which is full of his emotional conflicts, is terrifyingly personal (62), yet it touches the despair of others. In *Despair* he

7.26. The Shriek *by Edvard Munch.*

7.27. The Kiss *by Edvard Munch.*

expands distances to stress the frightening isolation and loneliness of man, and places an almost unbridgeable distance between the subject and the two indistinct anonymous figures in the background. But distance is Munch's only protection; permitting himself to get close, as in *The Kiss,* provoked the danger of being absorbed and melting away.

A painting by one of our schizophrenic patients (color plate 2), though lacking the artistic appeal and emotional impact of Munch's paintings, resembles them in structure. The twenty-five-year-old male patient had been hospitalized for four months, complaining that others were aware of, and able to control, his thoughts. This fear led him to avoid social contacts and become a recluse. Others regarded him as strange and were discouraged by his aloof, superior air. But he preferred to be alone, as it offered protection from his fears of the world around him, and he kept himself aloof as a protection against external hostile influences. His emotional withdrawal, as it appears in his painting, would have been considered contrived at the time, were it not for his disturbed clinical behavior. The composition, shading, and forms make his previous art training obvious. As his personality was not severely disintegrated, he maintained control over the form and structure of the painting. The woman's face in the foreground shows good shading, which makes it come alive; but in contrast, the right side of the face is empty. The face, half blank, is dramatically emphasized by its placement on a desert landscape on whose horizon rises a pyramid. The painting shows the ambivalent feelings of the patient: the partially blank face is disturbing yet otherwise almost serene; it lacks the distraught feeling of many of Munch's works.

Munch's defenses against his fears of being consumed by a hostile environment result in attempts to escape into isolation. He paints long barren roads leading into endless distances from which there is no return (62). The emphasis on spatial distance appears also in paintings by patients who have made a marginal adjustment, reflecting the beginning of their personality disintegration (Table 2). They

7.28. *Painted by a patient during an episode of acute schizophrenia, this picture exhibits elongation and emphasizes depth. Eyes observe from behind the clouds.*

can be highly self-conscious in their relation to others. As they watch with great apprehension their growing involvement with others, they keep their distance in order to protect themselves from emotional trauma. Being on the brink of an overt psychosis makes it difficult to handle minor stress, and this creates an atmosphere of impending disintegration.

The paintings of a twenty-two-year-old patient suffering from an acute schizophrenic episode (Case 112) have as their recurring theme a road leading to the horizon, all activities revolve around the road. The patient was hospitalized when he panicked after being approached by a homosexual. He became acutely delusional, agitated, restless, and unable to sleep. He believed that God spoke to him in an angry voice, accusing him of being a homosexual, although he had never had homosexual experiences or fantasies. While in the hospital he became withdrawn, had difficulties in concentrating, and was preoccupied with his inner thoughts, showing little interest in his surroundings. During interviews with his therapist, he talked fairly freely about his preoccupations and delusions, but his talk was vague and his thoughts rambled. When he was offered art materials, he started to paint without hesitation. His first watercolor established the basic structure of almost all of his work with the exception of his last picture. The space is divided by a road leading to the horizon which is extended on a horizontal line on the upper third of the paper. The initial graphic (illustration 7.28) shows a male figure, in the midst of the road, being attacked by two arms that emerge from the fields flanking the road, holding daggers in their hands. The blood dripping from the daggers seems to indicate that the figure—only its upper part emerging—has been stabbed. The man leans back as if to avoid further attacks. The road leads to a house on the distant horizon that is located in a valley between two mountains; the mountains are shaped like breasts. Two clouds appear in the sky, with eyes appearing behind each one, the left eye is blue and expressionless; the right eye is red and prominent and belongs to the indistinct green head of a threatening

7.29. *This painting has a structure similar to that of the previous one. However, the content is clearly more threatening.*

animal-like figure that the patient describes as being a monster.

The first illustration is followed by a scene of the same basic structure (illustration 7.29). The road has a black surface until it reaches a fence; behind the closed gate the surface changes to white. The two mountains that flanked the valley in the previous watercolor are now lifted into the sky; their shape is maintained but they appear as clouds. The eye that in the previous sketch peered threateningly from behind the cloud is replaced by an eye on top of an arched tree trunk. The left part of the trunk is rooted in a brown field plowed in parallel rows. The right side of the arch is short, ending in an arm holding a saw. It has started to cut into the tree, and the trunk below the cut is blood-red. A branch that spreads from the trunk ends in a skull (often seen as a warning on bottles of poison). Three arms emerge from the skull: the muscular upper arm holds a dagger in a threatening gesture; the hairy lower arms pour liquid from a bottle into a funnel that is connected to a tube surrounding the lower part of the red trunk. The bottom of the trunk also has a pair of hands, one holding the tube, the other gripping a cup. Upon questioning, the patient commented that the skull means death and the bottle contains poison. The saw tries to "cut it off [and] tries to get away from it." According to the patient's own comments, the tree represents the blood-red penis which has to be destroyed. It is apparently a substitute for the male figure that had emerged in the road of the previous drawing, where it was attacked by the two daggers. The tree is cut off by the saw, stabbed by the dagger, and finally poisoned to assure its complete destruction.

The patient develops the theme of annihilation in his drawings spontaneously and without outside encouragement. The omnipresent eye is struck by lightning (illustration 7.30); a crown of sparks radiates from it; blood drips to the ground, taking the shape of a very obvious penis with testicles, which grows in the location of the male figure that appeared in the first drawing. In this drawing, the phallus covers the road that leads into a tunnel between the first mountains,

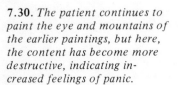

7.30. *The patient continues to paint the eye and mountains of the earlier paintings, but here, the content has become more destructive, indicating increased feelings of panic.*

112

showing a gradual decline. The first mountain range appears to extend like limbs into the foreground. Behind the first range, a second range appears, in the breast-like shape of the previous drawings. The patient's comments on this watercolor suggest that lightning struck "his eye . . . [and] blood falls from the eye on a road leading to the tunnel." The painting shows blood dripping on the road forming the penis; it is reminiscent of the Greek creation myths in which Cronos, the son of Uranus and the Earth Goddess Gaea, cuts off his father's penis at the urging of his mother. The penis falls into the sea and Aphrodite is born from its union with the oceans.

The patient's clinical condition had improved following the last watercolor; the picture "was something real to him"; it was part of his life, as he told his art therapist. Clinically, he was able to establish better social relations and appeared less withdrawn. He had become far less anxious and less agitated; the hallucinatory voices had subsided and he began to question their reality. The church in this picutre is the one where he was married (illustration 7.31). It had no doors and no windows, for he considered religion something private. The white road, no longer blocked by obstacles or threatening figures, passes the church and extends into the center of one of the blue eyes on the horizon. He stated that his wife's eyes were blue. The road leading by the church (which he considered a "private affair") seems related to the patient's personal relationship to his wife. The watercolor transmits an air of tranquility, no longer conveying the many threats of the earlier graphics. He followed the watercolor relating to his marriage with one named *Test Tube Baby* (illustration 7.32). In it, an embryo is submerged in a test tube and is connected by its umbilical cord to an eye; before reaching the eye, the cord becomes covered with hair; on the other side of the eye, it terminates in a hand with three fingers that supports the test tube. The patient commented that he had wanted to be a scientist and to have a baby in a scientific way, but that he should stop dreaming and adjust to life as it is: he should be with his wife and have children.

7.31. *As the patient improves, the content of his paintings becomes less threatening. While the spatial structure is similar to that of the other paintings, it contains no destructive elements, and obstacles no longer block the road.*

The patient's drawings and their sequence seem almost contrived, but they reflect the intuitive insight the schizophrenic has into his inner life and conflicts. Their content, as confirmed by his own statements, centers on his sexual conflicts. Being approached by a homosexual activated uncertainties over his sexual role. He reacted with panic, which precipitated an acute personality disintegration. His first watercolors depict the fear of annihilation at the beginning of his psychotic episode and the eventual calm when he realizes that the attack on him, symbolized by lightning striking his eye, did not result in the destruction that he had anticipated. Blood dripping from the injured eye to the road leading to a tunnel produced a test tube baby, recalling the Greek myth of Aphrodite's birth.

The spatial structure of his paintings showed a consistent pattern, emphasizing a moderate elevation of the horizon which resulted in a slight vertical projection (Table 2). The space between the figures is empty; the objects are two-dimensional, lacking in depth. The entire structure reflects the clinical picture of early personality disintegration in marginally adjusted patients; they often realize that a distance exists between themselves and others. At the same time, individuals to whom they relate appear to them only as shadows, like the mannequins that filled de Chirico's world. The world of the schizophrenic, reflected in his graphics, appears at best as a depersonalized, unreal stage rather than a full-blooded three-dimensional world. The content of these paintings seems more personally motivated than those of many other patients, while the spatial structure is not yet severely disorganized. These graphics convey the extreme discomfort of the early schizophrenic who becomes highly disturbed by the disintegration taking place within him, while the expressions of the chronic, severely disintegrated patient show an indifferent, emotionally flattened response reflected in his regressed spatial patterns.

The defensive exaggeration of depth is depicted not only in the elongations seen in paintings by schizophrenics during the early phases of disintegration, but

7.32. *In "Test Tube Baby," the former images of destruction give way to images of creation.*

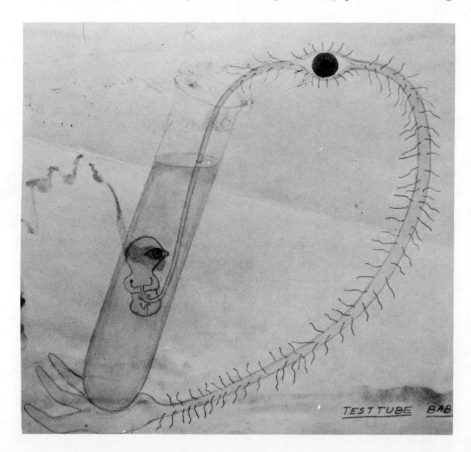

also in the disappearing conceptual boundaries. Munch's faces are not only emptied of facial features, but personal consciousness melts away in the passion of love: *The Kiss* (illustration 7.27). Love to Munch was a threatening experience that implied losing one's identity without retaining personal significance, culminating in the fear of being lost in nothingness. Love, in its physical closeness, dissolved one's personality and permitted one to be absorbed by another (62). In a previously discussed case (Case 115), one of our patients showed similar apprehensions in his relationships to women. The "softness of woman's hair, closeness, warmth" were disgusting, they caused him to panic; he wanted to annihilate the world before being destroyed. "They (women) are worse than the empty nothing of space." He, like Munch, had fears of being destroyed by women, who did not consider men "partners in the same venture of love." But, unlike Munch, he defended himself with fantasies of destroying beautiful women to save himself. In Munch's *The Kiss,* the faces of the lovers melt together, the man surrendering his identity to the woman. The woman pictured in his *Vampire* bears down on the man by burdening him with her love, crushing his creative strength and causing his spiritual death (62). Our patient must escape the love of women in spite of being attracted to them. When a girl "threw herself" at him and kissed him, he had to run away, but he felt trapped in his loneliness; he was frightened, and he fantasized about destroying her. His watercolor of the flag (illustration 7.3) shows a pink figure melting in the "incandescent heat" around it (indicated by the surrounding white space). The concentric short strokes surrounding her represent heat waves. The shape of a female figure, her head already melted away, is indicated by its wavy outline. Both Munch and the schizophrenic patient show these disintegrating boundaries in their art works.

If personality disintegration produces regressive changes in the spatial structure of graphics, the improvement of the clinical condition should also be reflected in the patient's concepts of space and reality. The reintegrative changes may be seen in a twenty-seven-year-old male patient who became acutely disturbed and delusional; he was unable to sleep and his speech became incoherent. As he noticed the first changes within himself, he became perplexed and very anxious; he "tried to escape reality by religion . . . My greatest desire is to be above everybody." He searched for answers in religious mysticism, as in Swedenborg's writings.[8] Not finding a satisfactory solution made him more disturbed; he verbalized the conflicts and the characteristic *ambivalence* of the schizophrenic: ". . . there is God and I can't go to Him because I have evil in me. . . . There is the Devil and I can't go to him because I have some good. . . . Isn't that Hell?" And changing from his usual voice, he added in a high falsetto voice: "No, this is Heaven. . . ." He evidenced considerable conflicts about his sexual identity, which made him feel effeminate and believe that he was pregnant. However, his voice, often falsetto, resumed masculine characteristics when his girlfriend visited him.

The patient painted watercolors during the course of his psychosis, which enabled us to correlate his clinical reintegration with the concurrent changes in his graphic expressions. At the height of his psychosis, at a time when he was completely unable to organize his thoughts, his watercolors revealed the poorly integrated structures (illustration 7.15) which we have discussed earlier; they consist of short random strokes without adequate direction (50). As he seemed to improve, he grouped the short strokes into parallel lines, straight and curved,

8. Swedenborg, Emanuel (1688-1772), the eminent Swedish scientist and theosophist. In later years, he claimed to having been admitted to the spiritual world and reported on his visions of Heaven and Hell. Kant and other philosophers renounced Swedenborg's *Heaven and Hell* and *Dreams of a Spiritual Seer* as illusionary notions.

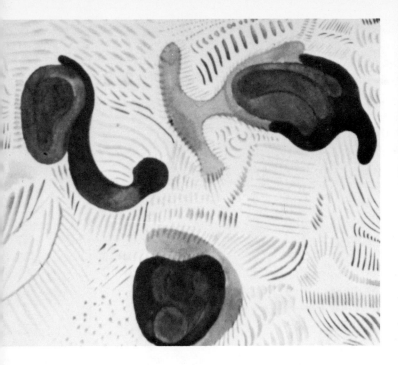

forming small entities; abstract, poorly shaped designs appear between them (illustration 7.33). In the next watercolor (illustration 7.34), integrative patterns begin to develop: the rays of the sun seem to penetrate the surface of the ground, forming petal intrusions above a masklike face in the lower right corner. A round blue eye is supplemented by a crescent eye; hornlike protrusions appear on the upper side of the face; the red face seems flame shaped. The patient's ambivalent feelings over being in Heaven or Hell seem to find expression in the sun melting the earth which harbors the Devil.

Further clinical progress produced a landscape (illustration 7.35) consisting of the short strokes that appeared in his first graphics. He was now capable of arranging the short lines into recognizable landscapes containing specific objects. A curved road leads to a small house; the trees become smaller as they recede into the background; the sun and its rays are shaped as in the previous watercolor; the fire on the mountaintop and the smoke rising from it resemble the face seen

earlier. The patient's watercolor, in spite of his attempts to give it depth perspective, remains essentially flat. He uses a style similar to the pointillism of Signac and Seurat, a technique of deliberately breaking up lines into fragmented parts. The patient's graphics up to this point are childlike, but not because he lacks artistic ability. The later drawings integrated markedly as his illness improved (illustration 7.36). He painted four different animals that are highly sophisticated; the grace of their movements is in marked contrast to the rigidly painted landscape. The final watercolors (illustration 7.37) show a purposefully stiff formality which resembles commercial art. As the patient recovered from his mental illness, the short strokes, at first arranged at random, became linked and merged into cohesive structural patterns.

As we followed the progress of this patient from a highly disintegrated state to the level of clinical recovery, we correlated his clinical condition to the spatial structure of his paintings. Other cases observed during their clinical reintegration added regressive patterns not shown in the previous case.

The progress of a young schizophrenic woman's clinical illness was closely paralleled by her graphics (Case 102). In the first watercolor, the figures stand on a single baseline (illustration 7.38). As she established the first tentative interpersonal relationships, she painted a house on the baseline but with its front expanding slightly into the foreground (illustration 7.39). Next appeared a landscape divided into three baselines (illustration 7.40). The large trees show some gradation of depth, and the sun throws their shadows into the foreground. The final charcoal drawing, made at the time of her clinical recovery, exhibits a three-dimensional landscape that presents a chiaroscuro effect (illustration 7.41).

The regression of the disintegrated personality makes the patient unable to distinguish between himself and his environment and to draw distinct borders between his concepts. This regression does not seem disorderly or arbitrary, but seems to follow preestablished levels parallel to the phylogenetic and antogenetic development of man. In graphics, that assumption is supported by the progressive development of spatial organization in children's drawings (92) as well as by art patterns that appear during the phylogenesis of man from prehistory to the sophisticated use of space of modern man (50).

The earliest impressions made by man appear on pebbles and bones dating from the Magdalenian period. They consist of parallel lines, paired in groups, crossing

7.36. *By now, the patient has improved substantially. He paints well integrated animals, which are, however, still isolated images.*

7.37. *Clinical recovery: the patient's images are integrated. However, the figures are still somewhat rigidly drawn.*

7.38-41. *A severely disturbed Western patient created these graphics as her personality was reintegrating.*

7.38. *Baseline: severe psychotic regression.*

or running zigzag. The "absolute freedom of direction" (50) of early primeval art reveals the conception of oneness with the world. All the directions available to Paleolithic man were of equal importance (50). The nomad was able to move in any direction to hunt his game and gather his food. During the Paleolithic period, the hunter's senses were sharpened by observing the habits and the habitats of animals, their tracks and their sounds; to survive, he had to ponder and to plot his hunts. His total dependence on his bounty and the unpredictable hazards of life caused him to seek relief by attempting to predestine the outcomes of his hunts by making images of what was to occur. Eventually, his developing skills produced amazingly sophisticated paintings and carvings that brightened his dark caves. Similar multidirectional concepts of space characterize the infant (92,

7.39. *Tentative extension into space.*

7.40. *With the patient's improvement, her drawings begin to indicate depth.*

137a, 137b) and the most disintegrated psychotic who has regressed to a level where all differentiation has dissolved.

As primeval man attempted to extend his world, he had to reckon with the impact of the often invisible forces in his surroundings that forced him to recognize and accept limits. He abandoned the nomadic life that had enabled him to supply his needs by gathering food and hunting. Settling on homesteads required that he make fundamental changes in his attitudes. He no longer needed the keen observation and sensory sensitivity of his ancestors; instead, he planned for future crops and for enlarging his herds. He replaced his concern for immediate problems with planning for the future; he learned to abstract. As man turned to domesticating animals and to planting food, he attempted to become independent of the

7.41. *The patient's social recovery is paralleled by her use of three-dimensional perspective in her drawings. Similar patterns are found in the art of widely separated cultures.*

119

changes and caprices of nature. The world of the Neolithic farmer and cattle breeder became circumscribed, restricting him to a more limited area that he could cultivate and where he could safely keep his herd. The nomadic hordes of the Paleolithic period settled in stable, organized communities (59).

The newly acquired need for organizing spatial concepts, which replaced the unrestricted wanderings of the nomads, appears in the art of Neolithic man. Multi-dimensional designs yield to abstract designs, representing the need for an organized system that would establish an ordered reality within a circumscribed area. Concepts are reduced to geometric abstractions symbolizing the original idea rather than representing the naturalistic likeness of an object; the artist may represent a human figure simply by drawing a vertical line to indicate the body and two semicircles for the head, arms, and legs (59). Similar geometric forms appear independently in countries widely separated and with no possibility of historical contact. We see similarities between ancient Greek pottery of the eighth century B.C. (illustration 7.42), early American Indian baskets woven around A.D. 900 (illustration 7.43), and New Guinea bark paintings made only a few years ago (illustration 7.44). Being made in such different times and places, these similar designs were produced independently from one another, but they are characteristic of corresponding levels of conceptual development, suggesting universal factors in the establishment of reality concepts.

During the first high civilizations of Egypt and Mesopotamia, when man moved out of caves into the open plains and began to build dwellings, he had to recognize the forces of gravity, if he were to erect his buildings in an upright position. The earlier concepts of multidirectional space were replaced, and the organizing principle of spatial structure became the vertical. Man's struggle with gravity made him perceive the space above him as unreachable, unobtainable. He soon endowed it with ethical values, making all that he could not reach into his various concepts of heaven. He erected the obelisk and the pyramid; the obelisk enabled the divine power of the sun to descend to earth, while the regal personage of the time, the Pharaoh, ascended from the top of the pyramid into the sky where he joined the sun god (see Chapter 2). The ancient Egyptian interpreted the upward, vertical motion as a divine privilege to establish a "link with invisible powers" (50). The horizontal became the line of repose, which supplied stability and a base on which action was built.

The influence of gravitational forces affects innate biological patterns, as seen in the early fetal movements of vertebrate animals (28). Infant behavior is determined by these forces as first horizontal and then vertical movements are progressively segregated out of random disorganized movements (137) (as they must be to satisfy basic needs of survival). Just as gravity, exercising its constant influence, controls the basic biological orientations of vertebrate life, it forces man to formulate the concepts of direction that will enable him to build shelters that will not collapse. In the same way, it directs his artistic creativity according to the structure of space. Vertical and horizontal directions form the basic two-dimensional principle from which the behavioral development of all vertebrates originates. Loeb (91) believes that the early behavior of the infant develops into the adult's communication system by the addition of one simple movement after another. This aggregation of building stones results eventually in the characteristic behavior of the organism specific for its species.

The prevalence of two-dimensional spatial conceptions is confirmed in children's drawings (92), and is repeated in the regressive patterns of disintegrated patients. Objects are built on a baseline that frequently extends horizontally

7.42. A Greek vase of the eighth century B.C.

7.43. A pattern woven into American Indian baskets around 900 A.D.

7.44. Abstract designs which are still being used in present-day New Guinea.

across the lower two-thirds of the paper (illustration 2.11); the figures are two-dimensional, flat, and strictly limited to the baseline; nothing extends beyond it. A similar spatial arrangement appears in a crayon drawing by a patient from Kenya (illustration 7.45).

In the more severely disintegrated personality, conceptual boundaries are very poorly organized, causing the patient to produce "inarticulate structures" (see Chapter 3). Disproportionate in size and lacking detail, they are rigid, frozen, and without motion. In spite of his illness, one of our patients realized the poor articulation of his picture and named it, at first, "a primitive thing . . . an amoeba of a man" (illustration 7.14). Lacking the ability to form stable concepts, he later changed his title to *A Mechanized Prussian Approach to War* (the painting was produced during World War II); finally he called it a "kind of gargoyle type." Although the patient changed the title of the painting, he was aware of its grotesque distortion. He knew that his ideas were distorted, in spite of a long, chronic illness that was marked by episodes of delusions, hallucinations, and bizarre behavior. His normal mood was emotionally flat, lacking adequate shadings of emotion; his thoughts were poorly formed, and his verbal expressions were indecisive and vague.

As the reintegration of the defective personality progresses, the fragmented concepts become linked in increasing realism. Basic outlines of the human body appear, but at first its proportions are distorted—some parts are elongated, others shortened or omitted. The weakened personality structure cannot adequately maintain and delineate realistic borders for its concepts; the flow of energy bridging the fragments is inadequate and only partially successful in linking them into completed wholes. As a patient's personality becomes slightly better integrated, the distortions may be less marked; he maintains the basic proportions of the body, but significant parts may be elongated or shortened according to their emotional charge. A nineteen-year-old male patient (Case 124) who had been mentally ill for eighteen months painted a watercolor that he identified as a self-portrait (illustration 7.46). The arms were elongated in the extreme, ending in a snake's head and a rattlesnake's tail. The absurdly long penis reached to the ground, striking fire; the excessively long ears ended in sharp points; the mouth bared its teeth. The entire watercolor reflected the patient's desire to appear aggressive, but the highly exaggerated body parts made it seem absurd. The patient

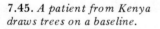

7.45. A patient from Kenya draws trees on a baseline.

had fantasies of being in love with a young, attractive girl to whom he had hardly spoken. He was "in a great rage" because she had rejected his delusional sexual advances. He had sought protection from his disturbing delusions by turning to his father and explaining to him that he desired to assault the girl and wanted to be locked up. The father had recognized his son's emerging illness and suggested, "How about hypnotizing you so you can't do it?"—a milder restraint than locking him up. He pretended to hyponotize his son in order to weaken his arms, preventing him from aggressive acts. The father repeated the procedure three times before the patient felt that he had lost control over his arms. The boy, apparently having ambivalent feelings about his aggressive thoughts, expressed them in the concrete manner of schizophrenic thinking: "I didn't want a conscience . . . my father gave me one by making my arms weak." It was not a physical weakness that had affected him, but his weakened personality boundaries offered inadequate protection and limit for the highly emotional material that he had expressed in his fantasies of sexual assault. The patient, like many schizophrenic patients, demonstrated considerable insight into the dynamic conflicts within his personality. Being subjectively aware of his desire to restrain his fantasies, he wanted to surrender to outside controls imposed by the authority of the hypnotist, his father. The aggressive threats of his fantasies appear in the form of the head and tail of the rattlesnake attached to grotesquely overextended, repeatedly folded arms. Their length renders them completely ineffective. The absurd length of his penis, almost half of the size of his body, suggests impotency by virtue of its unusable size, rather than virility; the incongruous extensions seem to express strong desires for power by reaching beyond realistic limits, but only result in ineffective

7.46. An American patient elongates parts of this figure due to their emotional significance.

7.47. As the patient regresses further, his paintings display more poorly articulated structures.

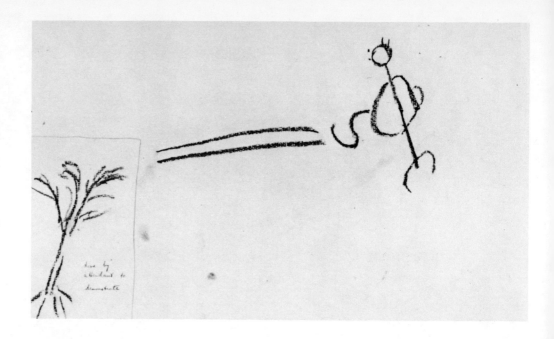

7.48. *A patient from Kenya uses elongation to represent strength. While the figure's left arm is small and shriveled, the right arm extends to reach for a snake (two parallel lines at left).*

7.49. *The long nose of a Sepik River mask symbolizes masculinity.*

weakness. As the patient's clinical condition regresses further, his disintegrated concepts form poorly articulated structures (illustration 7.47), showing considerable similarity to watercolors painted by a disintegrated patient from an isolated New Guinea area, the Gulf District (illustration 8.19).

A similar wish to express strength through elongation appears in the drawings of a disintegrated patient from Kenya (illustration 7.48). The body of a spirit-being is schematically drawn in the form of a circle; a straight line connects the head and legs. The left arm is almost withered, while the right "arm of the spirit reaches for the snake." The arm is folded over but not as extensively as in the painting of the previous patient.

If body parts are extended to unrealistic extremes, it may indicate unusual, at times magical, powers, as in the telescopic eyes of masks carved by members of the African Poro Society (illustration 6.6). The elongated noses of New Guineans from areas in the Sepik River signify masculinity; such noses decorate many of the regional masks (illustration 7.49). Elongations and distortions of the human body and of other objects occur frequently in primitive art, for the conceptual boundaries are not fixed by external reality. The primitive artist is in a stage of societal development that does not require him to test his concepts against what exists around him but rather against what exists within him; he conceives reality as a system controlled by emotionally significant factors, by what has proven important to him and his group, rather than by what it is. His interpretations of what seems to exist have outweighed fact; he submits to a subjective system constructed by expectations; if realistic concepts interfere, reality must surrender. Primitive concepts are rooted in past experiences, often expanded by elaborations meaningful to the society from which they originate. Having established conceptual boundaries, these concepts are rigidly enforced and do not readily submit to newly gained experiences.

The psychotic personality is unable to set up efficiently functioning boundaries that restrict concepts according to realistic limits. The concepts that he does develop are confirmed neither by testing them against realistic experiences, nor by the societal systems from which the psychotic originates. The inefficiently functioning boundaries result in disproportionate and distorted concepts, in inner fears, fantasies that are imposed on the external world. The work of the primitive

artist has societal meaning to the group within which he functions, while the psychotic patient has little societal interchange, and feels increasingly isolated (111). Superficial similarities between psychotic expression and primitive or contemporary Western art are deceptive; they could be misjudged in cases of mild disintegration. But structural spatial changes due to mild personality disintegration may be just as difficult to diagnose clinically. Graphic expression by disintegrated patients (Table 2) runs the gamut from slight spatial distortions to undifferentiated scribbles and splotches, as has been shown. Above that level, concepts retain some realistic elements; the proportions of conceptual outlines are maintained only in the most inarticulated forms (illustration 7.14). Severe pictorial distortions can easily be differentiated from the work of tribal or contemporary artists, and even from the feeble artistic attempts of the unskilled nonpsychotic. Less obvious distortions elicit feelings of strangeness in the viewer, even if the productions are not always identified as those of psychotic patients. The loosening conceptual boundaries make walls invisible (illustration 7.11); bodies become transparent; essential parts of a person are seen in twisted perspective (illustration 7.10); various elements are placed on top of each other in vertical projection.

Vertical projection appears in the art of various cultures. Asiatic art, from Persian (illustration 7.50) to Japanese paintings (illustration 7.51), uses the technique to illustrate spatial relationships instead of Western perspective; foreshadowing and the converging of lines to the horizon are not used (105). Figures or objects in space are placed vertically; figures in the distance do not necessarily appear smaller, but what is far away is on top. The size of a person is not deter-

Vertical projection is used to render the illusion of distance in the art of many cultures.

7.50. *Persian Miniature— sixteenth century.*

7.51. *A Japanese painting from the Ippen Shoni Scroll, late thirteenth century. Tokyo National Museum.*

125

7.52. *The Mikado. Tokyo National Museum.*

mined by distance but by his social rank. Unimportant peasants in the foreground are often smaller than important courtiers, generals, or the Mikado, who may appear in the center of the painting (illustration 7.52). Pictorial relationships are shifted and rearranged according to their societal significance. Various views, front, side and top, are combined; nothing is omitted that is worth knowing of an object or of an event fitting into the cultural system. These artists neglect what is inessential within the context of their universe, regardless of the importance the omitted details may have for a Western artist.

A patient's delusions of world destruction reflect the chaos that he feels within himself. The anguish of his own disintegration is reflected in the world that surrounds him. Munch's *Despair* depicts a scream that cannot be heard, a feeling of frightening isolation. One patient, a twenty-five-year-old woman, became aware of the change in her environment. As with many schizophrenic patients, she expressed her personality change in concrete terms; she felt, as did one of the previous patients, that her world was destroyed; she and everyone else had died. She was surrounded by a deep silence that she could not penetrate. When she attempted to touch her brother to find comfort, his hands were cold; they were the "hands of a dead man." The schizophrenic's images often express destruction. The splitting of the globe (illustration 7.2) symbolizes the cosmic extension of the patient's inner feelings; his ambivalence, based on his anger, reacts with the feeling of rejection and guilt that he felt, ending in self-destructive feelings. His individual conflicts, as in many disintegrated patients, attain cosmic significance. Only if his personality restitutes, at least partially, even if defectively, will he be able to establish some relationship to others. He will feel less isolated and reality will assume meaning (130).

World destruction seems to be an archetypal, recurrent motif in many religions and mythologies, but there it differs significantly from a schizophrenic's delusions. Frequently, as in Indian philosophy, the dissolution of the individual is not final. The end is the proper finish of the life cycle in which the individual participates. His "transient, frail existence . . . [is part of] a dynamic radiation of the Self Eternal." Lord Shiva, the supreme divinity, is the same essence appearing in three attitudes: God Brahma, the Creator; God Vishnu, the Maintainer; and God Shiva, the Destroyer. Shiva effects not the final destruction of the world but a state of dissolution followed by recreation. Being divine, he transcends the limits of time and space. He maintains the life cycle by the round of life flowing forth, "fruition, dissolution and re-emanation" (151). This wheel of life maintains the creative vitality of existence rather than being destructive. In contrast, the lifeless, zombielike existence produced by the disintegrating ego-boundaries of the psychotic appears in the paintings of the tortured painter. It eternalizes the patient's feelings of living death. His fantasies and imagery reflect the finality of his disintegration; there is no chance of redemption as long as he remains ill.

8

Schizophrenic Expression and New Guinean Art

We reported in the last chapter the changes which appear in the structures of graphics by Western, mostly North American, schizophrenic patients. The spatial concepts of their productions reflect the levels of personality disintegration which appear during the various stages of regression (Table 2). We attempted to correlate those changes to equivalent developments in the history of art.

The imagery of art produced by the psychotic and the nonpsychotic alike emerges from the unconscious part of the personality. Images are then shaped into cohesive and socially relevant concepts by the integrated personality, while the disintegrated individual lacks the faculty to transform them into well-organized entities. The drawings of psychotics remain poorly articulated, maintaining highly subjective and solipsistic value.

It is possible that Western man's concept of space grew when he came into contact with foreign values; as he conquered other nations, he absorbed some of the new ideas of the conquered people (see the discussion of the Crusades in Chapter 2). Nonwestern conquerors, such as the Mongols and Arabs, amassed large land areas but their penetration was temporary and they assimilated few of the aspects of host cultures. In spite of geographic expansion, most conquerors have remained isolated within their own cultural and scientific horizons, confined in their traditional ideational concepts. They have conquered geographically, but they have been defeated by their sociocultural stagnation. Overcoming the stagnation of an isolated culture is exemplified by the pace with which Japan changed from a feudal system to a modern nation. When American sailors forced their way into Japan, they brought with them an entirely foreign culture. Traditional patterns changed rapidly. The change was not forced upon the Japanese; their own cultural values were respected and the dignity of their traditional life was maintained; they preserved their independence and self-respect. In contrast to countries that were colonized by foreign powers, the Japanese were able to absorb much of the Western life style without destroying their own. Western technology did not intimidate them as it did African nations or the people of New Guinea; they applied themselves not only to imitating Western technical knowledge, but also to developing many refinements. Marked economic changes eventually influenced their societal organization. Gradually family patterns became restructured, but religious attitudes were slow to be given up. Momentous historical and cultural changes force revisions of existing societal patterns.

Major historical events do not appear to be incidental, but seem to be created by societal needs and by the minds of men. These events often coincide with artistic innovations since both are prompted by similar concerns; changing attitudes cause art to precede many crises. Art's emotional impact may become so powerful that it may become a threat to the established institutions of a culture. During the eighth century, the Catholic Church oppressed any homage to sacred images as idolatry, and in A.D. 754 the Council of Hieria ordered the wholesale destruction of all images (74). The Church's fears grew out of miraculous and magic powers being attributed to the holy images and icons; the exceptional growth of icon worship had caused great controversy within the Church hiearchy, creating a dilemma for many theologians that was rooted in the basic conflict over the representation of an object being identified with the object itself, the image of Christ being worshipped as Christ. It was the worshipers' limited horizon and the clergy's interpolation that created a frustrating distance between the individual and his God. Exalting the image of the Savior and the Saints allowed the believer to have direct access to his Saints, who could then intercede in his behalf. Artistic images fulfilled his needs and enabled him to extend himself beyond his own boundaries to infinite eternity. The parent who extends himself through his children, expecting to fulfill ambitions through them that he never reached himself; the artist who fulfills his fantasies in his creations; the worshiper who throws himself in deep devotion in front of the relic; the psychotic who creates his delusion—all of them, dissatisfied with their mortal destiny, attempt to step beyond the limits of their narrow existences and find fulfillment in their creations. Man's insatiable thirst to surpass the bland boundaries of his life has caused him to push back the spatial boundaries around him. He set out to expand from the world as it existed in the days of the primordial hordes whose involvement did not reach farther than their eyes could scan, to the nearly unlimited space of the twentieth century.

Man's view of space has been dependent on his experience and knowledge. It is reflected in his works of art from prehistoric days, when no prevailing spatial direction was established (50), to the Renaissance period of the Western world. The painter in primitive society, who had been restricted to the narrow horizons of his immediate geographic or spiritual surroundings, created symbolic images representing thoughts and fantasies rather than the real nature of things. He created images of great spiritual power; their shapes and coloring were strictly regulated in tribal societies, as they were in Western societies, even if for diametrically opposed reasons. In primitive society, the spiritual being resides in the sculpture, making it mandatory to maintain its traditional aspects. The images cannot be altered since basic changes would destroy their ancestral character. In contrast, the Church hierarchy of the early Middle Ages was disturbed over the same process of identification, feeling obligated, as guardian of the faith, to prevent the idolatrous worship of the image.

The widening of man's horizons and the many scientific discoveries of subsequent centuries promoted a naturalistic approach to life that modified the spatial organization of paintings. The newly acquired knowledge let objects appear in proportioned depth, three-dimensional perspective reached its height during the first half of the nineteenth century. Constable and Turner nearly exhausted the possibilities of naturalistic landscape painting by replicating the infinite space of nature on canvas (74). Contemporary artists, searching for new forms, turn away from naturalism, and during the last century have had vast options at their disposal, finding alternatives in abstraction and geometry, to the three-dimensional painting of the past.

The artist's search for a new way of seeing reality has often been repressed by established institutions as by the Council of Hieria, as by the Inquisition or by the potent spiritual beliefs of tribal societies. Removal of such restrictions can lead to a wave of experimentation which, if undirected, may result in an eventual deterioration of the arts. The loosening of religious controls under the rule of Akhenaten enabled the artist to unfreeze the traditional *perspective tordue,* in which a figure was painted in a work of art in both front and side views simultaneously. The ready acceptance of a three-dimensional style by educated local nursing personnel in New Guinea's Highlands (illustration 8.76), and the markedly Western style by the disintegrated but basically acculturated patient from Buka (Case 510), also indicate the ability to adopt concepts if the latent potential for such development exists.

Art plays an essential role in the life of the people of New Guinea. The elaborate displays used in the ceremonies are greatly responsible for that art (40 b). This art has become highly developed and has gained wide renown. The motives were handed down from generation to generation, and originally had great spiritual significance, but, as with most sacred art, were formal and restricted. Later, as the spiritual significance of these art objects lessened, the designs began to appear on secular articles of domestic use (129 a).

The art styles vary in different regions. Wood sculptures and masks find the highest level of development in the Sepik River area; the Gulf of Papua region produces impressive plaques up to twenty feet high; the Highlands excels in body painting, wigs, and headdresses. For the Highlanders, the painted face becomes a mask representing the spirit whose expression is alive and highly expressive; it is not the limited, static expression of the traditional wood masks (93, 48).

It may be of interest to determine if the local place talk, which limits verbal communication to a narrow geographic area, has encouraged the use of nonverbal expression. Art seems to reach the highest level of sophistication in areas where many different languages are spoken, each of them reaching only a few hundred people. In the Sepik River region, with its many languages, verbal communication is far more limited, and the art more highly developed, than in the Highlands, where as many as sixty thousand people share the same language.[1]

During the nineteenth century, foreign governments occupying various parts of Papua and New Guinea attempted to force westernization on the people. Only the Highlands were spared the forceful penetration by outside powers, as the region was considered impenetrable at that time. The coastal area and offshore

1. A similar relationship between verbal and visual language is stressed by H. Read (118) and others. He infers that visual language existed prior to verbal language. He questions if during the Paleolithic periods a language even existed. There is certainly no trace of it left, but the art of that period is highly developed, and survived in the remarkable cave paintings of Lascaux.

islands lost many of their traditions under the impact of Western ideas. Traditional practices such as cannibalism and head-hunting were outlawed, and villages involved in raiding parties were burned. Hamlets of sixty to eighty people were encouraged to merge with other villages into larger communities, reducing the cultural and linguistic isolation, but also loosening the sociocultural identity of the people and causing a decay in the traditional life styles and art forms (129 b). The styles and designs became disintegrated and contaminated by outside influences. In contrast, traditional designs were maintained longer in the Highlands, where the people had few outside contacts prior to World War II.

The productions of artists and patients alike must be considered within the contexts of their sociocultural settings. As long as the patients are not too limited by their personality disorganization, their paintings express culture-bound material and maintain the structural characteristics of their society. A Western patient was influenced in the content of his watercolors by the figurations of his own culture (illustration 7.38), but he developed the customary three-dimensional spatial concepts only after he had improved clinically (illustration 7.41).

Our study compares the graphic expressions of disintegrated Western patients with those of patients in New Guinea. A comparison of the two cultures is particularly significant because many of the Melanesian patients lived during their formative years in an isolated culture, nearly uninfluenced by Western contacts. Hopefully, this study will shed some light on the structure of reality as reflected by the artistic structuralization of space, and the effect of the disintegrated personality on forming ideastional concepts, in two totally different cultural settings.

The patients participating in this study came from various parts of New Guinea, including offshore islands such as Bougainville, Buka and New Britain. The area had been under Australian administration until independence was achieved in 1974. All patients except one were hospitalized either at the Psychiatric Hospital at Laloki (near Port Moresby, the capital) or on the psychiatric service of the General Hospital at Goroka (in the Eastern Highlands). One man (Case 511) was interviewed at the maximum security section of the Bomana Prison outside Port Moresby. Patients from rural sections were usually hospitalized for the protection of their fellow villagers; the treatment aspects of hospitalization were of little concern. Westernized patients from larger towns were more frequently hospitalized for treatment. The graphics were drawn principally by male patients, who are hospitalized in far larger numbers than women. In general, the mentally ill person is tolerated in his comminity as long as he does not disturb others or interfere with community activities. Needless, unprovoked violent acts directed against one's own village are particularly unacceptable, and the person committing them is considered "long-long." Not all violent acts are necessarily signs of pathological behavior. But the villagers recognize culturally deviant attitudes and readily determine behavior as being "normal" or pathological (2). The courts have often considered that violence is a cultural factor in the lives of the islanders, allowing this consideration to mitigate sentences. The Australian law has been bent a little in the remote areas of the Highlands where "killing is still a moral obligation," while the law is far more strictly enforced in the costal areas where where there has been longer Western contact and a higher level of sophistication is assumed (127). Only recently, the *Papua-New Guinea Post Courier* reported that a sentence for payback (the killing was to avenge a fatal automobile accident) was reduced since the offenders spent their formative years in the southern Highlands where payback was customary.

Our interviews with patients were conducted with the aid of interpreters, who had various degrees of psychiatric experience—a psychiatrist, psychiatric nurses, and medical students. Unless the interpreter could speak the local language, more than one interpreter was necessary; few patients could speak neo-Melanesian pidgin, increasing the difficulties of obtaining adequate translations of the interviews. Translators experienced in psychiatry and the local place talk had no difficulties with neurotic or other psychiatric complaints as long as the personality structure, and therefore the verbal expression, were integrated. Understanding the schizophrenic's vague and incomplete verbosity in one's own language is often difficult, but a translation from the local place talk of a schizophrenic patient into neo-Melanesian and then into English is almost totally incomprehensible. The translator experienced in psychiatry and neo-Melanesian was often frustrated in translating schizophrenic language, with its vagueness, neologisms and difficulties in conceptual organization. During the interviews, a patient might talk for a few minutes, but only one short sentence would be translated. As we pressed for a more detailed translation, the usual answer was that the patient's statements were vague, inconsistent, often incoherent, interfering with the verbatim translation. Some of the interpreters who attempted to be accurate found the experience very exhausting. The translation difficulty itself seemed to reflect the pathological thought disturbances and was helpful in establishing if any personality disintegration was present.

Nonverbal expressions are of value not only in overcoming the linguistic limitation in New Guinea, but also in understanding the schizophrenic patient anywhere (14 b). Verbal language is a complex system depending on an adequate interaction between the individual and others. The schizophrenic personality disintegration limits the capacity for interaction; the ability for linear sequential thinking (4 b) becomes reduced. Patients of any culture become aware of their inability to establish a sequential order to their concepts; Many thoughts appear simultaneously and patients may feel unable to handle the impact of all these impressions crowding in on them. They feel perplexed and helpless (14 b). One of our patients said repeatedly, "I just can't say what I want to say; there is too much." She painted to overcome her limitations in verbal communication. Her landscapes lacked three-dimensional aspects; her thoughts were expressed by perseverating emotionally significant materials—she painted two suns in a landscape instead of a single one.

Schizophrenic patients attempt to find substitutes for their limitations. They often begin to draw spontaneously during the course of their illnesses (14 c). Graphic expression enables them to represent simultaneous thoughts even if these have to be put on paper or canvas in sequence; ideational processes can be continuously modified and altered when expressed graphically. If the personality structure reintegrates, the sequential and linear thought processes are reestablished; the need for nonverbal expression becomes reduced and patients often lose the need to paint (14 a).

Our material may be considered limited since all of our patients were institutionalized. However, hospitalized patients were possibly less influenced by outside factors than they might have been if they had painted in their own villages. The curiosity of other villagers and their critical comments might have hindered the spontaneity of the productions. Moreover, psychotics in their home villages would probably not have been allowed to paint. Few activities are private in the villages; most work—the raising of crops and the hunting—is shared by the community; the whole village participates in spiritual rituals. Art alone is produced by a special few, and artists are a group unto themselves. It would have been difficult for someone who was long-long (psychotic) to use art materials, which are reserved for a small, select group of men. Finally, the very fact of outsiders coming to the village to contact a particular member of their community would have created enough excitement to interfere with the privacy of any evaluating process; many unpredictable variants would have been introduced.

In the hospital, the patients were offered various art materials: commercial paints, brushes, crayons, and pencils—quite a change from traditional Melanesian art, in which colors are limited to red and yellow ochre, white, pink made from a rare form of limestone, and black made from burnt umber. Feathers and twigs served as brushes in the past. In more recent years, commercial paints and brushes have been substituted in most areas. Most patients had served and sometimes assisted artists in their home villages using paints and brushes, but they had not used such materials on their own before their hospitalization. They had no difficulty in making proper use of the material however, and they painted with apparent ease.

We attempted, as with the Western patients, to correlate structural changes in the graphics with the clinical changes of personality disintegration. The clinical records were reviewed, and we interviewed the patients participating in this study. The sessions were tape recorded. Since large numbers of the patients were hospitalized as a result of violent behavior—assault or murder—we wondered if such selected clinical material would introduce significant variations. However, as pointed out previously, the patient's behavior has to be considered in its social context. Until recently, killings (cannabalism, headhunting, war parties) were within the cultural norm. A murder committed in Western society is a definite violation of the accepted code of behavior, while killing, in many areas of New Guinea, performed a ritual role in the lives of the people. Violent behavior was accepted, and often prestigious, before European standards were forced on the population; killing of at least one man was considered in some groups to be a prerequisite to distinction as a warrior. Within the context of New Guinean society, therefore, the large percentage of violent-behavior patients among the cases studied does not seem to introduce a significant variant, nor does it seem to change the validity of our material applicable to the standards of personality disintegration on a cross-cultural basis.

As the patients regress due to their psychotic disintegration, they frequently use in their own graphics traditional designs which are no longer in use. They regress to the early periods of their formative years when such patterns were originally used (Cases 506, 550). The regression to traditional art forms is most marked in the drawings of patients from the Highlands, as they have been subjected to few cultural changes. Traditional cultural influence remains strong where an individual has undergone vigorous initiation ceremonies, and most of the patients, who are now middle aged, have been influenced to some degree by these customs. Some of the younger patients and those of mixed racial origin have had little traditional instruction. In order to appraise the patient's symptom formation properly, the cultural influences on the content of his delusions must be evaluated (155, 2). Culturally conditioned beliefs may control the delusions and hallucinations of patients from areas where foreign contacts have taken place only recently. In such cases traditional patterns may continue to appear in patient's graphics. As the patient's personality regresses, the graphic material reflects cultural determinants less often; universal factors common to regressed patients, regardless of cultural background, turn up. It is not the content, but the spatial structure of graphics that reflects the state of disintegration. This is borne out by schizophrenic patients of African, Japanese, and European descent who show a highly similar spatial framework in their drawings.

In order to distinguish the cultural from the universal elements of psychotic graphic expression, we shall arrange our material according to the geographic origin of the patient. The population groups of New Guinea are highly diversified, which can be seen from the fact that over seven hundred different languages are spoken. The linguistic isolation and varied ethnic background limit the art styles but these are not necessarily restricted to a specific language group (110 c). It is assumed that tribal wars and limited food supply caused migration and resettlement of large groups, which may have been responsible for the existence of related art styles in geographically separated areas. The rings around the eyes of a large face painted on the Abelam men's houses (Sepik River, illustration 8.16) give their figures a strong resemblance to those on Papua Gulf plaques (illustration 6.3). The stylistic diversities are noticeable even within a single clan where individual artists carve and paint figures and plaques, while in other villages a master artist supervises the work of several assistants at the same time (Abelam). Before the availability of commercial paints and brushes, the greatly diverse material used in producing the paintings contributed individualistic variations to the basic style. Art forms were also spread by headhunters, who raided neighboring villages, looted, and brought home spiritual figures, carvings, and decorated pots, contributing to the cultural exchange.

The patients' cultural and regional background, including their art, may have influenced their graphics, but as their personality disintegration advanced, the pathology of their concepts played an increasing role in the final product. The lack of a uniform road system and the great variety of the existing trade routes made the degree of Western influence vary from village to village.

CENTRAL DISTRICT

A few of our patients came from the Central District located on the South Coast of Papua; the country's capital, Port Moresby, is located here.

Case 503
The first patient belonged to the Mekeo clan of Central District; he had had considerable European contacts during his teens. A study of the 1930's describes this area as isolated, but undergoing economic change. Agricultural development had long been encouraged, but traditional sociocultural patterns persisted. Frequent quarrels caused fighting among the Mekeos; they sought protection by forming alliances with neighboring groups, and when they failed in their defense, they abandoned their villages. Some Mekeos escaped by moving to Port Moresby, but they continued to maintain family ties with their homes. In the capital they acted as family agents in the betel nut traffic.

The Mekeos underwent many changes in recent years, attempting to face their many dangers and insecurities. Like people in other parts of New Guinea, they developed strong beliefs in sorcery. The sorcerers among them grew powerful, suspect and feared by their own group; but these men remained a potent force in spite of their destructiveness. Each sorcerer was skilled in a specialized craft that was handed down from generation to generation. The belief in sorcery substituted for the Mekeos' customary ways of settling disputes, the headhunting raids and cannibalism which had been outlawed. Having been deprived of the traditional ways of handling their spiritual needs, they invested a great amount of faith in *puri-puri* (sorcery). Sorcery protected the people from a disintegration of their social order without disrupting basic cultural patterns. No significant art originates with the Mekeos. They produce only a few forehead ornaments consisting of the universal geometric designs of wheels with radial spikes or concentric herringbone patterns spreading from the center of a circular ornament (illustration 8.1).

The patient on whom we report came from a small village of the area. He was the oldest of four children; their mother had died when he was thirteen. Her sudden death was attributed to magic brought on by a sorcerer. In spite of the family's having joined the Catholic Church, they continued to believe in sorcery.

After attending eight years of primary school, the patient moved to Port Moresby to become a student at the technical college, learning carpentry. Soon after leaving his home village, he became confused and developed difficulties in concentrating. He accused another student of having placed a spell on him to chase away his mind. He talked about having visual hallucinations of a European man telling him to "forget bad things and think about good things."

In spite of his strong belief in sorcery, the patient's father recognized his son's

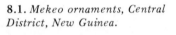

8.1. *Mekeo ornaments, Central District, New Guinea.*

symptoms as an illness. He dated the onset of the illness to when his son moved away from home and entered college in Port Moresby. Apparently, his illness had been precipitated not only by his conflicts between traditional magicoreligious beliefs and Christianity but also by the stress of moving to the city. He had felt secure within his home environment, where he had an assured position in his social group. In moving from his small village to Port Moresby, he abandoned his familiar boundaries and exposed himself to the seemingly limitless area of an unfamiliar and potentially threatening environment. Tenuous relationships, mostly with strangers, were an inadequate substitute for solid ties within a tightly controlled community.

Some of his clinical symptoms were suggestive of his cultural background, such as the belief in sorcery. Delusions of thought control may be culture bound, but they are also found among Western patients (18, 22). The affective disturbances and the disintegrated thought processes go beyond culturally conditioned behavior and are indicative of a disorganized personality structure. The patient's crayon drawing (illustration 8.2) shows Western influences. The house in the center seems to be one of the prefabricated government buildings frequently found in various parts of New Guinea. Two small figures dressed in European clothes are in front. On the left are the four directions of the compass (incorrect). The entire drawing lacks Melanesian content and indicates the Western orientation

8.2. *A patient's crayon drawing shows Western influence, in spite of the disoriented compass.*

of the patient. His personality disintegration is reflected in the structural design, as previously described in schizophrenic graphics of other cultures (14 a, c). The human figures are disproportionately small in relation to the compass. The designs are rigidly constructed; motion is absent; the monotone colors lack shading.

Case 513

The first crayon drawing (illustration 8.3) by a patient from a small village in the Marshall Lagoon Subdistrict shows considerable regression. The two principal concepts, the pig on top and the woman in the center, are isolated and unrelated. Parts of both figures consist of fragmented short strokes, a characteristic of a disintegrative process (see Table 2). In an attempt to organize space, the patient has placed the main figure on a baseline and flanked it by two trees. All figures are in frontal view; three-dimensional depth is lacking, although later graphics by the same patient illustrate that he is capable of indicating depth.

The next drawing (illustration 8.4) shows the beginnings of reintegration; the various figures are no longer fragmented, but are formed by complete, uninterrupted lines and show increasingly realistic features. The concepts are unrelated to

8.3. *The patient places her figures on a baseline, and uses short, interrupted strokes instead of continued lines.*

135

8.4, 8.5. *The drawing by this New Guinean patient is quite similar to one drawn by a Western schizophrenic.*

8.6. *As the patient's condition improves, his drawings become increasingly cohesive. Here, the patient combines Western with traditional material.*

one another, however, and form independent images standing on the baseline (see Table 2). A woman with European features is the central figure in this drawing. (The drawing has considerable similarity to the portrait drawn by a European schizophrenic which has been reproduced in the classical Prinzhorn collection [illustration 8.5] published in 1922.) Our patient's figure is rigidly drawn and two-dimensional, but it possesses some cohesiveness. Traditional Melanesian zig-zag designs are placed on the right and left edges of the paper.

The crayon (illustration 8.6) that follows is far more cohesive and integrated, in spite of some distortion. The elongation, in contrast to the more disintegrated earlier picture, shows a milder form of disintegration. The features and hair styles here too are European, but traditional Melanesian triangles frame the facial contour.

A landscape (illustration 8.7) painted by the same patient is in the European tradition. It is far better integrated although regressive signs of subjective space appear in the mixing of planes (92, 14 a). The lake and land surrounding it are seen from above, while objects, although in proper proportion, are seen from the front; depth perception is lacking. As a rule, landscapes are an infrequent subject of primitive art (39 b). This series of drawings shows continuous reintegration, from disconnected and unrelated objects to well-integrated concepts, even if some regressive characteristics remain (mixing of planes and lack of adequate depth perception).

This patient, twenty-eight years old at the time of his last hospitalization, had continuous European contact during his early years. He joined the Seventh Day Adventist Church and abandoned many of his early beliefs. When he became psychotic, his delusions revolved around the coming of the Millennium—not brought about by ancestral spirits, as New Guineans often believe, but not in itself a pathological belief among followers of the cargo cults. The deeply seated Christian beliefs of this patient made him attribute his salvation to the second coming of Christ. He asserted that he, the patient, had been crucified twice. He spoke incoherently about living in a civilized world where "we must learn about economy. . . ."[2] The content and style of his graphics, as of his delusions, are

8.7. *The patient has improved clinically and his drawing is more cohesive. The mixing of planes is more a cultural than a pathological characteristic.*

137

A series of drawings shows the integrative change of the subject from taro roots to a human hand.

8.8. Disintegrated personality structure.

8.9. Consolidating of conceptual fragments.

greatly influenced by European cultural contacts and show little of traditional content. This patient's graphics, like those of others (Case 510), seem to indicate that prolonged Western contacts during the developmental years of an individual affect his conceptual structure even if his personality disintegrates.

Case 548

This patient comes from a village in the Central District. He had only limited outside contacts as a young child, but traditional rituals were no longer practiced in his village. The area had Western contact for forty or fifty years; cannibalism, tribal wars, and initiation ceremonies had been successfully repressed. In spite of long missionary work, Christianity was of little more than superficial significance; the belief in spirit-beings remained strong.

Little is known of the patient's illness except that he was acutely disturbed at the time of admission to the Laloki Psychiatric Center. The diagnosis of schizophrenia was made when he was admitted and it was retained as his discharge diagnosis.

The first of the patient's drawings (illustration 8.8) shows designs resembling the tubers and leaves of a taro plant. In the next drawing (illustration 8.9) the tubers are pulled together; the center has developed into a stem from which five oblong objects originate. The colors and shapes used in the previous drawings emerge as a hand in the final drawing (illustration 8.10).

The patient's merging of the taro plant into the design of a hand raises interesting questions about the cultural significance and influence of traditional art on a mental patient's drawings in nonliterate societies. The taro plant, a staple food in New Guinea, has been the source of various cults. Because the taro is necessary for survival in a country with meager food supplies, cults have developed around the worship of spirits which control the taro's growth, and with it, the prosperity of the community. The success of the crop depends on many

2. One of the basic current issues in New Guinea deals with converting an economy based on subsistence farming, into a cash economy.

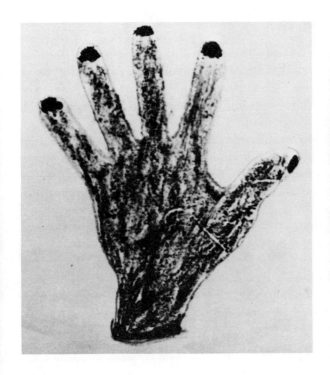  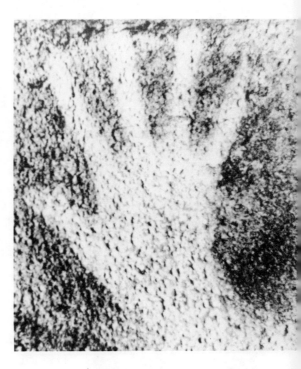

incalculable factors beyond the reach of the individual. When man feels helpless and at the mercy of powers he does not understand, he may try to placate them by the use of magic. Not having direct access to these spirits, the people of the area ask for the help of the Taro man, a sorcerer living among them. The Taro man is able to make the taro grow by commanding the rain to fall or the sun to shine. If the taro grows, the sorcerer's power spreads. The Taro man is not to be offended. Not to show him the proper respect means to abuse the spirit he represents. When angered, the spirit can keep food from growing; he can cause famine and can make people sick. The spirit enters the body of anyone thoughtless enough to show disrespect, and causes sickness. During the taro rituals, the queer practice of universal handshaking takes place to keep on good terms with the Taro man (147 b). The hand, particularly the upraised hand, appears frequently in New Guinean art of many regions, as in other widely diverse cultures (50).[3] The raised hand wards off evils; the laying on of hands has a healing quality.

The sign of a hand appears frequently in prehistoric and nonliterate art (50). We found it unexpectedly as the only decoration on the outside wall of a hut in the patient's village in the Eastern Highlands (illustration 8.11). None of the other huts showed any decorations or paintings. When we asked the owner of the hut, who had no privileged position in the community, for an explanation of the hand painted on the wall or its significance, he responded only with a blank smile. It seems that the meaning of his own symbolism was lost to the indigenous man, not an infrequent occurrence.

Our patient seems to express a symbolic union by making the Taro roots merge into the hand. This seems to reflect the regression of the disintegrated personality to culturally significant symbolism. The patient may have witnessed related cult activites during his formative years, but the practice may have been abandoned since that time.

3. The upraised hand appears independently in many cultures; it was discovered in the caverns of Peche-Merle in southern France (illustration 8.12); as it is attributed to the Aurignacian period, between 85,000 to 35,000 B.C., the time interval precludes any possible contact with the very similar designs on the hut in the Eastern Highlands of New Guinea; it is, far more likely, another indication that basic designs develop independently.

8.10. *Integration into cohesive concepts.*

8.11. *Hand painted on a hut in the Asoro Valley, Eastern Highlands.*

8.12. *The human hand is a design prevalent in the art of most cultures. This drawing from the Aurignacian Period was discovered in the caverns of Pech-Merle, in southern France.*

GULF OF PAPUA

Case 506

Another patient, a man in his early fifties, had been living in a small village in the Ihu Subdistrict of the Gulf area. Many villages of this district, including the patient's, had been completely isolated during the years of his early childhood. The area came under closer Australian scrutiny as the patient reached adulthood. Frequent patrols vigorously enforced the laws against cannibalism, tribal war, and payback. The people of the area accepted Christianity passively and gave up many of their traditional beliefs. As in other regions, the belief in magic continued, and sorcery increased in importance as ancestral ceremonial activities diminished (95).

Missionaries had suppressed the old initiation ceremonies. They had burned the ceremonial houses and the spiritual art works which were kept in the sacred shrines. Early evangelists lacked the sophistication and the sensitivity to realize that their arbitrary disregard for the traditional beliefs of the people caused consternation and great resentment which is still evident in the Gulf area. Old men talk with pride about fights against the government patrols who attempted to pacify the area. As recently at ten years ago, they talked about white and black men suddenly disappearing, and a few months later their bones being found (other parts of their bodies had apparently become part of a cannibalistic feast) (127). It seemed they were killed during ceremonies celebrating ancestral spirits. Even more recently, solitary strangers would enter small villages outside the coastal towns with some apprehension.

The Christian faith, as adopted by Melanesians, was adjusted to fit the beliefs in spirit-beings. Christ became a cult hero, remote but important to the general welfare of the villages. Ghosts, having a more personal significance, continued to be feared and were called upon for protection. Some parts of the initiation practices have been retained. The practice of piercing the earlobes and the nasal septum to attach decorations made from the tusks of wild boars and the teeth of dogs has survived.[4] Other ornaments—bracelets, anklets, and headpieces—are used today in traditional ceremonies as they were in the past. When a young man married recently, he was allowed to choose his own wife, in contrast with earlier customs, but the groom's family still paid the bride price. However, the price was paid in inflated Australian currency instead of in traditional shells and pigs.

F. E. Williams, in the *Drama of Orokolo* (147 a), gives extensive reports of our patient's home region during his early youth. Traditional beliefs dominated the lives of the villagers. Men lived in the men's house, the Evaro. Women and children were completely excluded from the area. The buildings were impressive structures: the fronts were more than fifty feet high. Religious and initiation ceremonies took place in the Evaro and religious relics were stored in the dark interior. When the men's houses were first built and not yet occupied, only men knowledgeable in the secrets of the Heheve masks were admitted. The bringing of the sacred masks and plaques into the house sanctified it and was believed to endow it with magic powers (147 a).

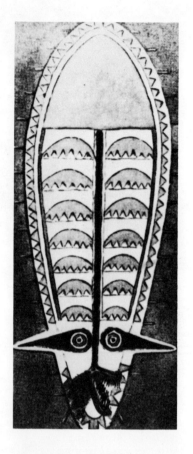

8.13. *Heheve masks of the Papuan Gulf represent the daughters of the sea monster.*

4. One of our drivers through the Highlands, a young man in his early twenties, told us in good English about the success of his family, referring to his clan. They owned several trucks and cars; they were contractors excavating for building roads. The young man was dressed in Western clothes, but his nasal septum was pierced, an indication of having undergone partial initiation ceremonies. New Guinea's Chief Minister Michael Somara describes in his recent book, *Sana* (136), undergoing the "third phase" of his initiation in 1973. He had not undergone the ceremony at the appropriate age of sixteen. Since his government duties did not allow a prolonged absence from the affairs of state, the ceremony had to be condensed to a few days instead of several months when it finally took place. In spite of the deviations, he considered the ceremony important if he were not to separate himself from his people and to maintain his identity at home (136). He recognized the importance for a newly formed nation to integrate its cultural heritage with the life of a modern state.

Our patient's childhood experiences took place during a period of cultural transition; consequently, his life reflects the conflict of beliefs; he did not undergo full intiation ceremonies, but his ears and nasal septum were pierced to hold the shell or boar tusk worn as ornaments during the traditional ceremonies. Warfare between clans was still practiced when he was a boy, but he did not participate in it. Illness and death, particularly sudden death, were supposed to be caused by sorcery.

According to his personal history, the patient had been considered a quiet, somewhat withdrawn child. He did not attend school except for a few months of Bible school. When working on a plantation he was considered a poor worker because he resented being supervised, but he supported himself and his family by working on his own as a subsistence farmer. During World War II, he was recruited as a runner for the Australian army, but being afraid of the invading Japanese, he ran away from the Angau (the Australian Civilian Administration).

The patient's psychiatric illness became apparent shortly after his wife's sudden death. On the day of her disappearance she had gone fishing with two other women. According to the women's story, they were separated for a short time, and on their return to a prearranged spot they discovered that the patient's wife had suddenly disappeared, apparently in the river where they had fished. They assumed she had been killed by a crocodile. The patient suspected that his wife's death was conjured by a sorcerer. The wife's brother had previously run off with the wife of another man. The estranged man's family forced the adulterer to leave the village, and the patient believed that they also engaged a sorcerer to "pay back" for the shame that his dead wife's brother had caused. Supposedly, the sorcerer cast a spell on a crocodile, causing it to devour the patient's wife. The patient wanted to appeal to the Australian courts to punish the family of the abducted wife, since sorcery was a crime that was severely punished, but he feared putting the responsible family in prison since they could use sorcery against him.

As he brooded more and more over his wife's death, he started to lose interest in his activities. The villagers noticed a change in his personality. His behavior was considered highly unusual: he began to neglect his crops and stole vegetables and nuts to feed himself. He developed ideas of persecution. Fearing for his life, he no longer slept in his hut. His speech became vague and incoherent; his family and his neighbors could not understand why he imagined himself persecuted. He attempted to protect himself by always carrying his bow and arrow. One day, he broke into the hut of a man, threatening to kill him, as he held him responsible for his wife's death. Later he moved into the hut of his brother, whom he also threatened when he became suspicious that his brother and his brother's wife were trying to poison him. The villagers realized that this strange behavior was due to an illness precipitated by his wife's death; they asked the district officer in the village for help. After visiting the patient, he sent him to the psychiatric center at Laloki for admission.[5]

On admission the patient appeared confused, incoherent, and unable to formulate his thoughts adequately. He was restless, talking in a loud voice; he repeated meaningless phrases and was very delusional. Having lost his ability to express himself verbally, he started to paint copiously. The designs were repetitive and obviously influenced by traditional designs of the Gulf Region.

The art of the Papuan Gulf is distinguished by its plaques, used in ancestor cults. Related styles appear in the various regions of the area; the most spectacular are possibly the Heheve masks and the Hohao plaques. The traditional Hohao

5. The officer's letter to request admission appears in the Appendix.

boards are four to five feet high, oval in shape, and carved from broken canoes (illustration 6.3); they are painted in pale yellow or burnt ochre, and are decorated in white, pink and black clay. The face of the mask has prominent eyes surrounded by decorative chevrons. A headdress tops the forehead and the eyebrows are emphasized. The nose forms a long central axis ending at the open mouth, which displays two rows of shark's teeth. The body is usually incomplete and disproportionately small; the arms and hands are upraised in a protective gesture (110 a); the navel, symbolizing the center of the clan, consists of several concentric rings; the phallus is often prominent.

The Hohaos were believed to possess the dangerous spirits of powerful ancestors whose help was invoked before a hunt, a war raid, or during a crisis. The spirit of the Hohao, representing a mythical hero, would walk into battle in front of the warrior. The role of the plaques was ambivalent: they served the interests of the group but were also capable of destructive and dangerous deeds affecting the individual. They could cause illness and death, but they could also offer powerful protection in time of danger. Under the influence of the missionaries, many of the Hohao plaques were destroyed when the Evaros (men's houses) were set afire in an attempt to eliminate pagan customs. Some were saved from destruction and can be found in museums throughout the world.

Other traditionally important regional masks were those of the Heheves, which represented the daughters of a sea monster (illustration 8.13). These masks were twenty feet high; they were made on a cane frame, over which a bark cloth was stretched. The mouth, containing sharp, sharklike teeth, was their most distinctive part. It was made separately and protruded forward from the rest of the mask. Their symmetrical design varied, but it was cohesive and of tight construction, using the same colors as the Hohao boards. These masks were used in

8.14. *The revivals of Hohao designs lack the impact of the original carvings.*

8.15. *Hohao board, by permission of the Field Museum of Natural History, Chicago, IL.*

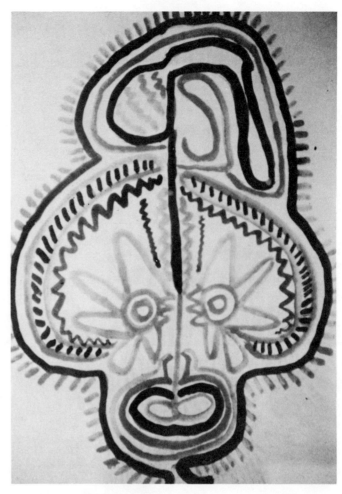

elaborate ceremonies; strictly regulated instructions for construction of the plaques were handed down from generation to generation; protected by magical powers, the Heheves were feared and respected.

Our patient spontaneously painted many figures resembling the traditional Hohao plaques. His personality function regressed to levels of early developmental patterns mobilizing earlier art styles that had not been part of his cultural activities during recent years. His designs, serving essential personal needs, were less integrated but far more authentic than the reproductions of commissioned artists (7). The products of commercial artists were more cohesive, but they lacked the impact of the original carvings (illustration 8.14).

During each of the recurring psychotic episodes, the patient's preoccupation with the spirit of his dead wife returned; his fears continued for years after her death, going far beyond the traditional customs for paying respect to the spirit of the deceased. The patient drew numerous figures resembling the traditional Hohao plaques; the cohesiveness of his designs fluctuated greatly depending on the level of his personality disintegration. He sought protection from the manifestations of his wife's ghost by painting plaques that traditionally shielded the individual from supernatural dangers. A fear of the ghost of a deceased spouse, and the wish for protection against its power, is a widespread custom among many cultures. Reminders of a deceased spouse, even among Westerners, often interfere with the development of a new relationship, and remarriage is possibly correlated with the practice of tie-breaking customs (124). The patient recognized

8.16. (left). *Painting in the Haus Tamberan, Abelam, New Guinea; courtesy of Anthony Forge, Canberra, Australia. Although this painting does not come from the patient's home district, it is similar to the paintings of his clan.*

8.17. (right). *Beginning disintegration.*

8.18. (top left). *Moderate disintegration: cultural characteristics (indentations) begin to disappear.*

8.19. (top right). *Increasing disintegration: condensations and elaborations of original design.*

8.20. (left). *Elaborations, condensations and perseverations of the original design. The face in this painting has two pairs of eyes, at the extreme top and bottom.*

that he was unable to break his emotional ties with his deceased wife; his fears controlled him even when his condition seemed to be in remission; he never remarried, as her spirit was "too strong" for him to free himself from her domination.

In all of his graphics, the patient used traditional structures, such as those of the Hohao board (illustration 8.15) and the painting in the House Tamberans (illustration 8.16). His first drawings display comparatively slight distortions, which progress as his personality disintegrates. The concept of the Hohao is preserved in his first watercolor, which is only slightly distorted in its overall design (illustration 8.17). The border of this plaque is reinforced by five to six layers, while traditionally it has only two or three layers. The symmetry of the plaque is still maintained, with the exception of the headdress, which evolves into irregular curves without definite pattern. The center line is surrounded by red and blue zigzag lines; the eyes and the encircling chevrons are exaggerated. The patient used primarily two colors—a reddish brown and a dark blue. A number of concentric layers are around the mouth, which lacks the customary double row of teeth. The rest of the body, which is not prominent in the traditional board, is completely omitted in the patient's drawings. The increased number of boundary lines and the asymmetrical headdress indicate the beginnings of distortion of the basic concept.

The concept of the next watercolor (illustration 8.18) is tightened; the indentations have disappeared; the entire design is more condensed but considerably distorted. The border consists of zigzag lines; ovals form an enlarged headdress; disproportionately large triangles encircle the unusually small eyes; the mouth contains the traditional double row of teeth; other segments of the body are absent. The colors are untraditionally bright—bright reds and yellows in addition to various shades of blue.

As the patient's personality disintegrates further, he aggravates the distortions by condensing some parts and elaborating and perseverating others; the reinforced boundaries of the first drawing begin to disintegrate (illustration 8.19). In spite of considerable disorganization, the basic structure is still preserved; parts of the original design have disintegrated—the boundary of the lower part has disappeared while the upper part, the headdress, is enlarged by the repetition of numerous curved and zigzag lines and triangles. The remainder of the traditional board has been highly condensed; the annular eyes are surrounded by simplified chevrons;

8.21. (left). *The dissolution of the patient's ego boundaries is reflected in the fact that the borders of his design are lifting off, attached at only two points.*

8.22. (right). *Condensed, impoverished design.*

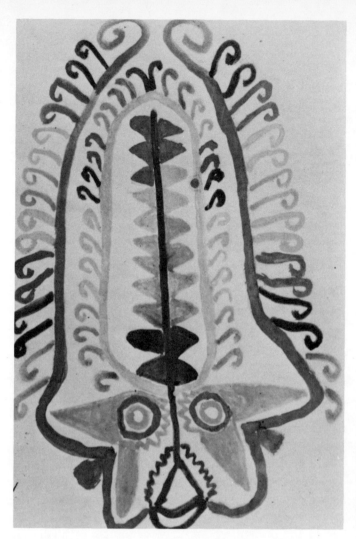

the central straight line ends at the mouth, which has become a toothless, empty cavity. The remainder of the body is missing.

Psychopathological features in the form of elaborations, condensations and perseverations appear in the next graphic (illustration 8.20). While the outline of the plaque is maintained, the border consists of more than the usual number of layers of zigzag lines, a characteristic that appears frequently in graphics by schizophrenics from New Guinea (illustration 8.36). It may represent an attempt to compensate for the loss of protective *ego boundaries* that customarily establish a distinct border between the individual and his environment. The drawing's top and bottom show elaborations of decorative curlycues; the central axis of the board is preserved. The eyes are surrounded by the traditional chevrons, although increased in number; a pair of eyes is displaced to the top while another pair is at the lower end just above the mouth. While repetitious patterns appear frequently in Melanesian art, a perseveration of eyes does not occur in the Hohaos and must be considered a pathological concept.

The dissolution of ego boundaries becomes still more advanced in the next watercolor (illustration 8.21). The patient can no longer maintain his attempts to compensate for the disintegration of the conceptual boundaries by reinforcing them as in the earlier drawings. The borders appear lifted off, becoming detached except for two anchoring points; they end in decorative curlycues, purposeless perseverations, similar to the repetitious lines of a Western schizophrenic patient (illustration 7.46). The interior of the board is reduced to geometric figures with-

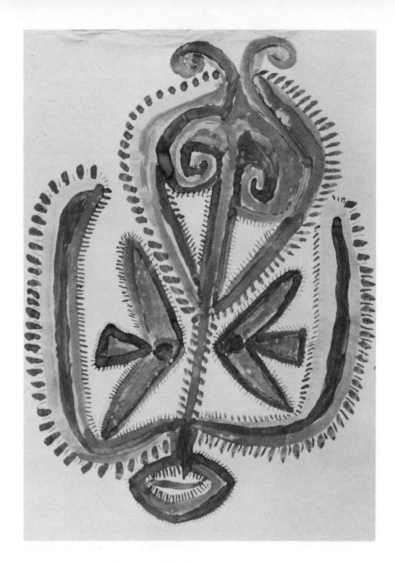

8.25. *The patient suffered another psychotic episode. Conceptual disintegration recurs.*

8.23. (left). *Reintegrating design with border absent.*

8.24. (right). *Conceptual reintegration.*

out symbolic meaning. In place of the eyes is an oval figure surrounded by small dark blue triangles. The central axis is missing but an open triangle ending in curlycues is attached below the upper oval. A larger oval figure replacing the mouth is surrounded by black, red, and yellow curved lines. The usual double row of shark teeth is displaced to the right outside the central design, and is also drawn in curlycues. Some parts of the design are missing altogether; others are condensed. The distortion of the basic design, particularly the displacement of parts that originally conveyed strength (shark teeth) to insignificant locations, and the perseveration of curlycues weaken the original power of the plaque.

The most advanced state of condensation and of highly impoverished design is reached in the patient's next graphic (illustration 8.22). The vertical axis, which originally represented the nose, is continued and perseverated by a horizontal line forming a cross. Crosses appear repeatedly in various art forms throughout New Guinea; Newton (110 d) attributes them to designs related to fertility rites. The continuous black, yellow, and red lines surrounding three arms of the cross are separated from the upper vertical arm; they form curved lines ending, as in the previous graphic, in curlycues.

The next watercolor shows a reintegration resulting in a return to the basic Hohao design; the figure is without a border and seems to be floating in space. The central axis is maintained, flanked by eyes with characteristic chevrons. The headdress is composed of wavy lines; at the lower end of the axis is an open mouth without teeth; no other part of the body is shown. The colors are untraditional, varying from red to green and from purple to blue (illustration 8.23).

Prior to his leaving the hospital, the patient painted well-integrated masks resembling greatly the traditional Heheve plaque (illustration 8.13). The annular eyes and the surrounding chevrons are designed like the traditional works; even tassels are added to the lower part of the face. Only the shape of the mouth is altered, and the colors show the greatest deviation from the original plaques (illustration 8.24).

The patient's clinical condition responded favorably to chemotherapy, enabling him to return to his village following his discharge from the hospital. As there are no treatment facilities outside the larger towns, the patient did not continue his treatment; his condition relapsed soon and he had to be readmitted to the hospital several times. Each time, he attributed his illness to the reappearance of his wife's very powerful spirit, which had again gained control of his thoughts. During each hospitalization he began spontaneously to paint designs resembling those of the Hohaos and the Heheves. The Hohaos painted by the patient during his most recent admission show even less cohesive and integrated patterns than previously, which may be evidence of increasing personality disintegration due to his prolonged illness. The boundaries of the designs are dissolved, the painted lines broader and more coarse; the paintings are covered with perseverated short strokes without apparent significance. Curlycues, a frequent disintegrative design, appear with increasing frequency. The eyes are made of dots rather than concentric circles; the chevrons are formed by closed triangles instead of the open designs seen earlier (illustration 8.25).

Case 511

When we visited another patient, who had originally lived in a village of the Papuan Gulf, in the maximum security section of the Bomana Prison, we had an occasion to see the institution. A well-kept road led to the open buildings; tropical flowers and shrubs were planted along the paths and around the clean cottages. As we arrived, the prisoners were exercising; they appeared to be well nourished; they were dressed in clean, wine-red lap laps, a traditional shirtlike covering. We were told that the prisoners participated in a regulated rehabilitation program.

When we entered the maximum security section, we had to pass through three heavy steel gates. When we signed the visitor's book, even the prison director had to enter his signature. This section of the prison was patrolled by guards with police dogs, and the watch towers were manned by officers carrying machine guns. Any apprehensions that we might have felt disappeared when we entered a room in the main building. The room was austere, furnished with a small table, a few chairs, and a wooden cabinet, all impeccably clean. Two guards in smart military uniforms brought the patient into the room. The prison director seemed friendly with the patient, but correctly formal. The patient appeared at ease and seemed not to be intimidated by the director or the guards; he spoke freely. We interviewed him in the presence of the guards, who translated the local place talk into Neo-Melanesian.

The patient was a small man of approximately fifty years of age. Little is known of his early history except that he grew up in a small village near Kerema in the Gulf District. He did not attend school. During his youth, he had few, if any, contacts outside his village. As he approached puberty, initial Western contacts in his area led to significant societal changes. Without these changes, he would have undergone the customary initiation ceremonies. He was spared that

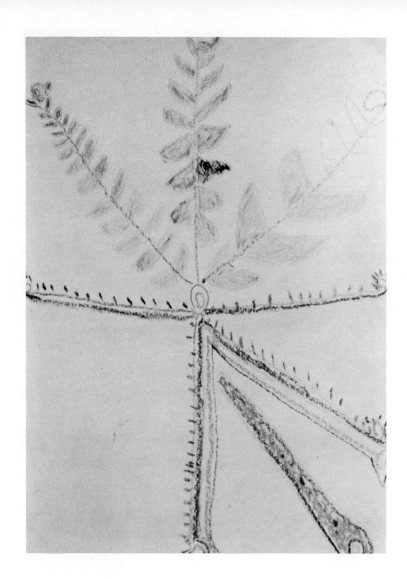

8.26. *Marked disintegration: rudimentary designs (Gulf of Papua).*

experience, but not all of the traditional rites: his earlobes were pierced so that he could wear ornaments important at ceremonials. When he became an adult, he left his village and found work as a janitor at the Port Moresby Airport. He married a woman from his home village who liked him at first, but soon started to complain that he did not give her enough money. They started to argue frequently; he became violent at times, and finally, during one of the arguments, he killed her with an ax. He was sentenced to prison.

During the early years of his imprisonment, he was "troublesome" and emotionally explosive. One day, without apparent reason, he attacked and killed a warden. When questioned, he stated that he heard voices that had told him that the warden had had an affair with the patient's girlfriend, who supposedly lived near the prison. It was soon discovered, however, that the girlfriend did not exist; she was a delusional fantasy. It was evident that the patient was mentally ill and he was transferred to Laloki Psychiatric Center. As his condition improved considerably with the use of psychotropic drugs (tranquilizers used in the treatment of schizophrenic reactions), he was returned to the correctional institution.

During our interview, the patient appeared overly talkative. His ideational processes were fairly coherent as long as he did not talk about his delusions. When he was dealing with his delusions, his thoughts became disorganized. He could not express his delusional ideas adequately, being distracted by many irrelevant details. His thoughts became vague, making the translation difficult. He became

8.27. *Beginning structuralization.*

8.28. *The patient's first anthropomorphic figure begins to take shape, although its borders merge with those of the surrounding geometric figures.*

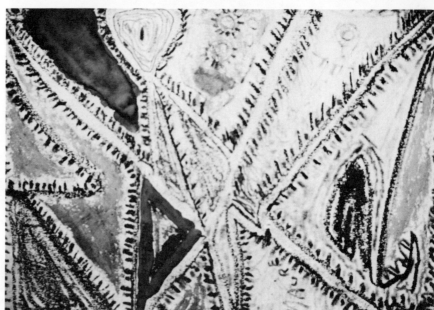

8.29. *The patient's culture begins to exert its influence on his art as the anthropomorphic figure becomes more clearly defined.*

150

8.30. *(see also color plate 8). The patient's condition has improved to the point where he is able to create a design resembling a Kokave mask of the Papuan Gulf.*

obviously tense, in contrast to the calm and indifferent attitude he exhibited when not dealing with emotionally charged material.

According to the information given by the prison warden. his affect, initially explosive, had gradually flattened, and he became increasingly detached from his environment. He told us that he heard male voices talking about his wife; these voices came from aircraft flying overhead, but he did not know where the planes originated. His Western contacts had modified the customary spirit beliefs; his work at the airport had changed his view of the ways in which spirit-beings behave. If he had held to his traditional concepts, he would have believed that the voices of his ancestral spirits came from stones, trees, and shrubs. But his hallucinations were modernized by his experiences, making him believe that the voices came from aircraft.

When we questioned him, he readily admitted that he had no regrets about killing his wife. According to the traditional belief, she was still alive in "another world," and lived near him. Customarily, the spirit of the dead stays in the home village for a few months, but his wife's ghost had stayed near him for an unusually long time—several years. His wife appeared to him dressed in white; she came regularly at four o'clock in the afternoon, always telling him, "You are my man." He was not disturbed by the vision, and her voice sounded tender and affectionate. Her actions were in contrast to the usual appearance of ghosts, particularly of female ghosts, who are feared as vengeful and dangerous.

The first of the patient's drawings (illustration 8.26) contains abstract patterns, part of which seem to be leaves. In addition, he has drawn horizontal,

151

vertical, and diagonal lines, and has placed short strokes on top of the lines. Similar designs appear frequently in graphics of the area, suggesting some cultural significance; otherwise, the total composition suggests little culture-bound material, but is more characteristic of regressive designs found among advanced disintegrated patients of any cultural background.

The lines of the next graphic (illustration 8.27) are organized in geometric patterns; the space between the individual forms is filled in with olive paint and purplish crayons; there is no shading.

Anthropomorphic figures are a frequent subject of New Guinean art. The amount of culture-bound material in a patient's art usually decreases as personality disintegration increases. But in the next watercolor (illustration 8.28), our patient attempted to recreate traditional artistic designs. A moderately cohesive figure leaning to the left is entirely shaped of triangles, including the head, which consists of concentric triangular lines. The outline of the figure is covered with the characteristic short strokes that are common in graphics of all regions of the country but that are often overemphasized in psychopathological expressions. As the patient integrates further (illustration 8.29), the anthropomorphic figures become more clearly developed. The concentric lines that shaped the head in the earlier graphics define the facial features more clearly. The arms are stretched out, and there seem to be two parts of legs. Geometric shapes fill the spaces between the limbs compulsively, suggesting horror vacui.

The final drawing (illustration 8.30) by this patient was completed when his illness had improved considerably. The design of the figure assumes culture-bound elements; it shows the characteristics of the traditional masks of the area (100 a). The masks of this part of the Orokolo Region consist of a squarish headpiece; banana leaves cover the sides of the figure. Williams (147 a) compared the portly posture of these figures to that of a Church dignitary in his robes. The patient's graphic seems similarly to convey the impression of a cumbersome figure, his feet limiting his movements. The head contains square phalanges which surround the eyes; they seem to be a perseveration of the usual chevrons; they are filled with dots, which appeared in the patient's earlier drawings. The entire figure is cohesive, although distorted, and resembles in its basic structure an exaggerated expression of the original concept of the Haruhu mask of Opau. The image of the portly, dignified figure mentioned by Williams is successfully communicated in

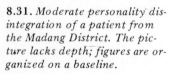

8.31. *Moderate personality disintegration of a patient from the Madang District. The picture lacks depth; figures are organized on a baseline.*

the schizophrenic's drawing. As in the previous case, the reintegrative capacities are displayed in the patient's graphics and correspond to his clinical improvement.

MADANG DISTRICT

Case 512

The Madang District on the northern coast exemplifies the vast differences among all aspects of New Guinea life. The people of the coastal region have had contacts with the outside world for over one hundred years. The Madang harbor has been a busy port in the South Seas and an important commercial center on the north coast, while the isolated mountain people continue farming, which barely supplies their daily needs.

The traditional art of the district consists of geometric designs, often signifying fruits or clouds (illustration 8.34). Our patient came from the mountainous part of the region. Having lived in an isolated village, he had few outside contacts during most of his life. When he was admitted for treatment, his thought processes were disorganized, his speech vague and moderately incoherent, and the interpreter encountered considerable difficulties in translating his statements. He had developed ideas of grandeur, believing he was Jesus Christ.

The content of his drawing (illustration 8.31) shows local characteristics. A man in traditional costume with a large headdress stands next to a sacred men's house; a tree stands in front of the house. The picture's lack of depth makes the tree appear to grow up through the house. In spite of the drawing's traditional content, its spatial structure is handled according to European principles. The traditional artists of the Madang Region, and those of other parts of New Guinea, depict geometric abstractions (57) or single forms (129 a), but they do not use a baseline or perspective to interrelate their figures; they remain isolated. Using a baseline as a foundation on which to build the scenery is a concept foreign to New Guinea art. Rather, it is found in the early pictures of high civilizations (50) and in European art. The spatial structure of the patient's watercolor shows the regressive patterns of a disintegrated patient from any cultural background (Table 2).

8.32. *Geometric design; disintegrated personality; Northern District.*

153

NORTHERN DISTRICT

Case 508

For the next case, we focus on a small town in the thinly populated Northern District. High mountain ranges descend sharply, first to the dense forests of the foothills and then to the swampy grasslands of the coastal area.

A large part of the population is made up of the Orokaiva people. The clansmen are steeped in cult activities, among these the Taro cult (147 b). The entire community participates in the ceremonials. This common activity establishes close family relationships and forms strong kinship solidarity. Outsiders are only slowly accepted, injustices are repaid with violent fights, and the Orokaiva people are known by their neighbors for their explosive nature.

The mountainous and forbidding inland sections were protected from outside contacts until World War II, when they were shocked into the twentieth century by suddenly becoming a battleground. The Kokoda Trail, famous during the war, led from the outskirts of Port Moresby all the way out to the Northern District. The local people were thrust into the conflict taking place on their soil. The Western forces conscripted them as carriers or messengers, but those who were caught by the Japanese were publicly decapitated for collaborating with the enemy. The fighting of alien forces on their ground forced the Orokaiva to abandon many of their embattled villages.

The patient, approximately forty-five years old, had witnessed many societal and cultural changes since his early childhood. Many ceremonial customs had lost their significance; initiation ceremonies that had taken place in several phases,

extending over a number of years, had died out under pressure from missionaries. By the time the patient reached adolescence, only his earlobes and his nasal septum were pierced so he could wear the traditional ornaments during ceremonial festivals, a custom continued in this area, as in many others.

He had no unusual conflicts until he married a woman who had promised to marry another man. His mother had argued against the marriage because family tradition disapproved of such behavior. Her efforts were fruitless, but she never accepted the daughter-in-law. The mother died a few years later. After her death, her spirit appeared to the patient, telling him that his wife had other men, and that his children were those of another man. After several appearances, the ghost told the patient to kill his son. The patient confronted his wife with an accusation of infidelity, but she denied any guilt. Their arguments eventually led to violence. One morning, after a fight, the patient took his son behind his hut and decapitated and dismembered him with an ax. He became very disturbed over what he had done. Becoming confused, he wandered aimlessly for days. On his return he was arrested.

During the psychiatric evaluation, the patient's statements were inconsistent; his thoughts were vague and poorly organized. He no longer seemed disturbed over his actions, but he appeared indifferent and emotionally detached; his affect was flat. He soon developed delusions of grandeur and hallucinations. Voices told him that he would marry the Queen of Australia. Lilliputian creatures one foot tall visited him. They were not ancestors; they were young, but not human children; they were spirit-beings who worked in gardens, planting vegetables. They were not disturbing to him. He asserted that he was privileged to see them every day, while others could see them only once a year, on Good Friday. In addition, women spirits from the cemetery visited him at night trying to entice him to do bad things, but he resisted their blatant advances.

His graphics show regression to geometric and abstract designs. One such abstract (illustration 8.32) shows a half-moon design framing the paper's edges; other half-moons adjoin each other to form diagonal lines, they form a circle in the center. The designs show no culture-bound material. Similar shapes have

8.33. *Beside his drawing, the patient imitates writing in an attempt to communicate his thoughts.*

8.34. Ancestor *is a traditional woven pattern of the Northern District. It is used here by courtesy of Dr. W. Moi, Laloki Psychiatric Center, Papua, New Guinea, as is illustration 8.35.*

8.35. War Council.

been drawn by Western schizophrenics, as reported by Prinzhorn (illustration 8.5; Table 2). Although illiterate, the patient tried to imitate writing in several of his drawings (illustration 8.33) in an apparent attempt to communicate his thoughts. The imitation lettering is combined with geometric figures placed on top of one another. The figure is somewhat suggestive of traditional New Guinea designs, but not specifically of the art from the patient's home district. The design appears in local weaving patterns but they are highly organized and symmetrical, as in a fabric called the *Ancestor* (illustration 8.34). It consists of three quarter-circles surrounding the ends of three rows of straight trunks that branch off the center stem. Another piece is composed of several circles, symbolizing rows of warriors surrounding the village in the center, plotting a head-hunting raid (illustration 8.35). The patient's graphics show traces of culturally characteristic designs of a general nature but not characteristic of a specific area. His fairly advanced personality disintegration prevents more distinct culture-bound material from being produced.

BUKA ISLAND

Case 510

Buka, a small island in the extreme northwest part of the Solomon chain, has had a colorful history. The Spaniards landed an expedition here during the sixteenth century, believing that they had discovered King Solomon's mines. Their failure to find gold did not dampen their spirits, and they named the island chain after the Biblical king. (The sailors' intuition was not entirely wrong—gold was discovered four hundred years later in parts of New Guinea.) After this initial contact, further communication with the outside world was sporadic until various European nations sent permanent expeditions to the islands in the 1820's. The Solomon chain, including Buka, has had longer continuous contact with Western culture than any other group in Melanesia.

The inhabitants of Buka have been described as the blackest people in the world (127). They are intelligent and imaginative (24 b). Germany and Great Britain have trained and used men from Buka as policemen in all parts of New Guinea; others have been taken to Australia as laborers. After their return, the natives told their countrymen of their experiences in the outside world. At first they admired the wealth and skills of the white man, but soon the people, increasingly aware of their own poverty, became resentful of the white man's material advantages. In the past they had been accustomed to sharing their fortune with others, and consequently expected to receive part of the white man's goods. When they did not receive what they considered their share, they became hostile, plotting schemes to attain that wealth. Thus developed the cargo cults, which had their beginnings on the island around 1910.

One of the most fascinating of these movements developed in 1954. In the village of Hahalis, a welfare society was formed with the intent to learn the necessary secrets for acquiring the wealth and power of the Europeans. The members believed that imitating the Australian's habits of eating and drinking, and his dress, would make them, too, wealthy masters of the country (127). They stopped their physical labor; their working hours became as leisurely as the white man's seemed to be. They pushed imaginary buttons on imaginary machines, spoke into imaginary telephones and adopted liberalized sexual patterns. A "baby garden" was set up, and a select group of young women were placed in special houses. Men who did good work for the Society were allowed to visit the gardens. Each woman had many visitors and the children born in the garden belonged to the Society and were educated to become leaders. The baby garden not only offered rewards for productive behavior, but also gave promise to develop a master race (127).

Our patient had become a leader of the Hahalis Welfare Society. Even prior to joining the group, while still a young man, he had been considered a "bigpela" (important person) by the clan. His family had held respected positions in the community for generations. The patient's uncle was a head man of the clan, and after his death the patient's mother became the group's leader. (Only exceptionally do women become chiefs, and then only if their fathers or brothers have held the rank before them; however, leadership is not inherited—it was passed along in families according to their role in the clan.)

The patient established contacts with Western civilization early in life. During his youth, he served as "number one boss boy" (supervisor) for a large Australian company, overseeing all indigenous employees in the office. He became increasingly successful and comparatively wealthy and respected. Eventually he owned four trade stores. Because of his respected standing in the community, the Australian government appointed him "luluai" (head man). He served in this capacity for fifteen years. He married three times but, at the interview, was vague about whether or not he was married to more than one wife at a time. (Polygamy was generally accepted.)

About five years before the onset of his acute illness, he became seclusive and irritable. He neglected his affairs. He became involved in fights, which was unusual for him. He was jailed for a short time after an encounter with a native policeman. Following that incident, he became openly angry and resentful toward the Australian government. He complained that he had not been paid for his services as head man of his clan. He turned against the established system and joined the controversial Hahalis Welfare Society. He was aware that such a move on his part would not be approved by the administration that had appointed him Luluai, a position requiring loyalty. Even those of his own people, who were loyal to the government, disapproved of many of his actions. As a convert, he began to preach about the coming of a millennium of wealth when the ancestors would return with a cargo of goods. He became convinced that in order to prove himself as the leader of the Society he would have to sacrifice a human being. The local council of the Society had supposedly approved the sacrifice at a secret meeting and had chosen as the victim the patient's sister's daughter's son, a sixteen-year-old boy who had always been considered weak and sickly. He was a safe subject, as the ghost of a deceased person is believed to possess only the strength he had when he was living (78); a weak man's ghost is less feared. The family accepted the sacrifice of the boy as a form of distinction. During a public ceremony, the patient cut the boy's head off. By virtue of the sacrifice, the patient considered himself god-like. He sponsored a great feast to celebrate, inviting villagers from the entire region. He paid for the feast both with traditional shell money and *pressing money* (Australian currency).

But the authorities arrested him for the murder of his nephew. He showed no remorse for his action, believing that what he had done was in the interest of his people. He accepted his arrest without surprise, realizing that the government would not understand his act as important to the salvation of his people, and as a protest against their inferior role. He was surprised, however, when the court wanted him to undergo a psychiatric evaluation even if the members of his own village considered him to be "long-long." During the psychiatric interview, the patient appeared indifferent and emotionally withdrawn (24 b). He attempted suicide on three occasions by cutting his throat in a manner similar to that by which he had sacrificed his nephew. The first suicide attempt was made after the preliminary court hearings. Soon after recovering, while he was still in the hospital, he attempted again to cut his throat. He tried a third time, after being informed that his oldest son had been killed in an accident. As the court procedures dragged on, the patient became annoyed. He felt old and tired; he wanted to escape his life on earth for a while by going into the spiritual world, with the opportunity to return when life was more pleasant. He was convinced that a legal trial was superfluous, only an intolerable, newly contrived, and ineffective method of putting things in order. He had no faith in the new laws and expected that the people would revert to the former traditional rules. As he considered himself godlike, he was beyond the reach of the courts.

Some of the patient's delusions were difficult to differentiate from the existing cultural beliefs; but other thoughts were clearly beyond the customary local tenets. His belief, for instance, that he could pass as the same person, in the same appearance, from this world to the other world and return at will, was not shared by others in his community. It was an indication of his pathological thinking (24 b). The traditional beliefs in spirit-beings assume that the spirit of a person who has died lives near the village in trees or behind stones (78) and visits the survivors. It may appear to them for a few weeks or months, but it is recognized as a different being—a spirit that is endowed with supernatural powers but that never joins the living again.

As the patient's illness advanced over the next five years, his delusions became fixed. He admitted to having committed four other sacrifices in addition to the one for which he was arrested. He could not accept that his human sacrifices failed to deliver the cargo, but was convinced that his people were not yet good enough to deserve the favors of the ancestors. He believed further human sacrifices might be needed to induce the ancestral spirits to deliver the cargo.

At the time of our interview, the patient's thought processes appeared fairly coherent, but his affect was shallow; he was seclusive and seldom associated with other patients. When we were at the hospital, he moved at the periphery of the

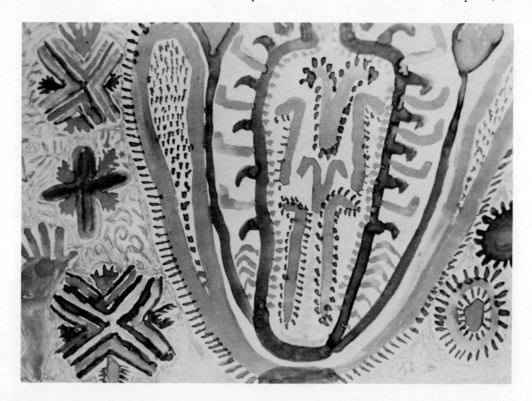

8.36. *Abstractions using traditional patterns; disintegrated personality; Buka.*

8.37. *The patient draws an anthropomorphic, ghostlike figure, overpowering and distorted.*

interviewing team, obviously waiting for opportunities to have further contacts that seemed prestigious to him. Such contacts would reflect his own importance. In spite of his self-assigned godlike position, he had to accept his daily infirmities, however lowly they might be. When we interviewed him, he pointed to his feet, requesting medical help for a fungus infection which he hesitantly attributed to sorcery. A sorcerer in his village had put a spell on him as he believed the patient had stolen palm leaves, which were used in chewing betel nuts, from his garden. The sorcerer supposedly put a potion into the patient's footsteps which caused the skin on his feet to peel and hurt. Such beliefs in sorcery were not beyond the customary cultural concepts, and the patient separated them from his more significant delusions. He emphasized that they had nothing to do with his role as cargo leader. He seemed reluctant to admit to such commonplace concerns, which would not be becoming to a godlike figure.

The patient's first watercolor was highly abstract and contained geometrical figures similar to traditional forms found in New Guinea (illustration 8.36). The individual designs seem unrelated to each other. The blue outline of the center figure suggests the outline of a Papuan Gulf plaque. On the right are mandala-like circles that appear frequently in the art of many cultures. The hand in the lower left is derived from the taro, its extensions forming the fingers and the root itself the palm (illustrations 8.8 to 8.10). Diagonals are seen frequently in indigenous art, as is the cross. The individual in New Guinea is not always aware of the symbolic significance of traditional designs of his own culture; he may be unable to give adequate interpretation and is apt to be influenced by superficial and arbitrary meanings.[6] Our patient associated the cross with the Red Cross, but this design has far earlier origins and is found in many areas of New Guinea (illustration 8.22). It has been associated with the yam cult and with initiation rites (110 d).

An anthropomorphic, ghostlike figure, overpowering and distorted, forms the next graphic (illustration 8.37). Similar poorly integrated figures have been

6. The symbolic meaning of art objects becomes lost due to the lack of any written history. The verbal report taking place from generation to generation distorts the original significance of many designs and of ritual customs.

described as "inarticulate structures" (35); they are poorly shaped and hardly recognizable as human. The facial features of the patient's graphic are incomplete and highly rudimentary: the eyes are simple circles; an empty oval structure shapes the mouth; the nose is missing. The rest of the body is suggested by the bare outline of the trunk; the arms hang from the neck. The other parts can only be inferred; the legs seem to be formed by M-shaped structures connected to the main body. The arms and legs are highly stylized, making the entire figure appear frozen and rigid. The three layers of color which traditionally form a figure's outline are perseverated to eleven or twelve layers. The many layers seem to be based on the patient's attempt to isolate himself and to compensate for the threatening dissolution of the boundaries between himself and his environment. Such boundaries are normally maintained to protect the individual from the impact of environmental controls. The lack of boundaries prevents adequate differentiation between one's self and the environment, which may lead to the fear that one's own thoughts and actions are controlled by others, as well as the belief that one has the power of controlling those of others (38).

The lack of boundaries between the patient and his surroundings precipitated the impression that he was able to leave this world (by suicide) and return at will when the world was ready to accept his ideas (24 b). The disintegrated boundaries are perceived by the psychotic as a lack of protection from environmental influences, a threatening feeling usually accompanied by intense anxiety. Our patient did not display such apprehensions. He seemed instead to compensate for his anxieties in his drawings by multiplying and perseverating the boundaries of the anthropomorphic figure, reflecting his defenses of shielding himself from exposure to others. The frozen rigidity, the perseverations, and the basically empty design are found in the highly regressed patterns drawn by patients of any cultural background (illustration 7.14).

The scenery of the next graphic (illustration 8.38) attempts to relate a sequence of events by drawing them in several layers. The technique being used here is not characteristic of tribal art, which usually deals only with a single principal idea. Tribal artists sculpt each ancestral figure as a single piece (illustration 4.7)

8.38. *The drawing of a psychotic tells a story with an arrangement of figures in sequential layers. A human figure battles with a snake.*

8.40. *Layered images are used here to show the menacing symbol of a two-tailed snake striking at a human figure. A helicopter flies overhead.*

or paint them individually on bark (illustration 4.8). They are condensed into single objects even if they represent several concepts. Parts of an art work may symbolize natural events or spiritual forces; indentations may represent clouds (110 a). The condensed tribal concepts in art are static, in contrast to the technique of depicting a continuous narrative sequence by moving from one layer to the next, as in certain Roman columns (illustration 8.39) and medieval illuminations (illustration 2.7). The patient's production matches the European style of developing a continuous story by moving from layer to layer.

The organization of our patient's drawing is loosened; objects are arranged on top of each other in vertical projection (14 a). The bottom consists mostly of curved lines, hardly identifiable, on which the second layer containing an oblong object, is placed. It is suggestive of a boat with trees growing out of it. The third layer is curved, topping the drawing with a snake, which seems to strike at a schematically drawn human figure standing in a defensive posture. The face of the figure appears in profile; the trunk and hands are clearly drawn in frontal view while the arms and legs are indistinct. The individual parts of the body are each drawn in their most significant position. This style known as *perspective tordue* appears not only in Egyptian, primitive, and contemporary art, but also in the regressive pattern of psychopathological expression (Table 2).

A similar stratification appears in the next drawing (illustration 8.40), which has three or four layers. The base, filling the lower fourth of the picture, again contains unidentifiable upright lines, some of which are curved; their meaning, as that of the geometric design on the side, is not clear. The second layer shows a chicken and a coconut tree,[7] possibly related to the cargo cult's agricultural plans. As the cult members built airstrips for their incoming planes (which never arrived), the patient drew a wind sock on the right to be used to determine the wind direction at airports. The top layer shows a double-tailed snake (in the same position as the snake in 8.38) apparently striking at an unidentifiable, ill-defined

8.39. *The Roman Trajan Column tells a far more intricate tale, but still uses the same technique of arranging its characters in a spiral sequence.*

---

7. The Welfare Society to which the patient belonged expected to grow coconuts as a cash crop. They demonstrated against the government to force building of roads to transport their copra crops to the seaports for export (127).

8.41. *Helicopters are a repeated subject of this patient's drawings.*

structure, substituted for the human figure. A double-headed (or double-tailed) snake symbolizes vicious and extremely dangerous spirits (147 a). In the top left corner is a fairly distinguishable helicopter dropping a bag attached to a gray line.[8] The crayon drawing seems to deal with the patient's preoccupation with the cargo cult. The helicopter drops the desired cargo while the patient expresses his hostility against the whites by attacking them with the double-tailed snakes.

Schizophrenic patients, often painfully aware of their disintegration, attempt to rebuild their personality structures, however incompletely. They force a defensive, rigid system of *obsessions* and *compulsions* upon their disorganized thinking. The patient's graphics demonstrate visually the defense against the disintegrative process by rigid, compulsively drawn pictures. The rigid symmetry is most evident in a crayon drawing of a meeting house (illustration 8.42). He built it on stilts and constructed it almost entirely of geometric figures; the colors are symmetrically arranged. On each side of the house are trees; the corresponding branches are carefully balanced. On top is a war canoe characteristic of the region. The canoe is arranged in almost perfect symmetry, as is the entire picture. The designs on the left of the canoe are similar to those found on the canoes of the patient's home village (17).

During the last two or three years, the patient's thinking became somewhat disorganized, his obsessive and compulsive concepts less adequately structured. The conceptual change is even more evident in his graphics (illustration 8.43) than in his clinical adjustments. The main concept maintains the basic theme, the assembly house of the welfare society. The symmetry is still present, but the compulsively precise drawing technique is no longer maintained: the house is unevenly drawn. The content deals with emotionally charged material, which no longer conceals his ideas of grandeur. He names the upper center portion of the drawing John's room, the patient being John, the Society's king or god, openly expressing his delusions. Underneath is the meeting room, flanked on each side by the rooms of the head man and the head woman, his immediate assistants. He

8. The patient had drawn helicopters that he identified as such on other occasions (illustration 8.41).

162

adds additional objects, mostly food, such as taro, tubers, a chicken and a fish; but the most important items are a cross used in fertility rites and an emblem of authority he names Morokiogo. The contrast between his earlier and more recent drawings seems most impressive. The earlier graphic is drawn in compulsive symmetry, the later crayon drawing, by contrast, is poorly organized, showing that his compulsive defenses are no longer effective due to the progressive disintegration of his personality.

We have discussed the patient's personal history, but it has to be viewed within the sociocultural framework of his group. Like many of his contemporaries, he found himself in a period of cultural transition. The patient grew up in Northern Buka, an area that was steeped in traditional beliefs. The European powers had penetrated the island about one hundred years earlier. The early

Drawings separated by an interval of two years demonstrate the patient's decline from an obsession with detail and geometric rigidity, to disorganized thinking and drawing.

8.42. *Rigid symmetry.*

8.43. *Disintegration of original design.*

8.44. *Figure from a traditional ceremonial paddle of Buka Island, used by permission of William H. Davenport, Director of the Museum of the University of Pennsylvania, Philadelphia, PA, as is 8.45.*

colonists were harsh masters and contributed greatly to the polarization between the islanders and the whites. The impact made on their stone age society caused a crisis profoundly affecting everyone's life. Conflicting influences were felt even within the same family. The patient's older brother underwent the traditional initiation ceremonies, but Christian missionaries had successfully stopped these practices when the patient reached adolescence. Within a few years, customs were profoundly altered, having a most confusing effect on a youngster of nine or ten years of age. He had learned to fear the ancestral spirits, but the missionaries cajoled the villagers to destroy their images. He had probably been aware of the destruction of some of his "false idols." The head men—his childhood idols—whose approach had been ceremonially announced by the warnings of bullroarers that frightened women and children away—were suddenly reduced to simple council members, obviously insignificant, appointed and discharged at the pleasure of a more powerful outside government. The real power was in the hands of European administrative officers who could wield their authority at will and could remove uncooperative village leaders (106).

The patient witnessed the crumbling of the prestige of his elders, who had ruled in the past by instilling awe and respect for traditional practices and had offered security against the dangers of a stone age society. Several members of his family had been regarded as powerful leaders. As he became older, the colonizers' hold became more apparent, and he watched the power of his elders pale next to the white man's wealth and ability to master all; the white man seemed invincible. Even the strongest among his own group appeared ineffective. As a child he had looked up to the village leaders as clever men, mighty warriors capable of communicating with the spirits. His own family had been accustomed to rule. He expected to follow his uncle's, brother's, and mother's leadership in the clan. But their power dwindled, and they became dependent on the will of people who could perform deeds more impressive than they or their ancestral spirits had ever imagined. Seeing his elders humble themselves before the white man must have created doubts and insecurities in the alert and intelligent youth. He lost some of his fear of their power, and with it much respect and considerable self-esteem. His conflict and confusion must have laid the foundation for his ambivalence toward his own group and the white man.

As an adolescent, instead of being initiated into his clan, he was baptized in the Catholic Church and assimilated some of its teachings, particularly the coming of a Messiah. However, the missionaries taught him that His coming, which would bring the millennium, could only be achieved through sacrifice, a familiar concept in the practice of cannibalism which had been part of his own beliefs. He incorporated the Church's teachings and bent them to fit the traditional beliefs of his people. To him the white man was obviously more successful; therefore, he reasoned, the sacrifice of Christ made the European's ancestral spirits more productive than his own. Such interpretations of Christianity were rampant in various Melanesian groups, but they did not really affect the patient's life until after he became sick. He started to brood about his life. He became aware, and possibly frightened, of the incipient disintegration of his thinking. In his preoccupations, he turned to spiritual beings to find an explanation for the puzzling changes taking place within him. As do patients from all cultures, the patient from Buka sought his answers in the supernatural.[9] As his delusions developed, he

9. Many Western patients turn to religion or the supernatural, often misinterpreting them disastrously. A patient in New Jersey, after becoming mentally ill, studied the Bible for months to find solutions for his own conflicts. He thought that he found the answers by discovering that the world was full of "money changers." He wanted to chase them out of the Temple; so he invaded a barbershop, killing eleven people.

was no longer satisfied with his former standards, but wanted to reach for the white man's fortunes. He joined the cargo cult movement, whose sacrificial aspects appealed to him. His beliefs, partly related to the formerly respected position of his family and partly due to his pathological thinking, made him decide that he was better suited than anyone else to lead his people into the millennium, and he prepared himself to make any necessary sacrifices.

The patient's drawings show progressive structural changes that can be correlated with the spatial structure observed in graphics by schizophrenic patients of many cultures (14 a, b). The inarticulated structures found in the anthropomorphic figure painted by the patient (illustration 8.37) have been described in Chapter 7 as "forms of severe regression" (14 b). These are characterized by a many-layered outline, frozen rigidity, and a basically empty design. The poorly structured figures are similar to those in drawings by Western patients.

The vertical projection seen in his drawings (illustrations 8.39, 8.41) shows that the disintegrated ego has regained a limited ability to organize concepts. The content of the drawings includes such traditional symbols as the double-tailed snake. He used dangerous, but powerful, spiritual forces in an attempt to acquire European standards and wealth. The patient, like other natives living in areas of prolonged Western contact (Case 513), has absorbed Western patterns in structuring the space of his graphics. The drawings no longer show isolated objects placed in space without connecting integrative background. The vertical projection and compulsively organized two-dimensional space express the pathological aspects of the patient's personality.

The traditional art of Buka and its neighboring island of Bougainville shows stylized and sophisticated designs, which can be seen in the ceremonial dance paddle (illustration 8.44). The conventionalized face emphasizes the prominent eys; the decorated ears stand away from the face; a large, conical headdress stresses the formal appearance of the carving; the mouth shows sharp teeth that seem to be gnashing; the head is more than half of the size of the total figure; the slim body contains no distracting details; the arms and legs are held in a traditional position. The total design is imposing by virtue of its simplicity.

The designs of a dance wand may run the gamut from geometric patterns, to simplified outlines of animal figures, to the traditional representation of spirit-beings (illustration 8.45).

8.45. *Traditional dance wand.*

Even less highly sophisticated designs from Buka (illustration 8.46) are integrated and stylized. They are tightly organized but form isolated images; the space between the figures is empty. These images do not build the integrative background that in Western art attempts to tell a story sequentially by bridging the space between the principal characters in the paintings. The patient's graphics show none of the specific traditional designs of Buka art. Even his first watercolor, containing symbolic designs that are found universally, cannot be identified with any specific culture. The cross, the mandala-like concentric circles, the herringbone designs, and the upright hand can be seen not only in any region of New Guinea but in primitive art anywhere.

On the surface, the patient we have been discussing wanted to return to the traditional magic beliefs of his ancestors in bringing back the cargo. He imitated the white man's methods to obtain his goals, and when he could not reach the omnipotence he desired through these means, he reactivated the magical method of human sacrifice. Prolonged contact with Europeans, whom he resented but admired, led him to adopt their structural approach in his art. It is reflected most strongly in the paintings that are almost devoid of traditional Melanesian designs.

He structured his concepts of reality as it is structured in Western graphics. He talked about Melanesian myths and principles, but he desired a European approach to life. His graphics are Westernized in their basic ways of structuring reality.

In contrast, in areas that have only recently made contact with the outside world, such as the Highlands, the subject matter of graphics is still culture-bound as long as the patient is not markedly disintegrated. Much work needs to be done to investigate the extent to which cultural elements are resistant to the psychotic process, and at what level they may start to deteriorate. Evidence available at this time indicates that personality disintegration in its recuperative stages is most likely to be culturally influenced, while more basic, perhaps universal factors, common to widely different regions, appear when the personality regression becomes more pronounced.

WEST NEW BRITAIN

Case 505

Talasea on the shores of New Britain has been described as the "Cinderella" of New Guinea (113). It has a great deal of charm for Europeans (106); the houses are well-kept and clean. Until just recently the area was isolated, and the lack of communication with the outside world made it possible for them to maintain traditional beliefs. Economic and cultural development have been slow to come.

Our patient, about thirty-five years old, was working on a plantation on the island as an indentured laborer when he became mentally ill. He became increasingly seclusive and indifferent toward others, but his apparent indifference was periodically interrupted by unprovoked emotional outbursts and indiscriminate

8.46. *This example of non-psychotic art from Buka Island is tightly organized but is made up of isolated, unconnected images.*

166

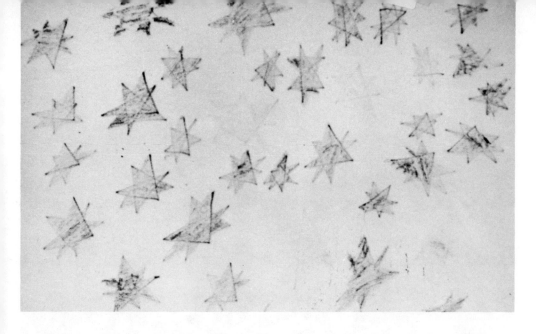

8.47. *A severely disintegrated patient perseverates a simple design; West New Britain.*

attacks on others; he would suddenly hit people without provocation. His unpredictable behavior continued after admission to the hospital. When interviewed, he appeared evasive and defensive; he denied having hallucinations but seemed devoid of outward feelings; his thoughts were vague and poorly integrated.

His drawings were simple, repetitive, starlike designs, all painted in light bluish green. He produced no cohesive pattern and made no attempt to connect the individual stars into an overall design (illustration 8.47). Phenothiazine therapy[10] led to a partial clinical improvement: his thought disturbances became less severe, and in his drawings he used fewer monotones, brighter colors, and more figures. A few stars still appear; a shadowlike boat and a house bring some variety to the crayon drawing. All objects are two-dimensional. The patient's productions are not culturally significant—similar patterns are produced by disintegrated patients from any cultural background.

THE HIGHLANDS

The Highlands of New Guinea has been isolated longer than any other area. It was long believed its rugged land and dense vegetation rendered it uninhabitable. In the early 1930's, prospectors looking for gold made the first contacts with the Highlanders (21). Even after this, contacts with outsiders remained rare, and the people were fundamentally unaffected by foreign influences until after World War II. As discussed more fully in Chapter 4, the traditional life styles of many people, including our patient, were not basically changed until they reached adulthood.

The customs and traditions of the Highlanders appear different from those of the people in the Lowlands (40 b); there are no great ceremonial houses with elaborate carvings here. The individual and his wealth are the focal point of the ceremonials; he displays his wealth by decorating himself with plumes and gold-lip shells (40 b) and paints his body, particularly his face, with intricate designs. Face paintings (illustration 8.48) become highly symbolic; colors have specific significance (141) and transfigure the participant into the likeness of a spirit-being. Other art forms are less important; they consist mainly of bark paintings, particularly in the Western Highlands (1), and of shields, spears, axes, and pipes decorated with geometric designs. These are not sacred items, but are owned by individuals. The decorative art of the Highlander stresses the significance of the

---

10. Phenothiazines are antipsychotic drugs commonly used in the treatment of various forms of mental illness, particularly schizophrenia.

8.48. *Face painting; Mount Hagen; Western Highlands.*

individual—the big man—over the group. This is in contrast to the art of the Lowlands, where masks and plaques are community property, as are the carvings of the Sepik River and the Papuan Gulf.

Several of our patients are from the Chimbu District of the Highlands, where Western influences remained insignificant until the early 1950's. Some of the men who were in their forties and fifties when examined had not had Western contacts until they were adults. Their ideas of the world were limited by their traditional beliefs. They showed little concern with the past or the future (their concept of time was restricted to the present), and their concept of space was limited to their immediate surroundings. They could only count to two; the numerals beyond two were handled by duplication—six is two and two and two, or just "many." The lack of conceptual faculties causes difficulty in conceiving of events within a temporal or spatial framework. Events take place in the present, the past is unimportant; if elders relate experiences from their past, they are ignored and often ridiculed (21). As we shall see, limitations of concept formation also seem to be reflected in the art of the area.

Geometric designs adorn artifacts from the Highlands. Used by permission of the Field Museum of Chicago.

8.50. *A comb of the Taidora people in the Eastern Highlands.*

8.49. *A stone axe from Mount Hagen in the Western Highlands.*

CHIMBU DISTRICT

Case 550

Even today, the Highlands of New Guinea are inhabited by people steeped in cultural tradition. Isolated until recent years, they still maintain many of their tribal customs. Their cultural identity may have deteriorated somewhat, however, as some of their essential practices have been almost completely abolished. Initiation ceremonies that established close ties with their spiritual past and aided them in maintaining the social structure have been greatly discouraged by Westerners, who considered them cruel and pagan. The economy of the Highlands is still marginal; the people are mostly subsistence farmers; a few coffee trees produce a meager cash income. Most men are reluctant to leave their villages, and only a few work in the surrounding towns. The belief in ancestral spirits continues to be strong; sorcery is still practiced (see Appendix); although cannibalism has almost vanished and headhunting has become rare, tribal wars still break out periodically, making international headlines. Just recently a battle in the Western Highlands was reported in the news all over the world. The UPI story[11] stated that war broke out between two rival tribes (actually clans). More than one thousand warriors fought one day at dawn near Wanpenamanda in the Western Highlands. The warriors' faces bore war paints, which has been customary for an untold number of years. They fought with axes, spears and arrows. Five clansmen died in battle, over forty houses were burned, and four hundred coffee trees were uprooted. The fighting was triggered by a "forbidden love affair" that was unacceptable according to the intertribal taboos.[12]

The art of the Chimbu District, as of other regions of the Highlands, differs considerably from the customary New Guinean art. Self-decoration (body paint-

11. The story was reported from Port Moresby dated November 1, 1975 (see Appendix).

12. Marriage taboos appear in most tribal societies; they are often made up of complex rules, serving as protection against incest by excluding marital bonds between a man and descendents of the mother's clan. Violations may be punished by severe punishment and even death.

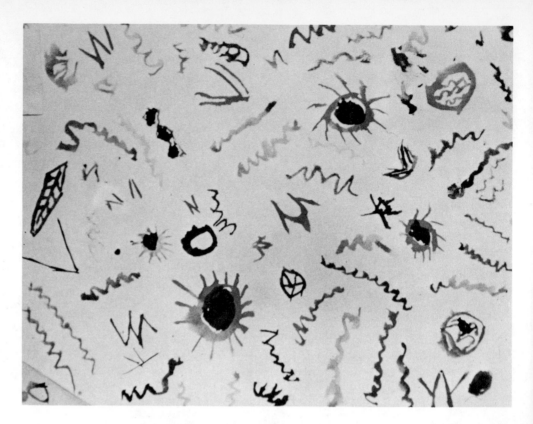

A patient from the Chimbu district draws mandalas, disorganized abstract designs, and anthropomorphic figures.

8.51.

ing) often develops highly symbolic, intricate designs (illustration 7.44), primarily embellishing the face. Axes, arrows, spears, and shields are adorned with geometric designs (illustrations 8.49, 50). The bark paintings seen in the Highlands are highly stylized and are considered personifications of local spirits (1).

The austere and forbidding beauty of the rugged terrain in the deep valleys and high mountain ranges of the Highlands was hardly accessible to outsiders. Natural barriers protected the clans from the overzealous European missionaries who destroyed local customs in most other parts of New Guinea. The original contacts, made by prospectors, were not pursued during World War II, for much of New Guinea was a bloody battleground between the Japanese and the Allied forces. It was not until the 1950's and 1960's that the fierce and warlike clansmen came into continued contact with the West, but by this time, the clans were allowed to preserve many of their traditions.

The Highlanders form the densest and most populous group of the country. In 1960, 180,000 people lived in an area of 2,260 square miles. The people live on steep hills and mountain ridges; the densely populated villages have lookout posts built in strategic positions for protection against enemy attacks (21). The women and small children live in huts some distance from the men. The men avoid close and frequent contacts with their women; it is considered unmanly and potentially harmful to their health to spend much time with their wives. Yet a man must provide well for his wives and children. He has the lowest status—yogo (rubbish)—if he cannot supply them with food and adequate amounts of shells, plumes and decorative material that can be used for exchange and ceremonials. Men who are active and productive, showing initiative and hard work, are most respected. They gain the right to speak up in clan affairs and to have others listen to them. In recent years, they have formed the local council, exercising influence in the affairs of the clan.

The white man had not established contact with the people of the region during the first twelve to fifteen years of our patient's life. Traditional customs

170

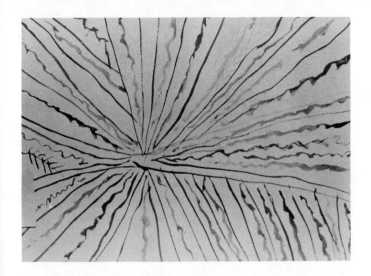
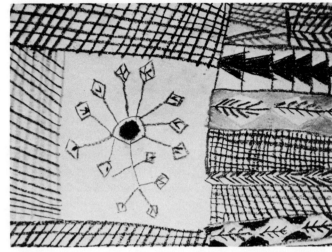

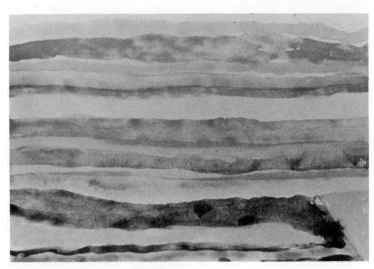

and beliefs in spirit-beings controlled his life during his formative years. Little was known about him personally; he had led an inconspicuous life until the death of his wife, when the Australian patrol officer for the area first noticed a marked personality change. The patrol officer reported that the Chimbu man had become confused and expressed contradictory (ambivalent) and inconsistent ideas; his speech became vague, disconnected and difficult to understand. A rumor spread in his village that he had had sexual intercourse with his dead wife, an act thought highly repulsive when committed with a woman of one's own village.[13]

The patient's behavior grew more bizarre; he abandoned his hut and wandered around aimlessly, armed with bow and arrow. This was unusual behavior; carrying weapons was customary only during times of war. Instead of providing his own food, he stole vegetables from the gardens and killed his neighbors' pigs. When he encountered a woman working in a garden from which he was trying to steal food, he shot and killed her with his bow and arrow. He was finally arrested after he killed a man from whom he had taken some pandanus nuts, falsely accusing the dead man of having stolen the nuts from him.

When he was examined at the psychiatric service, the patient's thoughts appeared moderately incoherent and vague; he had no insight into the reason for his hospitalization and wanted to return home. He spent most of his time in the day room of the hospital, indifferent toward others, sitting alone. He was evasive

13. Necrophilia committed with the women of conquered enemies was not uncommon in clan warfare (10a).

8.52.   8.53.

8.54.   8.55.

when questioned about his dead wife. His condition improved after several weeks of chemotherapy. He was discharged after two and a half years of hospitalization. Upon returning to his home village, he relapsed, as there was no follow-up treatment available, and he had to be readmitted. At each hospitalization his condition was diagnosed as schizophrenia.

While hospitalized, the patient participated in art therapy. His graphics basically show three different designs: mandalas, abstractions, and anthropomorphic figures. The first watercolor (illustration 8.51) shows small mandalas surrounded by chevrons and zigzag lines. Some of his geometrical figures are difficult to define. While this illustration shows little cohesiveness, he attempts in his next drawing to organize his lines, which radiate from a focal point in different directions (illustration 8.52). He next mixes culture-bound abstraction, appearing in the right upper corner of illustration 8.53, with a mandala below, accompanied by treelike designs, which become more clearly developed in later graphics; cross-hatching takes up the lower half. A mandala is the subject of the next graphic (illustration 8.54). Some of the chevrons that surround the circles form the mandala and are inverted; the circles are perseverated, forming six rings; the unusually bright colors are not customary in traditional paintings. The pattern is less cohesive than those produced by nonpsychotics of the Highlands (1).

The abstract designs originating from bandlike stripes (illustration 8.55) lack cohesiveness; their forms and colors do not appear in traditional drawings. The next drawing (illustration 8.56) more closely resembles the traditional designs of the Highlands; but the triangles found in traditional New Guinea art are solid. The

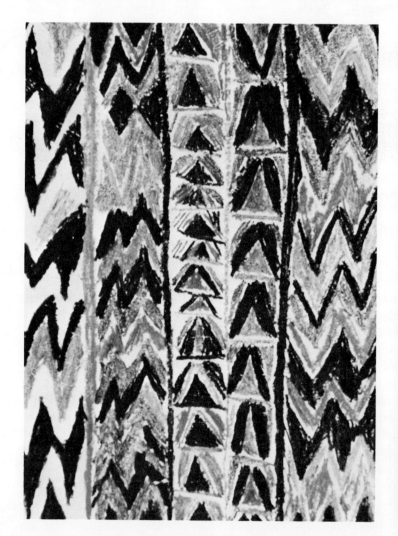

shapes drawn by the patient vary in size; he perseverates the zigzag lines forming the borders. In comparison, the traditional decorations (nonpsychotic) seen on a pipe from the same region show far better organization and cohesion (illustration 8.57). As the patient improved clinically and as his concept formation became more integrated, the figures in his graphics came to resemble local patterns more and more (illustration 8.58).

The third basic design has taken the form of the anthropomorhic figures commonly found in Melanesian art; they represent ancestral spirits. The patient's abstract designs and crosshatchings almost hide the figure in one of the early drawings (illustration 8.59). It is tentatively drawn; the various parts of the body are loosely connected in contrast to his well-defined later figures. The blue figure is shadowlike; the head drops on the right of the body; its bare outline is connected by a burnt orange line to the body. The rest of the drawing consists of geometric figures and crosshatchings. The head of the following figure consists of concentric rings around a dot; the body is narrow and elongated; the arms are missing, and the feet are inadequately developed; crosshatching surrounds the figure (illustration 8.60).

The graphic output of this patient is remarkable in its variety and quantity. This is particularly true when we consider that the art of the Highlands is far less dramatic, and there is far less of it, than in other areas of New Guinea. When our patient was severely regressed, his drawings consisted only of simple designs lacking culturally significant elements, in spite of his attempts at organization. As the personality reintegrated, culture-bound designs developed. At first, they were highly rudimentary, but a definite relationship to traditional forms was developing.

The patient's designs integrated further as his mental condition improved (illustration 8.61). The head of the next figure shows a mouth and eyes, features

8.58.

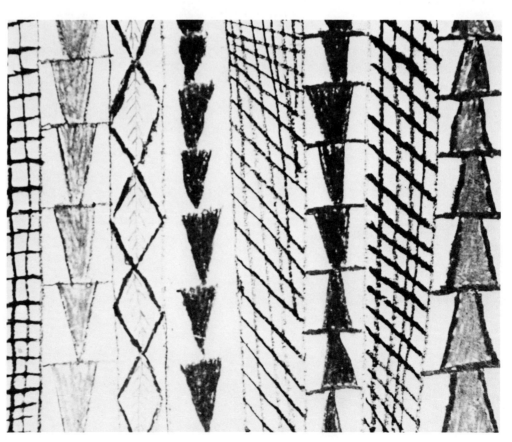

The patient's graphics become increasingly closer to traditional patterns.

8.56. (left).

8.57. (center). *A traditional cane flute is designed with solid triangles balanced tip to bottom. Used by permission of the Field Museum of Chicago.*

that had been missing earlier. The body is shaped by a rhomboid from which arms and legs spread apart. The limbs are bent at the joints, in the traditional position of New Guinea art (110 a). The integration of the central figure is deficient; superfluous details are added to the body; The top of the watercolor is bordered by red triangles, which appear frequently in regional designs. Stripes and mandala-like circles complete the drawing.

The rhomboid design of the main figure resembles the traditional Gerua board (illustration 8.62) of the same area, but the tribal plaque lacks the distracting details of the patient's drawings. The geometry of the basic design is perhaps more evident in the figures of the Taidora comb (illustration 8.50). The rhomboid figure is combined with crosshatching and other geometric designs.

The patient's clinical improvement was reflected in the increasing realism of his graphics (illustration 8.63). One of his last watercolors shows a human figure to the left of two lizards; lizards are a frequent subject of New Guinean art, with important symbolic significance. The patient has drawn them highly elongated, with their arms and legs bent in the traditional position (110 a). Elongation appears in traditional Melanesian drawings (illustration 8.64), but the elongations of disintegrated psychotic patients are far more pronounced. Such elongation is found in the graphics of patients from widely different cultures.[14]

Most of the patient's graphics find their basis in the cultural patterns of traditional art. Only a few of his watercolors, painted at the height of his psychotic disintegration, lack culture-bound designs; the structure of these watercolors is found universally in drawings by highly disintegrated psychotics. Even a moderate reintegration of the patient's personality results in patterns sensitive to traditional cultural designs that the present-day artist may have forgotten or repressed (as seen in the attempts to revive the Hohao boards (illustration 8.15). The moderately regressed psychotic is apt to reproduce inherent, culturally significant structure more accurately than the well-adjusted artist who is removed from his own

8.59. *There is the vague suggestion of an anthropomorphic figure at the right of this poorly integrated design.*

8.60. *The humanoid figure is slightly more clearly developed in this drawing than in the previous one.*

14. A patient from Kenya drew a very tall cowboy, elongated to the extreme. His concepts seem distorted not only when he draws the figures in the foreground, but the body contours of his herd of animals merge by flowing from one animal to the next (illustration 8.65). Giedion (50) observes the lack of definition of concepts in prehistoric art as they merge into each other. A schizophrenic patient, halfway across the globe in Austria, shows a very similar elongation in his ink drawings. His figure is disproportionately elongated and extremely narrow (illustration 7.7).

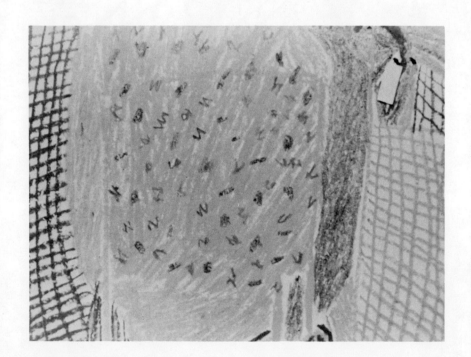

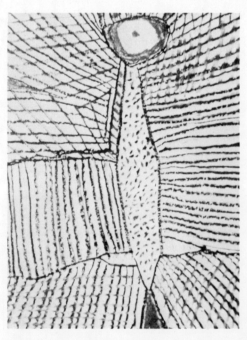

cultural past. The artist's patterns may be structurally cohesive, but they seem to be less authentic culturally than those by a patient, who can make the archaic past come alive, stripped of recently-learned foreign concepts. But, in turn, the patient's productions lack the necessary cohesion and integration to be artistically significant. Our patient's material exemplifies the point; the geometric designs, anthropomorphic figures, and mandalas appear to be intimately related to the traditional motifs of the Highlander's art, but they are structurally distorted by the patient's personality disintegration.

EASTERN HIGHLANDS

The Eastern Highlands, with its rugged terrain and mountains (the highest peaks are around twelve thousand feet), has remained isolated from outside contacts until recent years. As in the other Highland districts, the first contacts during the 1930's had negligible results. The area remained essentially undisturbed until twenty years later. Even then, Western penetration changed only the surface of the natives' behavior. Often, when there is personal or communal stress, it leads to a revival of traditional customs (see Chapter 5). But some changes started to occur in the 1950's. Local councils were set up to encourage a higher level of self-administration. A new road was built to the Highlands from the coast. It freed the area from its geographic isolation and enabled the farmer to find markets for his products. Schooling became more available; twenty percent of school-age children received primary school education, and a teacher's college was set up in Goroka.

We learned of the personal effect transition may play in the lives of the individuals. A young farmer (his paintings will be discussed at the end of this chapter), who had tended his small family garden, became ambitious and left his village to look for work in Goroka. It was not an easy decision, as many villagers find life lonely and difficult in a strange town. If they return home, they often become aware that they no longer fit into their former life.

The young man found employment as a janitor at the teacher's college. In cleaning the studio of the art department, he became more interested in the students' work than in his cleaning job. He started to paint, neglecting his job, and

8.61. *The central human figure becomes better articulated.*

8.62. *Gerua board, Eastern Highlands; used by permission of the Field Museum of Chicago.*

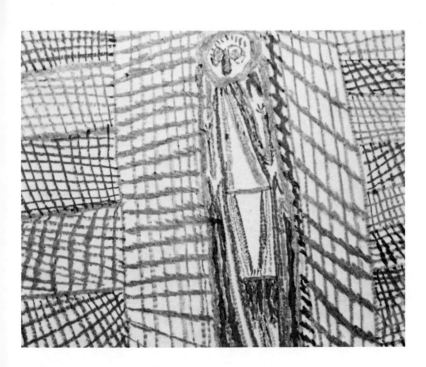

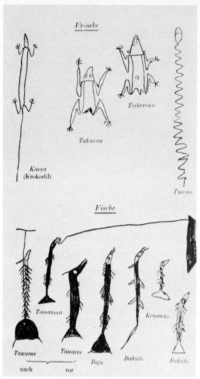

8.63. *The patient has improved to the point where he produces elongated figures very similar to traditional art.*

8.64. *Elongations in traditional art: Bougainville, New Guinea.*

8.65. *The drawing of an East African psychotic patient displays pronounced elongation.*

was eventually fired. The head of the department recognized his talents, however. He encouraged the young painter to keep at it, and bought his work. At present, this former janitor paints at the Creative Art Center outside of Port Moresby. He has become a recognized painter, and has held several highly successful exhibits in New Guinea and Australia.

Many societal and cultural transitions do not work out so happily. Sometimes they result in tragic conflicts, in which the local people are caught up by the impact of Western life and law on traditional customs (127). One such occurrence followed the murder of a young girl in the Eastern Highlands. Her family had captured the man whom they accused of the murder. They surrendered him to the local policeman, a member of the same clan, and demanded that he, as a law enforcement officer, execute the accused without a trial. They considered this his obligation to his clan. The policeman, indoctrinated with the white man's laws, tried to resist the pressure, but eventually submitted to his clansmen, cutting the prisoner to pieces with his bush knife. He was consequently brought to trial and sentenced to death.

The practical realism of the Eastern Highlanders (113) enabled them to be receptive to cultural change. Encouraged by the Australian administration, they planted coffee as a cash crop, helped in building roads to deliver their crops to Goroka, the district's center, and left their homes to earn more money in jobs on the coast. Still, many of the people have found it difficult to embrace the social, economic, and educational changes eroding their deeply ingrained customs. They have abandoned some traditional rites, but the force of centuries still holds sway in their minds. They may leave their villages to seek more income or better education; they may attend church on Sundays in white shirts and shorts. But under great stress the people have frequently reverted to the behavioral patterns of their ancestors. They seek magical solutions, for instance, and easily become provoked into quick, often violent action. An accident might trigger a tribal war if an entire village has been involved (see Appendix). The great need for magic in the Highlands and the relatively frequent tribal wars must make us realize that Westernization has not fully taken hold in their minds. The short period of Westernization has produced only a thin layer of twentieth-century societal influence.

8.66. *A village in the Eastern Highlands.*

Case A 570

A small village situated on a mountain ridge was the home of the next patient. Only a footpath gave access to the group of villages that formed his clan. Each village consisted of a cluster of huts. Some huts were square and built on stilts; others were traditional round houses (illustration 8.66). A fireplace in the center made the house very smoky, and had burnt the roof and rafters black (see Appendix). The inhabitants believed that they descended from a common ancestor.

The patient's illness probably developed twenty years prior to our contact with him when he was twenty-four. His family noticed that he acted strangely when his father sent him out to bring a chicken home. Instead, he returned with a huge sweet potato tuber which he had found on the road. The father, probably surprised, suggested to his son that he cook and eat the sweet potato. The son ignored the father's advice, an unusual action for a son, and gave it to the pigs instead. After that, his behavior became increasingly peculiar. He started to threaten people with his bow and arrow. His wife became afraid that he would cause serious trouble by shooting someone; she urged his family to cut off some of his fingers so that he could not tighten the string of the bow. His brothers refused; cutting off his fingers would interfere with his work in the garden.

His strange actions continued. He walked around the village shouting orders. He went to a nearby village, claiming to be a policeman or an administrative officer, and gave the natives instructions to chase the pigs out of their houses and to build fences to keep the animals in enclosures. The villagers recognized that he was sick but did not consider him dangerous. They tolerated his behavior, believing that a *masalai* (feared spirit) had bewitched him when he had gone to work in his garden. The capricious spirit must have affected his behavior.

He joined the Catholic Church and attended services regularly and conscien-

 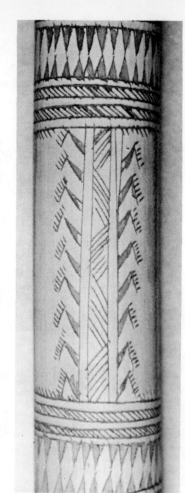

8.67. (left). *The patient's personality disintegration prevents him from copying traditional designs accurately.*

8.68. (right). *A cane pipe is decorated with triangles balanced top to bottom, and not back to back as in the patient's design. Used by permission of the Field Museum of Chicago.*

tiously, encouraging everyone else to attend and to become good Christians. At times, he grew very excited, telling people that he was Jesus or God. He ordered them to mend their sinful ways, to stop playing cards (outlawed in New Guinea at the time), to keep their houses clean, and to listen to the *kiap* (administrative officer).

He stayed away from others and walked long distances by himself, decorated in bizarre ways with grass and cassowary feathers (see glossary). On his walks he could be heard from far away because he was continuously blowing a police whistle. It had been given to him by a former district commissioner who was amused by his behavior and treated him as a pet. On one of his trips, he was arrested after shooting two dogs. He was admitted to the Goroka Hospital and later to Laloki, where he stayed for six months. Chemotherapy temporarily improved his condition, but his strange behavior returned after he had gone without medication for a few months, following his discharge from the hospital. Again he began shooting, and he killed two pigs with his bow and arrows on one of his restless wanderings. His condition was taken seriously only after he began shooting at people. After he shot several arrows at the driver of a construction truck, he was apprehended.

When he was examined at the Laloki Center, his thoughts were moderately disorganized and vague; he became evasive as he talked about being Jesus but seemed pleased about his role. Most of the time, he displayed indifference towards others around him; at other times, a sudden emotional outburst would interrupt his quiet behavior. While at the hospital, he participated in most activities, including art therapy. He drew many stereotyped geometric shapes (illustration 8.67). One picture consists of two rows of triangles placed back-to-back on a blue line. He fills the space between the two rows with rounded, double figures, connected by a necklike object. The figures are difficult to identify, but they vaguely suggest the flightless cassowary bird. Cones on the top edge of the paper and a single cone at the bottom complete the drawing. Its content is related to the traditional designs of the region, but the patient's perseverated triangles weaken the impact of traditional art. The design is one of empty repetitions. The patient's personality disintegration leads him to draw culture-bound material, but because it is inadequately organized, it conveys no meaning to others. In contrast to the patient's drawing, the triangles appearing in the traditional symbolic forms (illustration 8.68) are arranged with each triangle balanced on the tip of another. These triangles are few in number, while the patient's designs show considerable repetition.

Case A567

We visited another patient from the Eastern Highlands in his village, twenty-five miles from Goroka. The patient had been hospitalized at the General Hospital in Goroka, as the people in his village had become disturbed by his actions. At the onset of his psychosis, he complained that others were pestering and making fun of him. He believed that they imitated his facial expressions, and he overheard them telling others that the Devil (a Christian, not a traditional concept) had brought him into the world. He became perplexed when he dreamed of his dead father in the form of a short, fat snake, but being a male spirit, the snake was a kindly creature (78) and gave money to his son. At first the villagers ignored his conduct, for it was not disturbing or threatening. But his behavior became more bizarre. He would suddenly start to dance and shout. He heard voices that told him to go to a neighboring village to warn them that his village had planned to attack theirs. These voices encouraged him to negotiate peace between the villages; he saw himself as a big man, a skilled orator with the persuasive power to prevent war. The neighboring villagers believed his fantasies to be true, but instead of allowing the patient to arbitrate, they organized a preventive raid on his village, injuring several people. When it was discovered that the patient had caused the disturbance, he was hospitalized. This was lucky for him; in earlier years, he would have been killed for his actions.

Upon hospitalization he appeared hyperactive. His affect was inappropriate. He postured and made manneristic gestures. His thinking was disorganized; his speech was rambling and at times explosive. His facial expressions were either blank or grimacing.

When we interviewed the patient several months after his admission to the hospital, he had improved with chemotherapy. His mannerisms and posturing had disappeared; he was in better contact with his environment; his thoughts were still vague but less incoherent. He wanted to be discharged from the hospital, showing little understanding of his illness. When we told him about our plans to visit his home village, he wanted to join us. We allowed him to come along, but as has been detailed in Chapter 4, the villagers made it clear that they believed the patient to be dangerous, and did not want him to return. Our patient appeared dejected because of the welcome he had received from his family and the villagers. He began to rationalize that he really did not want to return home. The food in the hospital was more plentiful and better, and he had more physical comforts there than in the village. After his return to the hospital, he made many bids for attention by asking questions continually and by making numerous petty requests. He required considerable reassurance that—at least in the hospital—he was accepted.

The patient's crayon drawings consist primarily of scribblings (illustration 8.69), disorganized strokes lacking direction: these correspond to the multi-directional lines of drawings by severely regressed patients (Table 1). He attempts to organize the patterns of the next drawing (illustration 8.70), but is only moderately successful. He limits further expansion of the drawing by surrounding it with a frame. Setting such arbitrary borders seems to indicate the individual's attempt to compensate for his inability to differentiate between himself and his environment.[15] The drawing is in several sections, which are filled with brown parallel lines. The center, shifted somewhat to the right, consists of an ill-defined blue figure with an elongated head and protruding eyes. Below it, there seems to be a poorly outlined body with crosshatched lines. The patient's drawings indicate a pronounced personality disintegration, on which level all culture-bound material has disappeared. His drawings have regressed to haphazard scribblings. The second drawing suggests the vague outlines of a figure combined with the crosshatched lines, establishing a minimal organizational pattern.

The art of the Eastern Highlands, perhaps more than that of any other district in New Guinea, is limited in its expression. It is restricted to the decoration of arrows, flutes, and emblems (9), for which it uses mostly geometric patterns of obscure significance (129 b). Since European penetration into the Highlands, the designs have lost much of their traditional significance. When art styles no longer have an immediate link with their culture, they lose their impact and become colorless, empty imitations of past forms (7). When local people are asked to

15. Such inability to define space is frequently found in graphics by schizophrenic patients, regardless of cultural origin. Patients from the United States use similar mechanisms of framing spatial concepts (illustration 8.71).

8.70. *A frame also surrounds this slightly more organized drawing.*

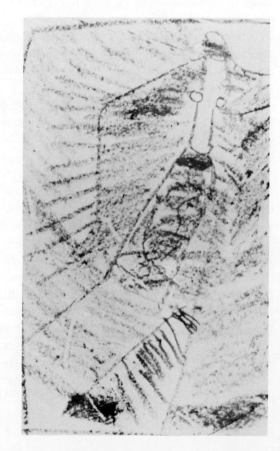

8.69. *This poorly organized drawing is enclosed by a frame—severely regressed patient.*

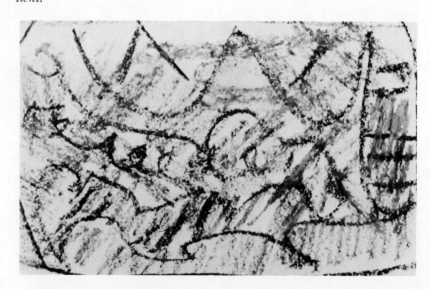

explain the meaning of the forms and symbols appearing in a painting of the past, they may become evasive, eventually admitting they don't know the meaning of what has been produced even by their immediate forebears. They have lost contact with their heritage.

Cultural influences on the art of patients from the Eastern Highlands are not very great. Their graphic expressions involve fewer culture-bound designs than the expressions of patients from the Papuan Gulf (Case 506, illustration 8.24) and the Chimbu District (Case 550). The cultural material used by the Highlanders consists primarily of geometric designs (Case A570).

8.71. *The use of repeated frames seems to compensate for the patient's inability to differentiate between himself and his environment. This drawing is by an American schizophrenic.*

WESTERN HIGHLANDS

Case 551

Our patient lived in a small hamlet perched on a mountain range in the Western Highlands (illustration 5.4). A man in his middle forties, he had witnessed tremendous social and cultural changes that had affected all aspects of life. The high mountains—higher than most others in New Guinea—and the terrain—probably rougher than in any other area—had kept the region isolated for many years. As a child, the patient stayed in the women's houses with other children, separated from the men. He saw his mother harvesting food and tending the gardens that were a considerable distance from their village. She had to walk for about forty-five minutes to her garden, where she spent most of the day. During the first years of his life, the boy seldom saw his father, who lived with the other men of the clan in one of the men's houses (usually located at a lookout point higher than the village to watch over the surroundings for attacks from neighboring groups). Headhunting parties and tribal warfare were a common occurence during the patient's youth, and he must have witnessed such attacks. When he grew older, he moved into the men's houses and underwent the early ceremonies of initiation. At first he was allowed to return to visit the women, but after he had shaved two or three times, and was considered an adult, he was no longer permitted to return there. Isolated in the large men's houses, he was told of the life of his ancestors, of the clan's spirits, warned of the women's trickery, and admonished to restrain his sexual activity as it would weaken his body for more manly tasks. It was impressed on him that he would have to take at least one head on a raid, whether a man's, a woman's or a child's, before he could be accepted as a warrior. Even at the time of the interview, he believed that cannibalism was still taking place occasionally. A recent news release confirms his opinion (see Appendix), but the practice is now severely punished by the courts (108).[16]

When we visited the area, we met some of the big men. A group of Mount Hagen men sat in a circle on the ground outside their villages (the men's houses had been destroyed many years earlier) having a discussion. No women participated in the meeting. Just as we arrived, a middle-aged woman passed by, obviously ignored; she did not stop, as a man would have done. She carried a heavy sack of vegetables home from a garden two or three miles away. Women supplied much of the staple food for the family, while the men discussed the important affairs of the clan. When the men saw us approaching accompanied by a guide who was a member of their clan, two big men broke from the circle and smiled, eager to meet us. Their clothing consisted of fur caps bearing their insignia as councilmen and laps laps, and a row of bamboo sticks (*omak*) on their chests

16. Tribal wars flare up periodically (see Appendix). The big men attempt first to negotiate a settlement over a dispute but if they are unable to accomplish it peacefully, the tribe goes to war. The surprise raids occur at night, but the tribal wars begin at daybreak.

8.72. *A geometric design suggesting plants was drawn by a regressed patient from near Mt. Hagen.*

182

which testified to their important role in the clan: each stick accounted for their sponsorship of an important feast (illustration 5.5). The big men were approximately the same age as our patient.

Earlier, when we had asked the patient about details of his initiation ceremonies, he had smiled and claimed that he could not remember them. We realized that we had transgressed into an area that should not be discussed. It did not matter that the patient had not completed the full cycle of the rituals; apparently he still felt captured by the secrecy of the ceremonies to which he had been sworn, and he feared the threats of harm if he were to reveal them. The changes that had occurred in the social structure, and even his mental illness were not enough to make him break the strong taboos of secrecy. Along with this strong traditional influence, he was also under the sway of his Christian beliefs.

As the European missionaries had gained influence in the area during the patient's adolescence, the traditional rituals had ceased, preventing him from completing his initiation. Instead, he was sent to a mission school, which he attended for three years. He must have had some adjustment difficulties, for he was expelled from the school for telling "false stories" about other children. We could not find out any details; he became defensive and evasive. During his teen years, he worked on a coffee plantation, and this was his first experience with Western ways.

His behavior started to change when he was in his twenties. At first he was ridiculed for wearing grass skirts, a custom completely foreign to the Highlands. Then he robbed the office of the coffee plantation where he had worked, stealing a stethoscope, an ophthalmoscope, and other articles for which he had no use. He was jailed for the thefts. After returning to his home village, he became increasingly excited and verbally abusive. When he began to believe that the Holy Spirit told him to kill people, the villagers became afraid of him. He attacked several villagers with an ax. They understood that his actions, occurring without apparent

8.74. *The hut on stilts displays elongation in addition to twisted perspective.*

motive, unrelated to payback or sorcery, must be due to a mental illness, and they arranged for his hospitalization.

During the interview at the hospital, he appeared emotionally detached. His affect was inappropriate, showing little fluctuation in emotional response. It was difficult to follow his thought processes since they were vague and incoherent.

The first crayon drawing (illustration 8.72) consists of parallel lines alternatively bright yellow, red and blue, forming a plantlike design on the left. It seems to be growing out of a red flower pot. On the right is a similar design consisting of parallel lines; several circles and triangles fill the remaining space. Some of the colors, blue and green, are rarely used in paintings indigenous to the Highlands. The geometric designs make the drawing appear rigid.

Isolated, disconnected images form the next graphic (illustration 8.73). The patient painted objects of disproportionate sizes, all in frontal view and lacking depth. A bird occupying the center is the largest figure; it is overly schematically drawn. In the lower left corner are a man and woman who hold their arms upward in the traditional gesture of New Guinean art (110 b), but their dress is European. The outline of a house appears on the right; the roof is unrealistically drawn; its sides are "folded over," (14 a) a method often used in schizophrenic drawings. The entire drawing lacks depth; the two-dimensional figures are isolated and detached from each other (Table 2).

As the patient improved clinically, the individual elements became more cohesive in spite of being distorted and disproportionate. The rounded hut is erected on high stilts (illustration 8.74). The folding over of the winding stairways and their elongation convey some conception of depth. Several figures are placed on the baseline (14 a) and are represented in perspective tordue.

The last crayon drawing (illustration 8.75) shows three huts standing on a baseline. The two-dimensional design is cohesive and fairly well organized, but the steps and pathways leading to the huts are not drawn in the proper perspective but as if viewed from the top. The patient's designs seem compulsively rigid, particularly if we consider a similar scene painted by a local nurse from the same

region (illustration 8.76). The patient drew three huts on a baseline with the space between the huts left empty. The landscape appears rigid and stilted, and the space is flat. The Melanesian nurse, on the other hand, painted similar huts in the foreground, but rather than being isolated images, they are interrelated by a common pathway and a field with flowers and other growth between each hut. Behind the yellow field in the foreground appears a greyish-white area, and above it is a mountain range. Although the nurse's watercolor is painted in vertical projection, the total design shows integration, flexibility, and cohesiveness.

Primitive art evokes images of fearful masks, carvings of distorted proportions, and paintings of contorted faces, but these are not characteristic of the Western Highlands of New Guinea. The villagers of the Mount Hagen area, the Engas, and the inhabitants of other parts of the rugged land are not carvers or painters of ancestral images as found in other parts of the country. The Hageners focus on elaborate facial and body decorations at festival time (illustration 8.48). The colors and designs of the paintings have specific significance; dark colors disguise the wearer, and warriors paint their faces black in order not to be seen; black also lends strength and power. Bright colors demonstrate fertility. The meanings of colors depend on the context in which they are used; red, symbolizing fertility in both male and female, is considered desirable, but it may also indicate danger or uncleanliness, as when connected with menstruation. Its brightness may endanger the warrior by making him conspicuous (141). The significance of color depends not only on its intrinsic value but also on the occasion when it is being used. Face and body paintings are part of the costume.[17] The patient eschews traditional colors. Another way in which Melanesian art is different from that of the patient is that local artists avoid landscapes in their paintings. New Guinea is besieged by volcanic eruptions and by ruinous earthquakes. The villagers often believe that these disasters are caused by spirits, who must be mollified with magic images. The traditional artist does not attempt to recapture the destructive scene or the volcanic landscape, as he fears that in recreating the catastrophe in the painting, he may challenge the ghost to repeat the occurrence. He does not report past events, which is a more Western approach to art.

Other art forms, such as the bark paintings of the Hewa group in the Western Highlands (illustration 8.77), primarily represent geometric abstractions consisting

8.75. *Huts on a baseline seem compulsively rigid, especially compared with the following illustration.*

8.76. *These huts were painted by a nonpsychotic male nurse from near the patient's home region.*

17. Feathers form headdresses and decorate the dancers at festival times; they are highly appreciated for their exchange value at festivals during which neighboring, rival groups attempt to outbid each other.

of triangles, diamonds, and X-shaped figures. They represent or personify bush spirits or spirits of the recently deceased (1). Similar designs are found not only in the Highland regions, but also in many other districts (illustrations 8.78, 79), on stone axes (illustration 8.49), Gerua boards[18] (illustration 8.62), ceremonial flutes (illustration 8.57), combs (illustration 8.50) and canepipes (illustration 8.68).[19]

The patient from the Mount Hagen area (Case 551) does not use traditional forms. Even his geometric shapes (illustration 8.72) lack any semblance of traditional abstractions. It seems that in spite of having experienced the rigors and pains of the initiation ceremonies, the patient valued Western standards more than traditional influences when he regressed during his psychosis. He heard the voice of the Holy Spirit, not those of spirit-beings. He did not steal pigs or vegetables as do other indigenous patients when they became psychotic. Rather, he stole prestigious European medical equipment for which he had no practical use. In spite of the patient's early cultural experiences, his graphics do not show basic characteristics of New Guinean art. Even if the content is somewhat traditional, the structuralization shows European characteristics. None of the regional designs appear in his graphics, which is unusual, even among patients who have been exposed to fewer cultural pressures.

18. The round and diamond-shaped designs of the Gerua boards symbolize the sun and the moon. The boards are displayed at large-scale ceremonies to favor the ancestral spirits (110b).

19. These objects show patterns similar to those painted by the highly productive Chimbu patient (Case 550).

8.77. Courtesy of J. A. Abramson, York University, Toronto, Canada.

8.78.

PATIENTS OF MIXED RACIAL ORIGIN

The population of New Guinea consists of 2.5 million Melanesians and about forty-five thousand nonindigenous people. In addition to these groups, a separate society of mixed Melanesian and white (possibly Chinese or Indian) racial ancestry represents a distinct category, clearly distinguished from the Melanesians and Europeans. Those of mixed origin constitute the least fortunate group (24 d). One of our patients was born in the mid-1940's in an area that had had considerable foreign contacts during World War II; the other mixed-race patient was born about ten years later, in the considerably more isolated area of the Papuan Gulf. Both were born at times and in circumstances requiring considerable determination or indifference to resist the social taboos against racial mixing. The mother and father had to cope with ostracism from their families and from the social environments of both races. Not only did the parents have to meet and resist many pressures, but they were often regarded with resentment and anger as well because they had transgressed the social limits against such unions. Their children were exposed to even greater discrimination, often being rejected by both the European and the Melanesian communities. The specific consequences of being of mixed ancestry may vary in different parts of New Guinea, but individuals of mixed race always move on the periphery of society (24 d). They are extremely self-conscious in the presence of Europeans; their marginal social role promotes

Traditional designs use geometric figures: diamonds, triangles and crosses.

8.79.

8.80. *Winged hearts is a Western design drawn by a patient of mixed race. This is two dimensional, and drawn in twisted perspective.*

anxiety, suspicion, and insecurity; paranoid states are not uncommon among such individuals. The mixed-race status creates considerable social pressure. Moving on the fringe of both societies interferes with the development of sufficient confidence in interpersonal relationships. The parents, having left their own cultural group, often lack the security needed to give emotional support to their children. Being under continual social pressure, they may eventually regret their marriages and displace their resentments onto their children, intensifying the children's feeling that, if they are not acceptable to their own parents, they can expect even less acceptance from others. The prevailing social attitudes reinforce their anxieties and apprehensions, the feelings of uncertainty, ambivalence, aggression, hostility, and suspicion which are very evident in such groups. This is the emotional climate that existed during the formative years of our patients. Apparently, it supported their view of the world, even though mixed-race status has improved considerably in the last ten to fifteen years.

We wanted to determine to what extent patients of mixed racial backgrounds are influenced by either Melanesian or European cultural factors, and whether these characteristics are reflected in their graphic productions.

Case 514

One of our mixed-race patients was the twenty-nine-year-old son of an Australian soldier killed during the Pacific War. His mother was a Papuan of a fairly prominent family. Following his mother's death, when the patient was eight years of age, he was adopted into the mother's family. He spent his youth in a town in the Milne Bay District, an area that was booming during the gold rush of the late nineteenth century; it has had Western contacts continuously since that time. During World War II the whole area turned into a bitterly contested battlefield, as the Japanese landed their invasion force (113) there. The patient was born at the end of the war and probably never knew his father. He lived with his mother's family but was not fully accepted by them. In spite of the fact that they adopted him, he did not become "one of them."

He attended a mission school for nine years; his scholastic work was outstanding, but he made a poor social adjustment. To avoid rejection, he stood aloof, never giving others the opportunity to befriend him. After leaving school he was employed as an apprentice pipe fitter for a petroleum company. He worked at the job for about two years, during which he felt uneasy and suspicious of other people. In the belief that a change of scene would dispel his insecurities, he attempted to escape the situation by taking a job as a clerk in a government office in Port Moresby. His relief lasted only a short time. As soon as he became better acquainted with the other people in the office, his feelings of insecurity returned and he started to believe that people were conspiring against him. Again he quit his job. As his delusional beliefs intensified, he stayed in his jobs for shorter periods, and he became inundated by thoughts that people everywhere were spreading lies about him and arousing others against him.

He began to drink heavily to relieve the tension; finally he was unable to hold a job. He wandered around the streets. One night, while carrying a rifle, he started to fire it aimlessly; fortunately no one was hurt. After he ran out of ammunition, the townsmen tried to chase him down. He became frightened, surrendered to the police, and was jailed for three months. After his release from jail, he stayed with his mother's family for a few weeks. While there, he heard his father's voice telling him to put his hand on his sister's throat. Again he was arrested, but this time his mental illness was recognized, and he was hospitalized. He responded to chemotherapy and was discharged to return home.

Since follow-up treatment facilities were not available, his condition deteriorated and hospitalization became necessary again. It was during the second hospitalization that we interviewed him. He spoke English fluently, which facilitated the psychiatric interview.

8.81. *Unconnected images, twisted perspective.*

8.82. *Two-dimensional, unrelated figures, drawn in twisted perspective.*

At the time of our interview, the patient had improved somewhat, but his thought processes were still vague. He was moderately coherent, but his inability to organize his thoughts adequately led to inconsistencies and contradictions in his statements; he would remark that people were talking about him, and then later deny it. He was preoccupied with his religious delusions and believed that God had chosen him to have electric shock treatments. At this point his speech became very vague, but he seemed to express an ambivalence over having to suffer so that he would be resurrected. He expressed the expectation that being sacrificed (he apparently equated electric shock treatment with electrocution) would free him from suffering the constant persecution of one of mixed race; he hoped to be reborn racially pure. He seemed to have no apprehension or fear about his fate; he appeared emotionally indifferent, withdrawn, and at times perplexed. In spite of his superficial indifference, he followed us around for days after the initial interview waiting for signs of attention and interest.

His graphics express his preoccupation with love. He sketched large, winged hearts on several occasions (illustration 8.80). In the center heart he placed people looking opposite directions. Although their position may be considered turning away from one another, it is more likely a regression in handling the spatial structure, previously described as *perspective tordue* (14 a). In the upper-left-hand corner, the smaller hearts are perseverated and disconnected. The left heart bears the patient's initials; a halo radiates from the top, as found frequently in paintings of Christ (the patient is a member of the Anglican Church). The three figures remain isolated in spite of their common content; the entire drawing is two-dimensional. The apparent identification with Christ reflects the distinction of being chosen by God to be sacrificed by electric shock treatments for his salvation. The idea of sacrifice bringing salvation reminds one of the Melanesian beliefs of attaining the European wealth by participating in the rites of the cargo cults; however, the idea of being "executed" by the Western means of electric shock treatments shows an adaptation of Western practices to traditional customs.

Spatial distortion and lack of cohesiveness become more evident in the next drawing (illustration 8.81). A two-dimensional church is on a baseline; the side of the church is turned, and continues into the front, a distortion described as "mixing of planes" (14 a). The parallel squares of green, red, and orange colors suggest stained-glass windows. One of the crosses on top of the church is surrounded by a yellow halo. The profile of a man, with the trunk in frontal view, appears in the upper part of the church, and the roof seems transparent ("x-ray pictures," see Table 2). The upper structures are difficult to identify but seem unrelated to the main theme of the church.

The last watercolor of this patient (illustration 8.82) shows two flat trees reduced to shadowy outlines, and a twisted human torso. The connected, isolated pictures of the trees and the man, the lack of graduation, and the perspective tordue are all frequent characteristics of graphics by regressed and disintegrated patients, regardless of cultural background (14 b).

Case A547 (Mixed Race: Woman)

Our last patient is a young woman, seventeen years old, of mixed Indian and Melanesian parentage. She lived in the Gulf District, where traditional influences continue to control the lives of the local population to a substantial degree. The young woman spoke English fluently, obviating any translation problems. A year earlier, she had been hospitalized for four months and discharged in improved condition. She relapsed after six months and was readmitted to the psychiatric center at Laloki.

At the time of our interview, she appeared confused and incoherent. At first her affect was flat, but as the interview continued she broke into uncontrolled, aimless laughter when she attempted to talk about emotionally disturbing material. She repeated phrases compulsively. She fragmented words into syllables and rearranged them into new words, neologisms. She was concerned about a "pirate man" who forced her on a long journey from Africa, travelling across a wide magic river for miles and miles (travelling on rivers or wide waters appears as a culture-bound concept in the mythologies of creation of the Southern Indian and Melanesian people). She spoke haltingly, interrupting her thoughts, repeating some in a monotone voice which was unexpectedly broken by hysterical laughter

8.83. The painting by a patient of mixed race is severely disorganized.

8.84. Early spatial organization: mixed planes.

8.86. *Improved personality integration: isolated, unconnected figures.*

indicating fear, not amusement. Seconds later, she would resume talking in a monotonous, singsong voice. Her affect and thought disturbances were classic symptoms of schizophrenic personality disintegration.

In general, women from New Guinea do not traditionally use art material. Even after becoming mentally ill, and in spite of her personality disintegration, the Melanesian woman is still controlled by the cultural taboos and hesitates to participate in any artistic activity. Because she is of mixed parentage, this patient was exposed to more foreign influences than her Melanesian counterpart. She had had ten years of schooling, which included instruction in art.

The first watercolor (illustration 8.83) shows severe spatial disintegration; the heavy predominant lines extend verticallly, horizontally, and diagonally; the space between them is filled with meaningless marks, reflecting undifferentiated thought formation. The patient scribbles illegibly in the left margin while she writes her name clearly on the bottom of the page.[20]

Another watercolor (illustration 8.84) was a landscape, a subject usually not painted by New Guineans and other primitive people (39 b). The painting showed the characteristic monochromatic colors of schizophrenic paintings, with an absence of shading. The spatial structure is two-dimensional; the pond in the center is viewed from the top, while the mountains are seen from the front; such mixing of planes is a significant characteristic of graphics by schizophrenic patients of many cultures (illustration 8.85). As the patient's personality reintegrated, she painted several fairly cohesive watercolors of girls; their structure remained spatially flat (illustration 8.86). The three figures are unrelated in space; splotches of undifferentiated colors surround the figures, one of them covering the legs of the girl in the foreground. Painting over an object may be attributed to a lack of sophistication, but the disregard of realistic borders, causing parts of an object to shine through the natural surface (x-ray pictures), indicates a disintegration of the personality.

20. Part of her name is omitted to observe the patient's right to privacy.

The progress of the patient's clinical condition can be easily traced in her graphics, which advance from an undifferentiated state through the various stages of spatial organization, but never to an integrated three-dimensional level. This may be due to cultural factors (see Chapters 2, 7) or to her clinical condition which reached a fairly good level of reintegration but continued to show mild disorganization of thinking and some emotional withdrawal. It is significant that this patient of mixed racial parentage paints without concern for traditional art forms.

8.87. *Jakupa, a local artist, paints the legend of Namole, the one-eyed, one-eared, one-legged monster.*

CONTROLS BY NONPSYCHOTIC LOCAL AMATEUR PAINTERS

Case GOR 1 (Nonpsychotic)

It may be of interest to compare the graphics of psychotic patients with those done by untrained nonpsychotic persons of similar cultural background. We have collected paintings by a local man from the Eastern Highlands, and some by another painter from the Madang District. They have had no previous art training and have attended only one or two years of primary school. Being folk artists, they apply traditional concepts but often alter the original style and use commercial paints of unconventional color.

Jakupa, the first painter, lived in a small village outside Goroka. A young man in his twenties, he had been exposed to both traditional and Western influences. Like many other young people, he worked away from his village from time to time to earn cash money, but he always returned to tend his garden and remained at home until he needed money again. He was a janitor at the Teacher's College at Goroka. As he observed the students' work, he became interested in art and started to paint. He sold a few of his paintings, and after a few months he returned to his home village.

8.88. *The giant lumbered down from his home in the mountains, terrifying the villagers and pillaging their gardens. With a huge right hand, he swept vegetables into his net bag.*

He was not seen at the college for several months. When he came back, he brought sixty watercolors to sell. He needed the cash to pay the villagers for the damage caused by his pig when it raided several neighboring vegetable gardens. He chose a local legend as the theme for his paintings and adapted it to his own experiences.

Namole, a one-eyed, one-eared, one-legged monster (illustration 8.87) lived in the mountains. He had a huge hand which enabled him to steal vegetables, which he put into a net bag (illustration 8.88). Another man watched from behind a tree. (The vegetables, painted in black, lie on the ground.) In the next graphic, the villagers kill the one-legged and one-eyed monster (illustration 8.89). The characters of the story form separate entities with blank spaces between them. In

8.89. *But finally the villagers overcame their fear and rose up against Namole. After a furious battle, they killed him.*

194

spite of being part of a continuous narrative, the various figures are unconnected, a significant characteristic of primitive art. This isolation in space is also evident in the artist's later, more sophisticated work (illustration 8.90). In contrast to the conventional use of space, the colors, usually bright, differ vastly from the muted traditional colors.

Not unlike the giant monster, Jakupa's pig trampled the gardens of his neighbors and ate their vegetables. The people asked him to pay for the damage. Needing money, Jakupa painted the story of Namole because he had behaved as his pig had done.

The young folk artist began to realize his artistic interest and imagine the possibility of success. He neglected his job and was eventually discharged for inefficiency. His work aroused attention, however, and his artistic talent was soon recognized; his works are now at the Creative Arts Centre near Port Moresby that sponsors young New Guinea artists. He recently exhibited his art in several galleries, including one in Sydney, Australia.

Akis, the artist from the Simbai Valley of the Madang District, had a background similar to that of the previous painter. He had been a subsistence farmer who started to work as a translator and informant for an anthropologist working in the area. He came to Port Moresby, and was introduced to the Creative Arts Centre. He had no previous artistic experience, but within six weeks he produced forty drawings that show a remarkable stylistic resemblance to the watercolors of the previous artist. The content of the paintings of both artists deals with traditional topics—the cassowary, lizards, snakes, pigs, butterfly men, monsters, and mythological figures. The paintings are two-dimensional and lack shading. The characters remain isolated in space, although they may gesture toward other figures, or one figure may be attached to another in the telling of a story (illustration 8.91). As in most tribal art, a background connecting and establishing the scenario is missing; the story depends solely on the individual characters.[21] Dec-

21. C. H. Berndt (9) describes the dramatic performances of the Krina of the Eastern Highlands, where emblems and masks are single images representing spirit-beings. Each mask or emblem tells its story individually and independently from the others. There is no background scenery connecting and integrating the individual characters.

orated paddles from the Solomon Islands, for example, depict single deities without elaborations or connecting links. In early social organizations, the essential strength of the people rests in the individual supernatural being who is responsible for man's failures and successes. Because the tribal artist seeks magical help only from the being he portrays, it is superfluous to relate it to other beings.

As discussed in Chapter 2, once man has established a firm relationship to the world around him and has securely anchored his concepts in a hierarchy, he feels less overwhelmed by the surrounding space. His increasing control over the environment allows him to see the world around him as a comprehensive whole, and his art reflects this security. The concepts in his paintings are no longer single figures hardly related to each other; now they become part of integrated, cohesive entities. The empty space between separate figures is bridged by interweaving scenery that becomes part of the painting's basic concept, and the painting becomes a new, complex entity, essentially different from the art forms of the past. This is in marked contrast to the graphics of Westernized nonpsychotic painters from the Highlands (illustration 8.76). Many of the graphics of the artist from Madang show transparencies (x-ray pictures, illustration 8.92), which are used in the art of Australian aborigines and the South African bushmen, in association with hunting magic.

The carvings, plaques and masks of New Guinea fulfilled a ceremonial purpose; they were the concrete representatives of the spirits that were carried by the clansman into the ceremonial; he acted as a puppeteer and brought life to the carved and painted object. By his measured movements, his dance steps, he made the spirits inhabit the plaques, and only then did they take full possession of the

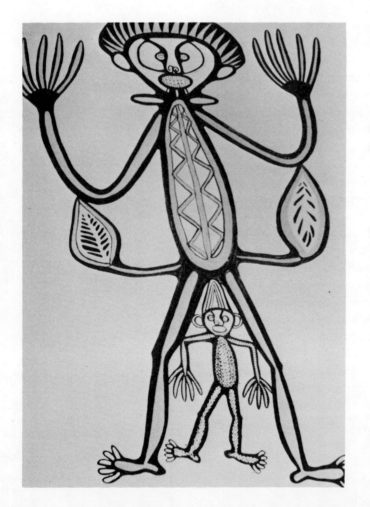

8.92. *A painting by Akis.*

8.91. *Another New Guinean artist, Akis, painted this "transparency."*

ancestral boards and ceremonial masks. The traditional carvings seemed immobile because of their impassive expressions and static sameness; but when they were set in motion by the ceremonial dancers, they moved with such force that there appeared to be no escape from their magic control. Some ceremonials imbued them with such power that they had to be destroyed after the rituals, as were the Heheve boards (147 a).

The forceful paintings of the Sepik River area, looking down from the walls of the Haus Tamberan on the assembled warriors, seem immobile; their magic power rests in their enduring constancy. They are highly stylized, adorned with geometric designs (illustration 8.16).

As mentioned previously, the graphics of Westernized Melanesians differ markedly from those of non-Westernized and traditional artists. Our art samples were supplied by the nursing staff of the Goroka Hospital in the Eastern Highlands. The staff was composed primarily of young men ranging in age from twenty to the early thirties; they were born in the late 1940's and early 1950's, when European influence had just become dominant throughout the Highlands. They were exposed to considerable Western schooling, which set them apart from the New Guineans who continued to live in their home villages and had few outside contacts. Being professional workers, they adopted Western cultural values. In contrast to plantation workers and laborers, they established firm roots in the towns and did not return periodically to their home villages.

Their graphics also show a thoroughly Western style; they primarily paint landscapes and sceneries, subjects seldom seen in tribal art (39 b). The spatial structuralization becomes Westernized, although traditional content appears in a few of their watercolors. The landscape by a Melanesian male nurse shows a peaceful scene including a volcano (illustration 1.1). The horizon is somewhat lifted (14 a, 119) so that the entire perspective appears slightly distorted. Such objects as the house and the outrigger appear partly in frontal and partly in side

8.93. *An amateur painter from Goroka arranges images in three-dimensional space.*

197

view. This mixing of planes indicates that the existing concepts (14 a) are not yet firmly organized. The lack of three-dimensional perspective is not necessarily pathological; even though Western influences have accustomed us to accepting three-dimensional depth as the only form of spatial realism. Realism has not always been restricted to the viewpoint that images have to be painted in a sequence that is determined by a given moment. Chinese silk paintings, Persian and European medieval miniatures (illustrations 7.51, 2.7) employ a less structured technique that permits a more comprehensive view of a scene; figures in the foreground are seen in their totality, and the objects behind them are raised, allowing for a fuller and more complete view of the scene.

Showing the essentials of a concept is characteristic of other techniques, such as perspective tordue. Egyptian wall paintings depict the head of a figure, while the body appears in frontal view and the extremities are painted from a side view. Mixing of geometrical planes is also used by contemporary Western artists; an outstanding example is Picasso's *Woman Looking into a Mirror*. The amateur painter from Goroka (illustration 8.93) loosens the conceptual boundaries and arranges the images in space according to their significance. His scenes are cohesive and integrated, while the same subjective mixing of places by a disintegrated personality results in a disconnected drawing that lacks inner cohesiveness and conceptual relatedness of images.

Art in New Guinea has played a great part in the cultural life of the people. [22] New Guinean patients who have spent their formative years in comparative cultural isolation continue to be influenced by traditional styles and produce culture-bound material as long as they are not severely disintegrated. Even if traditional images of the patient's cultural past have been abandoned, his psychotic regression seems to reactivate them.

Patients with similarly moderate personality disintegration who lived in a region that has had considerable European contact over many years, as in the offshore islands (Buka), are dominated by the more prestigeous Western cultural patterns. One of our patients, the cargo cult leader (Case 510), captured Western concepts in his paintings even during his psychosis. He wanted to acquire the European's status, and his drawings show a spatial structure (vertical projection) which is found in Western graphics. In spite of an apparent emphasis on his cultural past, he had adopted the concepts of Western infiltrators whom he hated but whom he sought to imitate.

Patients of mixed racial parentage show similar characteristics to those Melanesians who have had prolonged European contacts. Their concepts of space differ only slightly from those of Western patients.

As personality structure disintegrates, the patient's drawings lose more and more of their basic cultural characteristics, until universal designs replace culture-bound characteristics. The patient who had painted the Hohao plaques regressed to patterns free of cultural influences. They became abstract, geometric forms (illustration 8.22), more rudimentary than those drawn by a North American schizophrenic college student (illustration 3.5).

The integrated three-dimensional perspective of Western art developed fairly recently, during the Renaissance Period; it reflects Western attitudes about the structure of space, based on a scientific approach to reality. It establishes a hierarchy as it integrates the individual fragmented elements into cohesive entities, interweaving them with background material of lesser significance. Bridging the

22. The most outstanding art flourished along the Sepik River and in the valleys of its tributaries. Its carvings have been appreciated as some of the most important contributions to the world of art.

space between the primary concepts, it establishes a continued consistency (illustration 7.41). But the three-dimensional space flattens out when the personality disintegrates. As long as the disintegration is slight, the various components are connected and maintain their cohesive patterns even if the individual parts become changed, elongated, distorted, or condensed. Gradually the interval between the individual parts becomes extended, leading to an upward extension of spatial concepts in a vertical projection (Table 2). Such a representation of depth was accepted in the European Middle Ages (illustration 2.5), as it was in Oriental art (illustrations 7.51, 52). Further personality disintegration, causing increased withdrawal from the environment, empties the space between the principal elements; individual figures appear isolated and unconnected; the differences between the spatial structure of Western and non-Western graphics begins to fade. The patient's graphics leave empty spaces between the principal figures (illustration 7.38), reflecting an inability to put concepts into a logical sequence. Instead, the concepts remain isolated. Not related to a stable, cohesive, total structure, they tend to omit significant links, resulting in arbitrarily established concepts, determined by superficial appearances and similarities.

The regression to common universal patterns in severely disintegrated patients, regardless of cultural background, suggests a common basis for the development of personality structure and spatial concepts. Significant cultural differences in the structuring of the individual's personality and in the appearance of the world as he conceives it, are formed by patterns characteristic of the particular society within which he functions.

9.1. *Alchemists applied concepts that were related only superficially in their attempt to transmute base metals into gold. In a sixteenth century illustration, the lovers in a pond represent opposite metals merging in a crucible. Their wings stand for the volatility of the metals. From the* Rosarium Philosophorum; *sixteenth century; City Library, Vadinia, St. Gallen, Switzerland.*

9

Magical Thinking

Magical beliefs attempt to resolve the mysteries beyond rational thought. Whenever tolerating the unknown becomes unbearable, and rampant fears must be harnessed, magic attempts to provide explanations for the unexplainable. The impenetrable mysteries of life and death create needs for supernatural solutions. The cessation of life is the most difficult of all life's designs to accept, and the most puzzling. As we live with a person, we form an image of him based on our relations and interactions with him. A close, intense relationship has produced a vivid representation in our minds, and that image lingers on. It is difficult to exclude the image from our thoughts just because he has died. Sudden death, especially death by violence, accident, or suicide, appears almost unbelievable. The survivors' guilt makes them search for justifications for outliving the dead; they may accuse themselves of not having cared enough, of having failed to take actions that may have saved their lives.

To compensate for this feeling of guilt, we make the dead live on. We who survive create an image of their souls, often based on our reactions towards them during their lifetimes. They continue to appear in our minds in the images that we have shaped; some characteristics may be stressed, others suppressed. If they have failed us, we may make them endure tortures in our fantasies. These tortures serve also as a warning to others.

If the death is a result of violence, some cultures believe, the shadow of the dead person wanders restlessly in this world. He can rest only if his death is avenged: an apparent projection of our fears, of our need for protection, and of our unwillingness to allow a misdeed to go unpunished. Fears and conscience of the living do not permit the ghost to go to his resting place until the "foul and rotten" deed is avenged—Hamlet avenges his father's death at the cost of his own life. The ghost of a haunted house is finally placated when its death is vindicated by the punishment of those responsible for it. It is our guilt over permitting a violent act that makes us feel forced to retaliate for the unjust deed; only then is our conscience satisfied, and only then can the ghost find rest.

In the West, sudden unexpected death may be perplexing, guilt-producing and, at times, may cause one to suspect a criminal act; but in New Guinea death is considered an act of magic or sorcery unless it is the natural and expected death of an elderly person (78). The sudden death of a young woman in an automobile accident spread consternation; her ghost made those present fear her wrath and they withdrew with apprehension (Chapter 5). Even natural death may be associated with strange and uneasy forebodings; rituals honoring the dead are necessary, not only to respect their memories, but to offer protection to the survivors from their spirits.

Following the burial, the closest relatives of the deceased who are the chief mourners, must show their deference by fulfilling strictly prescribed customs. These may vary in different regions, but they are always intended to placate the spirit of the dead one, who remains close to the village where he lived. He stays in a tree or behind a stone for three to six months—rarely longer—after his death. During the mourning period, the family is not allowed to participate in the village's daily activities; their bodies are painted with lime or ashes, their heads covered with cloth. Their actions acknowledge the continuing presence of the spirit among his people. After the prescribed period of mourning has ended, all ties with the dead are broken. Funeral ceremonials force the spirit, who has been respected until now, away from the mourners. He is driven from the village by beating the mourners who represent his presence, by washing away the lime and the ashes, which are the signs of mourning, and by changing the clothes of mourning into colorful costumes. The spirit is driven out of the village to the happy islands of the dead (136). The ceremonial rites free the family and the village from further fears of the ghost, providing peace not only for the soul, but also for the survivors who have dislodged him from their memories.

If emotional ties persist or if feelings of great guilt are connected with the dead person, his spirit becomes distorted and endowed with an unusual tenacity to haunt those who have been close to him. Some of the patients described in the case material (Chapter 8) had considerable difficulty separating themselves from the images of the deceased. The man from the Papuan Gulf (Case 506) became very disturbed after his wife's disappearance; he felt responsible for her death, as he had assumed part of the guilt for a misdeed committed by his wife's brother, who ran away with another villager's wife. Even though his brother-in-law was exiled from the village for the illicit act, the patient did not consider the banishment a sufficiently severe punishment to expiate the violation. When the patient's wife (the offender's sister) died, the husband was convinced that her death was the work of a sorcerer who was hired by the family of the eloped woman's husband. Although not involved himself, the patient felt implicated in the plot leading to his wife's death, as he experienced part of the guilt of the family, and also considered himself cowardly for not having reported the sorcerer to the courts.

The patient had been lonely in the past, but never mentally ill; now he withdrew even more from his surroundings. His guilt, and fears of his wife's ghost, activated several psychotic periods. During each episode his dead wife's spirit filled him with severe apprehensions for which he could find no adequate solution. He was unable to remove himself emotionally from her image. Even after many years, he never dared to marry again since he considered his wife's spirit "too strong" and always present. Periodically he felt overcome by his conflicts and fears; according to his clan's tradition, he believed that invoking the magic forces of his ancestors would protect him. He looked for them in the Hohao plaques, ancestral boards, widely used in ceremonials of the past (illustration 6.4); they were reported to possess great spiritual powers that could offer protection in times of danger. The patient, feeling exposed to the wrath of his dead wife's spirit, painted many watercolors of the Hohaoes; even when his personality was severely disintegrated, he was still aware of the threats facing him, so he continued to paint the plaques. But at such times he could only produce abstract reminders of the powerful original designs; they became crosses and curlycues. Repeated to the point of absurdity, they were all that remained of the commanding symbols of the plaques (illustration 8.22). As his condition improved, his designs reintegrated, coming close to the original cohesive patterns (illustration 8.23).

His psychotic fears revived images of his cultural past; as he sought protection from a threatening presence, he regressed to the patterns of earlier customs. As in many primitive societies, his past is based not only on interpersonal relationships, but also on cultural experiences, which play a significant role in the individual's life—apparently more so than in the life of Western man. The patient's regressive patterns, considering his age, reactivated childhood experiences as they existed in the 1920's or early 1930's, a period when the Stone Age traditions were displayed in their full drama (147 a); a period when New Guinea was still substantially untouched by the white man's influence. During his childhood, carvings and masks were made to control threatening spirit-beings. Later on, when he became disturbed, the ceremonial use of the Hohao had been abandoned as a pagan custom, but because of the insoluble conflicts within him, he needed the magic protection of the archetypal spirits that had flourished during his formative years. As he regressed, he was able to produce designs very similar to the traditional plaques. The patient's productions were far more authentic than the carvings imitated by commissioned artists in a recent attempt to revive the traditional arts in the area—a revival that was initiated by the Catholic priests (7). The commissioned carvers produced cohesive and well-integrated patterns, but having lost contact with their cultural history, the carvings had lost their spiritual significance. A patient from the same area (Case 511), also regressed during his illness to the traditional influences of his early years; he, like the other patient, produced graphics that contained the potent designs of the Hohao. Both patients called on the magic power of their ancestors to combat their conflicts, and in doing so, reproduced historical images of great significance. In their regression to earlier levels of personality function, they seemed to be able to conjure up authentic plaques that were residual archetypes. The content of these productions carried the authenticity of the past, but their distortions of structure betrayed the disintegrated personality of the psychotic patient.

The psychotic is motivated and controlled by inner needs. In contrast to magic practiced by societal groups, the magical thinking of the psychotic is in a state of continual flux.[1] His disintegrated personality prevents him from focusing on stable goals, or even ideas, interfering with any attempt to find relief from his underlying anxieties. The magical thinking of the schizophrenic is often interwoven with beliefs from his own cultural past which he, as an individual, may have given up as he assimilated Western standards. His regression[2] may reactivate concerns with ancient symbols and religious views that were important to earlier

1. Societal magic, in order to attend to the needs of the group, is a highly integrated and conservative system, not subject to ready changes.

2. As pointed out previously, the psychotic's condition is not simple regression but the disintegration of his personality. The patient may be aware that his thoughts are unstable; their elusiveness and formlessness

generations and may still be practiced in rural areas of his country. A young woman from India was admitted to a psychiatric hospital in the United States, where she had lived for three years. Her family had been well educated, financially successful, and socially sophisticated; the patient had graduated from a college in New Delhi. She married a professional man whose work caused him to move to the United States. Having been emotionally dependent on her family, the patient was reluctant to move. At first the move caused some mild anxieties; then the tensions increased, intensified by her husband's preoccupation with his job. Two years after her arrival in the United States, she became highly delusional; her thoughts became incoherent; she reiterated phrases compulsively. When given a few sheets of paper and a pencil, she began to draw, producing disorganized scribblings.

As the woman's condition improved and her concepts became more clearly organized, she became able to verbalize her delusions of being Shakti, the Consort of the Supreme God Shiva. She considered her drawings to be endowed with magic forces which could alter the state of the universe. After additional clinical improvement, her paintings became less abstract and better integrated (illustration 3.4). When asked at the time of her improvement about her earlier graphics, she refused to comment except to say, "they don't mean anything any longer . . . it was a dream . . . I can't say anything about them." Earlier beliefs, even if founded in cultural attitudes that are still operative for some, had lost their meaning for the patient. She felt emotionally detached from them, treating them as if they had happened to someone else.

Channelling magical thinking into activities that are accepted by social groups that embrace one's beliefs, may not be beneficial only to the disorganized individual; it may also offer relief to others who are not capable of finding emotional security within themselves. This was the case with an Indian medicine man in Guatemala whom we shall call Gabriele (16). He was highly respected in his small Mayan community, where his strong beliefs and his fervor made him the most eminent of five healers. In superficial contacts (those were the only ones that he would permit), he seemed fairly well integrated; his thoughts were unusual, but he sounded convincing when he talked about his ideas. For example, he asserted, apparently without doubts, that the vaguely perceived butterflies that he saw in psychological test cards (Rorschach Test) were not mere pictures of animals, but that they were actually bewitched people who had been transfigured into lower creatures as punishment for not having respected their mothers, their fathers, or their ceremonial kin. His self-confidence persuaded others that he had found supernatural solutions for their problems and ills; his neighbors were a receptive audience, prepared as they were by their culture to be responsive to miracles. His delusions facilitated his convictions—they enabled him to speak with the authority of the psychotic. He appeared sincere and his low-level symbolism[3] made him convincing. On testing, his basic personality structure appeared

---

frightens him. The disintegration of his personality prevents him from forming an adequate view of the world, and he can accomplish only a defective restitution of his concepts. The result of this restitution ranges from delusions and hallucinations to socially aberrant behavior.

3. Low level symbolism implies the direct and simple substitution of one object for another, some substitutions are based on superficial similarities existing between the objects; others are arbitrarily named replacements, as those used by the Guatamalan medicine man. Low level symbolism does not demand the abstractive faculties necessary for shaping gods who have specific characters, and symbolize a myriad of qualities desirable or feared in the societal group which they represent. The abstractive faculty reaches its highest form in monotheism where the spiritual and moral order is derived from a single deity who incorporates the multiple divine attributes that had once been contained in many gods.

characteristic of schizophrenia, not only according to the findings obtained from urbanized patients but also compared to the test results of members of his own community. His concepts were vague, ill defined, and appeared to be controlled by preconceived ideas; his disintegrated personality was not capable of testing them against established concepts. This led to arbitrary, often delusional interpretations of happenings around him. He adhered rigidly to a vivid fantasy life, with blind determination and undoubting conviction. The other four medicine men in the community showed far fewer pathological characteristics when tested; their magical thinking was culturally determined rather than being part of their basic personality structures. Lacking the force of a delusional support system, their curing sessions were less compelling and less effective.

Gabriele's unshakable faith in his delusions gave strength to his pronouncements and brought him acceptance for his predictions. It was of no concern to those who believed in him that he had had an unhappy childhood and a very poor family relationship that led him to withdraw from contacts with others, or that he isolated himself and appeared distant and guarded. Not being part of the community, he lived literally on its periphery, in a small hut at the outskirts of the village; his way of life was considered somewhat strange, but appropriate for a man conversant with the supernatural.

We administered psychological tests to one of his clients. She was a forty-year-old Indian woman who had suffered from *espanto,* a form of extreme weakness accompanied by a variety of physical complaints, that had lasted for several years. Her personality tests showed that she was a highly insecure individual, excessively responsive to emotional stress, a reaction she could not adequately control. Her thought processes appeared poorly defined; simple images appealed to her when presented in a direct, convincing, forceful manner. But the emotionally highly charged ideas which appealed most to her were those which were vague and general. Superficial similarities outweighed well-conceived concepts. Her personality structure caused her to respond readily to the simple symbolic acts used by the curer, as he broke eggs over her body and incanted in singsong promising that a new and healthy life would be born from the eggs, and that a new spirit was blown into her body by the spray of alcohol from his mouth.

The therapeutic relationship between Gabriele and the sick woman can be understood on the basis of their psychological interaction. Her feelings of inadequacy, pain, and discomfort undermined the functioning of her personality. These also reduced her discriminative judgment, and she became receptive to the suggestive powers of the medicine man. She readily accepted the quick solutions of magical suggestions, for they relieved her of responsibility for her illness by attributing it to supernatural forces that she was unable to resist. She surrendered the control of her behavior, subjecting herself to the will and actions of the medicine man; she readily subscribed to his procedures and made his ways her own without testing them against existing value systems. The healer's conceptual boundaries, loosened by the disintegration of his personality, formed vague, often all-inclusive images. Being endowed with excessive emotional energy, these images expanded beyond their natural limits and assumed magical proportions, as they could stretch conventional spatial and temporal confines. The low-level, uncomplicated symbols fitted into the conceptual patterns of the dependent woman, and through them, Gabriele imparted strength and potency.

Life in the isolated Mayan village was beset by fears of the unknown. Gabriele's magic thinking enabled him to offer needed support to the community; he felt no pressure to bring his drive-dominated fantasy life under more rigid control.

The prevailing fears and insecurities in meeting incomprehensible happenings allowed him to substitute simple concepts for the inexplicable complexities of life. He offered solutions to socioreligious problems and supported the village's stable family structure by condemning unappreciative kin as inferior, animal-like people who were bewitched into butterflies for their misdeeds. His powerful convictions, even if highly subjective and pathological, brought him recognition and rewards, enabling him to establish an emotional balance that he would not have been able to achieve in a differently structured society. It is improbable that he would have been able to function in a cultural setting that did not accept the magic of his thinking. A lack of acceptance would have caused damage to his self-image, contributing further to the disintegration of his personality.

The Indians of the village look at magic as a way of explaining illness and unexpected events. Magical illness is caused by a bad wind cast into a sick person or by the commonly occurring spell of the evil eye (16). Magical power is needed to counteract the spell, and only the native curer possesses the proper skills. The efficacious medicine man must be engulfed by his magic faculties; his loosened concepts, unrestrained by conventional ideas of overriding realistic intercessions, are essential to forming images free of the pedestrian limitations that circumscribe realistic concepts. He finds his ready-made audience in the believer who is frightened of the pervasive unknown, just as the astrologer, the exorcist, and the spiritualist release Westerners who are trapped in their insecurities and in rigid conventions that demand uniformity and monotony in their daily lives. The sameness forced on them by tradition may prove to be as disturbing as the unknown is to Indians, and may cause them to seek adventures away from the regimented routine.

Magic beliefs may appear under stress among Western as well as primitive people. A college-educated mother in a North American city seemed sad, but not overwrought, by grief following the accidental death of her daughter. Her friends admired her courage in accepting the tragedy, attributing it to the sound relationship that had existed between her and her daughter. The mother continued with her customary activities, but two weeks after the funeral, she noticed strange occurrences in the house; the daughter's photograph fell from the wall, shattering the frame; chairs felt warm, as if someone had just sat in them; there were creaking doors in rooms located in other parts of the house. The woman convinced the other members of the household that it was the daughter's ghost who caused the disturbances. The experiences with the supernatural affected only a segment of her functioning. The ritualistic thinking of the villagers, on the other hand, controls all aspects of their lives; they are not to participate in any functions of the clan during the period of mourning, and the very existence of the bewitched among them may bring them under the sorcerer's spell (see Appendix). In contrast, the strange experiences puzzled and alarmed the American woman, but they did not interfere with her customary activities; she attended to her usual chores. After a few weeks, the ghostly manifestations disappeared. She had been able to assimilate the daughter's death, and the tragic event became a sad memory. The adaptive mechanism of the personality enabled the grieving mother to accept the death of her daughter.[4]

The magic of primitive society manipulates an uncertain reality, a potentially hostile world. Magic bridges the space between the individual and his environment. Such transcendent beliefs lead to customs such as the couvade, which

4. In many cultural groups, including some in the West, ghosts must be exorcised by the proper procedures before they vanish. Hawaiian newspapers report periodically that following fatal accidents on building sites, the disturbed local workers refuse to return to their jobs until a Hawaiian priest drives the spirit of the victim from the site by magic rituals; the procedure protects the workers from the wrath of the avenging ghost.

demands that the father of a newborn child remain completely inactive. "The men's childbed," as the ritual is also called, requires the father to retire to his bed after the child is born. It is believed that any activity would transcend the space between the father and the newborn, thereby injuring the child.

Magic serves the demands of its society; it is a highly integrated and conservative system, not readily subject to changes. Crises that force changes of wide scope in the lives of individuals are likely to meet resistance not only in tribal organizations but in almost any social group. In confrontations with spirit-beings, in the fear of a nuclear attack, in the loss of personal or national prestige, man turns to supernatural powers that appear stable, consistent, and removed from apparent control; he surrenders to unchanging, universal systems: to the stellar constellations or to the obscure forces of nature that surround him. When man turns to supernatural solutions, he replaces logical deductions by similitudes (Table 1). He does not feel humiliated if he cannot fight insubstantial apparitions, whom he knows to be evasive and outside his grasp. In times of social crisis, sophisticated, urbanized Western people turn to astrology or to eloquent cult leaders, even if it leads them to destruction.[5] It seems that man is blinded by his panic at times of social or emotional crisis, feeling impotent and helpless, he follows face-saving devices to escape his discomfort, regardless of their eventual failure. In societal crisis, even entire nations may turn to fantasies of becoming a superrace.

In his desire to transcend the forces that control him, man is willing to enter into a pact with the Devil. Faust is the archetypal figure who faces the end of his life filled with frustration; all the efforts of a lifetime appear to have been useless. In his desperation, he offers his soul, his eternal life, to Mephistopheles in exchange for the return of youth and the possibility of success. In seeking to regain his youth, he claims a divine right, and were he to succeed in reaching it, he would become godlike, a violation of his earthly existence for which he must be punished. The desire for unending life condemns Faust's soul, the spiritual image of himself.

Still, man attempts to pursue unreachable goals, and when he fails, he often seeks expansion in his thoughts. Turning to fantasies that appear unrealistic at first, he surpasses conceptual limits, allowing him to overcome doubts and insecurities and to persue objectives that would otherwise be unattainable. Man's desires for expansion encourage him to venture into new regions that formerly he didn't know existed.

Man's unfulfilled ambitions, and the desire to overcome his doubts and insecurities, motivate him to look for more challenges, and he often seeks to master them through magic. According to Roheim, the basis of magic lies in the desire to succeed when the odds are low, in the belief and trust in one's mission, and in the courage to pursue distant goals. Magic appears to lie halfway between reality and fantasy (122 b), depending on powers that man considers greater than his own. "Whoever hopes against hope, whoever dreams by day and builds castles in the air, has already magic in his heart" (147 b). In many respects, magic is related to science: it gives man the strength to "pit his powers against the world" (122 b) and the motivating force to forge links to new experiences outside the range of traditional knowledge (Table 1). Magic can not prove the correctness of its claims by logical evidence.

The unknown, having always been a potential challenge or threat, has pressed

5. Publications by disillusioned insiders of recent social mass movements such as Speer and Gehlin (49), and the theoretical classic treatises by Le Bon (81) and Freud (45), reveal that leaders who control entire population groups, using fully unrealistic devices, seek to avoid humiliation, even at the price of final destruction.

man to conquer it—to find solutions, whether sound or pseudoscientific. Misguided endeavors using magical procedures have probably preoccupied man far more frequently during his history than systematic scientific pursuits. One of the longest and most persistent of man's efforts was the alchemist's search for a way to transform base metals into gold. The attempt to link unknown, unmatchable fragments into a forced, pseudosequential order seems to be one of the most prominent examples of magic's resulting in defeat. The insistence on applying entirely unrelated concepts and excessively concrete ideas are classic features of sympathic magic, in which similarities between objects substitute for a consistent, underlying philosophy based on empirical fact. The illustrations from a sixteenth-century manuscript show the symbols used by the alchemists of the period (illustration 9.1). The images of royal lovers in a sexual embrace evoke the merging of opposites, the wings on their bodies represent the volatile state of metal (73). The insistence on mysticism and allegory made alchemy ineffective (71 b). But out of the alchemist's laboratory developed the science of chemistry. (Even its name, shares the syllable chem with its ancestor.) Fittingly, the subordinated branch of alchemy, chemistry, makes possible by its newest discoveries the transmutation of metals from one form to another. It is not the magician or the alchemist, but their scientific cousins, the nuclear chemist and physicist, who eventually supply the scientific answers with the aid of ingenious and creative, but also systematic methods of filling in the missing links. With logical deductions they find solutions that can be reproduced and give the same results. Science is not satisfied with the easy explanations of magic.

Scientists may lean, at times, toward excessive skepticism and tolerate new concepts with reluctance. A blatant example of mistaking scientific deduction for magic is an embarrassing episode in the medical history of the nineteenth century. Puerperal fever had taken a large toll among mothers of the newborn. A young physician, Ignaz Semmelweis, concluded from observing medical students that the killing infection might be caused by unsanitary conditions. Superiors ridiculed him, as they considered it inconceivable that the explanation could be so simple. It turned out, however, that handwashing by the attending physician could prevent the scourge of puerperal infection and the deaths of many women. The simple procedure filled the gaps in the principles of antisepsis. England's famed surgeon Lord Joseph Lister claimed that he would not have found the basis for antisepsis without Semmelweis's observations.

The mechanisms of magic make it difficult to separate imaginative magic (122 b) from the schizophrenic's magical thinking. The magic of primitive man usurps faculties beyond his means; he has appropriated powers that were originally not his, and must conciliate the gods by making adequate retribution. Much of the life of primitive people was built around ceremonies to please the gods. For years, the Mayans educated virgin maidens in nunneries for the ultimate purpose of offering them to the rain gods; ritual ball games ended by sacrificing the winning team's captain to the gods. Culturally accepted magic beliefs impelled the ancient Mexican priests to offer the hearts of thousands of victims in order to bring rain. In fairy tales, the pact with the Devil enables the common mortal to fulfill impossible wishes by setting aside space and time limitations, but the pact always brings with it the loss of his soul and eternal damnation. The Japanese farmer tried to stimulate the fertility of his farm land by having sexual intercourse on the freshly planted fields.

Such symbolic rites are not dissimilar to the schizophrenic patient's behavior; his pathological thoughts differ from the culture-bound ceremonies mainly by their goals. The ceremonial sacrifices are intended for the good of society. The patient's sexual activities serve only his personal needs (Chapter 7). He fantasizes about being omnipotent and capable of controlling the ecology of the nation; he withdraws the emotional energy with which he had endowed his surroundings, and invests it in his inner thoughts and desires. He cannot differentiate between his own thoughts and the outside world, and he believes that his actions or even his thinking of masturbating could bring destructive rains and floods. The schizophrenic punishes himself for his delusions by his fears of persecution. His paranoid delusions originate in a cruel, excessively punitive conscience.

Magic rites, ceremonial rites and prayers do not give man the power to master his frustrations in dealing with reality. Rather, they lend him the strength to dare to approach his goals. His limited skills and inadequate tools force him to seek relief from his disabilities by substitutive actions, and later by incantations and prayers that direct his efforts.

If a ritualistic act has proven successful in the past in dealing with the unseen forces of nature and their unknown causes, it must be repeated in the same manner as before. The compulsion to repeat effective acts, even if their effectiveness was purely coincidental, is not foreign to today's society. Many anxiety-producing events, even one so simple as a student taking an important examination, may cause a person to repeat incidental actions and behavior from similar events in the past. If the student has worn a certain piece of clothing on a previous successful occasion, he may insist on wearing the same article to ensure a favorable outcome in the present examination. His actions are not very different from those of the neolithic farmer or the European peasant who sought magic support in an attempt to control the elements that might hurt his crops. Such mechanisms, related as they are, differ from pathological neurotic or psychotic behavior, in which the individual hopes to reverse or undo the traumatic experiences of the past, even at the risk of causing himself pain and discomfort (Table 1).

The repetition of magical rituals reflects the need to maintain successful experiences by adopting successful formulae that are not one's own, and adding them to one's ritualistic system (89). New Guineans attempted to imitate the success of the Europeans with the magic aspects of the cargo cult. The movement, superimposed on the island's Stone Age culture, grew out of an encounter with a wealthier, more efficient technology. The Europeans' technology blinded the people to their own talents. As hunters and planters they had gained exceptional abilities that served them well in dealing with life; they had highly developed skills for observing the finest distinctions in nature that have meant the difference between survival and extinction (59). As the European invaded his world, the hunter's achievements became far less significant to him, and he began to deprecate his abilities. Sudden confrontation with a world of wealth and power which he had never known to exist resulted in his feeling humbled by the meager results of his efforts. The Melanesians, who had lived in constant fear of a surprise raid from neighboring villages, admired the white man's ability to sleep safely at night; he had the weapons and the means to protect himself from the unexpected. The Europeans lived in comfort and exuded confidence and self-reliance; the Melanesians felt overpowered and became filled with self-doubts.

Traditionally, it was the wealth and success of their own big men that the local people admired. Their wealth served entirely different purposes than that of European society; they displayed it to further their standing in the community by holding big feasts, having a large number of wives and children, and by growing larger yams than other farmers (24 c). The big men exulted in their success by carrying necklaces made of bamboo sticks, each stick accounting for having sponsored one feast—the longer the strand of sticks, the more respected its bearer (illustration 5.5). But the possessions of the wealthiest and the most powerful New Guineans paled beside the fortunes of the new European arrivals. Having been forced to accept that the power, knowledge and wealth of the new arrivals exceeded by far anything imaginable, the New Guineans attributed it to the supernatural abilities of the white settlers, considering some of them to be divine (77). Other whites caused resentment and hostility by being arrogant and exploiting the indigenous laborers, paying them extremely low wages of a few dollars for an entire year's work. The early colonist was met with considerable ambivalence; he was admired for his wealth, seeming to possess mysterious abilities to make big ships arrive, make "iron birds" fly, and make unknown goods arrive by speaking into strangely shaped black objects. He had boxes that could talk and make music, and machinery of limitless quantities and of many types. But the admiration for the Europeans was tarnished when some destroyed the dignity of even the most courageous and respected New Guineans, humiliating them with their condescending attitudes. The islanders felt defenseless against the white man's power and his often patronizing manners. They were puzzled and confused, and the white man's missionaries offered them a solution: salvation through conversion to Christ (see Chapter 5). The natives adopted Christianity but incorporated it into their own religious system, which was steeped in magic beliefs, making Christianity part of their magic. Christ became to them a black culture hero, thought to be held captive in Sydney. They believed also that the European's rich cargo had been originally destined for the Melanesians but it was diverted by the white man's cunning and never reached the coast. As magic was their way of life, so they intended to use magic to wrest the fortunes away from what they regarded to be the wicked intruders and to return it to themselves. They looked for means to compensate for their low self-esteem, resulting from their degradations and frustrations, through the magic of the cargo cult.

The followers of the cargo cults started to copy the Europeans' dress and behavior. They pushed buttons on imaginary black voice boxes, erected poles as imitation radio towers, and commanded imaginary cargo ships to arrive. As they no longer believed that they needed to work for their livelihood, they destroyed their food supplies, burned their fields, killed the pigs and, where crops had stood, built airfields and boat docks to prepare for the arrival of the cargo. Soon, they had to accept that the cargo would not arrive, and the movement collapsed.

Millenarian cults similar to the cargo cults have appeared in different parts of the world at times of great stress. The dedication of their followers and the sometimes ruthless disregard for their opponents leads to temporary success, but eventually to the inevitable defeat of such movements as the Taiping Rebellion in China, the Ghost Dance of the Paiute North American Indians, the Xhose Cult of South America, and even the *Thousand Year Reich,* the millennium of the Hitler movement. The common characteristics of such occurrences are crises caused by the stress of economic or social deprivation. The resulting conflicts produce an intense desire to assert oneself, to fight against odds, and this desire justifies all efforts to find compensation for having suffered from the wicked trickery of one's masters. It is magic that possesses the potential to transform the wishes of the disillusioned into reality; it bridges the limits of time and space, bringing greatly desired goods from far away, curing illnesses in a flash by the waving of a wand. Primitive man is controlled by his belief in magic, as is the religious fundamentalist who interprets the Bible literally and tests the strength of his faith in his conviction that "they shall take up serpents . . . [and] it shall not hurt them." By trusting that their faith will protect them, both the Melanesian and the fundamentalist never need to abandon their beliefs. Even if they fail, they attribute it to the individuals who lack sufficient faith, not to the cult itself (see Case 510).

The indigene is governed by rigid rules and taboos that assure the safety of himself and his community. He is not allowed the luxury of flexibility; his isolation and lack of experience prevent him from forming reactions that reach far beyond immediate happenings; the future is very limited. He has to interact with his environment as it appears to him at a given moment; the perceptions of his experiences are molded by expediency; having limited experience beyond his immediate environment causes him to depend on superficial similarities which are often incomplete concepts. He compensates for his uncertainities by rigidly defining and circumscribing his concepts. He resists the acceptance of new evidence at the expense of accuracy and effectiveness; his strictly regulated concepts establish unalterable guidelines that enable him to survive.

Even if at times reluctantly, the integrated personality is capable of adjusting the definition and boundaries of his concepts to environmental changes, of adapting to new findings and incorporating them into his total functioning. He possesses the potential to form life patterns that he can trust to remain basically constant, but modifiable under the influence of widening contacts with his environment. Inexperience may limit an existing image or belief but does not reduce its stability—and stability is a basic necessity in the individual's adjustment to his environment. The societal significance of reliable concepts is anchored in the constancy of their values; images may be incomplete, but further experiences will add to their growth. Like the Paleolithic hunter and the Neolithic farmer, the New Guineans sustained constant, cohesive, well-integrated concepts of themselves and of the world as they knew it; they could not have survived in the wilderness without being able to depend on such constant, though incomplete, concepts. They functioned well within their settings and they responded to their experiences as would any integrated individual—with goal-directed, purposeful actions; they coped with their experiences by applying the traditional means and tools at their disposal. Prior to the impact of foreign values, their sociocultural isolation allowed new experiences to be assimilated as long as they approximated their established systems; otherwise, the Melanesians rejected them as being inappropriate to them. But they became defenseless when a totally new experience, apparently efficient, was forced on them with great urgency, making them realize that the old standards and knowledge that they used were obsolete.

In most Western-oriented societies, magical solutions are separated from the daily activities of the people. The believer may submit to God, admitting his impotence and his inferior position, and asking for leniency if he has stepped beyond accepted and agreed limits. In periods of intense stress, or prior to precarious ventures, feelings of uncertainty and apprehension are likely to grow worse. Severe illness and unexplainable natural disasters intensify the believer's perplexity. The urgencies produced by such situations demand more forceful and rigid defenses, new taboos, and additional self-sacrifice, giving up pleasures, and even enduring physical pain inflicted on oneself or others. The believer's defensive reactions distort not the religious system, but the proper evaluation of the events taking place. Outsiders are suspect, as tolerance for any divergent opinion dwindles, and they become enemies, endowed with shrewd, unusual skills. They must be defeated by all measures as they are unscrupulous and dishonest conspirators. A "holy war" must be fought against them. The mob reaction of the group may determine the individual member's behavior, and societal pressure may force him to adopt the apprehensions and fears of the group. The group may react with a bitter intolerance and violence incomprehensible to the outsider. But the reactions are still confined to the specific conflicts and fears within the group. The individual's personality function is less affected and he continues to function appropriately on a personal basis.[6]

Small primitive groups organized in clans, moieties, or similar units, do not develop the same set of behavior patterns as large nations. The villager identifies and functions more directly within his own community; he becomes a more active, involved participant and develops a sense of belonging which he never loses (136). The small group is more immediately exposed to the surrounding unexplored world. Feeling individually inadequate, its members depend on group action to defend themselves against the external powers. The individual subordinates his personal interests to those of the group; he is locked into the communal rituals, ceremonials and magic that regulate his life in every detail, discouraging independent behavior. In contrast, Western man stands alone; he has isolated his spiritual behavior from his daily affairs. His prime concern lies with finding security and success within his societal structure. He competes for achievement and for social standing in his community. Even if he belongs to a religious, political, or other organized group, he acts as an individual; he primarily handles his own interests, and his personal life remains relatively untouched. The Westerner encapsulates his spiritual activities, not allowing them to consume his total life. The spiritual life of prehistoric and primitive man demands a total commitment. Its rituals, ceremonials and feasts are essential spiritual functions. The entire community participates in them, not as a multitude of individuals and separate worshipers, but as a group.

In his earliest days, man often recorded his activities on the walls of caves and on rocks. He has discovered that imitating an object, making it appear through his own faculties, conjures up strong feelings of power in him. As he did not know of gods, or even spirits or prayers, primitive man relied on powers of creation within him to model the objects of greatest interest. He experimented with crude forms, groping to find the proper images (50) until he developed accomplished artistic skills (illustration 2.16). He filled his caves with pictures of animals and hunting scenes; delicate shading and minute detail give witness to his talent for realism and his skill in observing action. Many of the paintings were placed in a single area of the cave; often, new pictures were painted on top of already existing scenes. This was not due to a lack of space, for there were many vacant spots in the caves, but to the fact that some specific areas seemed to possess special importance; images located in such positions were supposedly favored with greater magical significance (59).

Tribal artists carve and paint works that are highly significant to their group. Among many African tribes the ability to create spiritual images places their

6. During the Nazi regime, outstanding German physicians who grew up in a disintegrating economy and who were disturbed over the developing social disintegration of the 1920's and early 1930's, fell under the magic spells of leaders who offered them magic but unrealistic solutions—the restoration of their past glories and the new millennium of the Third Reich. Some became intoxicated by promises of regaining their lost significance, and they accepted uncritically the inhuman standards of their leaders. They became capable of committing degrading and inhuman pseudo-medical experiments on the "slave classes." (The experiments were later disclosed in the Doctors' Trial [see appendix].) These experiments proved to be valueless sacrifices of human lives. At the same time, the doctors proceeded, independently from what was adjudged genocide later, with their customary sound practice of medicine and pursued their urbane ways of life. They were connoisseurs of the arts, and showed concern in many endeavors considered to be highly sophisticated. Their conflicting behavior appeared beyond comprehension to the outsider. Some of them, later appalled by their own actions, committed suicide even before they were legally prosecuted.

makers in the role of religious leaders who are able to control the spirits. The tribal image-maker must possess the flexibility to create powerful icons, but he must also have sufficient control to make his work fit into the rigid forms prescribed by tradition. The latitude given to the artist is usually not allowed in other aspects of the life of primitives, who must accept the narrow standards of traditional behavior. The license taken by the poet and the artist to fill the missing gaps occurring during the creative act by similes and metaphors, shows that artists partake in magic. Creativity takes place on an archaic level of psychic organization (136); on such a level, the established, traditional boundaries between the individual and his environment become blurred. Realistic conceptual limits are loosened, and the viewer, like the spectator of the Kabuki play, permits himself to be carried away by the beauty of the moment (see Chapter 3).

Art, being related to magic, changes the appearance of the world. It transforms man's fantasies, unresolved conflicts, and apprehensions over an uncertain future into the reassuring completeness of visual images. As with magic, its creators condense and elaborate their personal concerns into examples of their societies' complexities. For active participation art substitutes apparitions on canvas, in wood and stone, on the stage, where the images interact to dramatize the observer's conflicts or desires. If art is meaningful and of social significance, it has to be created by artists with basically adequate personality integration. Recurrent reports of this or that artist having major psychiatric difficulties (93) have proven misleading in both Western and non-Western societies. The originality of creative thinking may set the artist apart from his social group but it in no way suggests that he is bordering on insanity. Severe psychotic regression causes a loss of creative abilities both for the artist and for the amateur; his restitutive attempts to link fragmented elements result in new but arbitrary forms that have meanings for him alone and not for others.

People of any societal group, Western or non-Western, develop doubts and insecurities in facing reality. Even if man has conquered much of the physical space around him, he cannot adequately govern the spiritual[7] world within him. Primitive man may have a greater need for magic and a "greater tendency to dramatize, to act out, than we have" (122 b); but the uncertainities of Western man, his self-doubts, and his inability to control the future, create a latent, ever-present need for magic. He may succeed in repressing such needs, but they will surface in times of danger and excessive strain. Personal stress or societal crisis often mobilize the latent tendency for magical solutions. Under overwhelming emotional or cultural stress, integrated people anywhere may accept vague, incomplete, and inadequately differentiated images that distort reality concepts. The images may transgress the customary boundaries of time and space; a spirit may rise and float through doors and walls, moving with unexpected speed from one place to another. The recent revival of interest in astrology, filling the bookshelves with galaxies of paperbacks on the zodiac, enables readers to become short-order astrologers. The various forms of occultism may seem to offer security in a world where rapid change isolates the individual from his societal group. That man seeks relief in the magic of the stars may be ironic in the face of the fact that it is his scientific exploration of outer space and nature that has caused his consternation. The cohesive, integrated personality succeeds in defending itself against stressful experiences by encapsulating and dissociating them from his total functioning. His

7. We define spiritual in this connection, not with religious or supernatural concepts, but with the functioning of the total inner being.

213

defenses serve to isolate the emotional pain, making it illusory; he can protect himself or his society by isolating the unacceptable, often unexplainable, traumatic experiences. At times, these experiences materialize in ghostly manifestions. As man's total concept of reality is otherwise preserved, magic becomes successfully compartmentalized.

The magic of the disintegrated psychotic personality, particularly of the schizoprenic, is a personal form of magic; it gives expression to the patient's own needs. Not affecting others, it lacks societal meaning. The New Guinean patient's graphics (Case 506), disintegrated into pseudoabstractions, retaining little or no culture-bound elements, are witness to his advanced disintegration. The artist who can still be productive even when suffering from mental illness is an exception. Van Gogh, Munch, and others continued to be creative until the climactic stages of their illness. Van Gogh's mental state is reflected in the chaotic turmoil of his last paintings; at that point he could no longer continue painting; he preferred to die than to live in mental chaos.

Magic thinking and artistic creativity are goal-directed; the nonpsychotic who uses magic concepts retains and reinforces them with rigid and strictly organized rituals. The schizophrenic's concepts are loose, inconstant, and lacking an overall objective; his thinking becomes directed by superficial similarities rather than by the deductive logic that directs the integrated individual. Concepts remain vague, overlapping, lacking in cohesiveness. A patient disturbed by her fragmented thoughts attempted to link them together, but she could only form unstable associations. Her poorly integrated personality panicked when it became impossible to link her thought processes tightly. Her fears found concrete expression in her feeling that she was an "amoeba floating in space" (Case 133). Another patient attempted to restitute the disturbing disintegration by any linking of her thoughts, however transient or unreal. As her condition improved, she detached herself from her disintegrated concepts, which no longer fulfilled or represented her needs, and she impatiently refused to deal with them, denying them any further meaning (Case 140).

The wish to find emotionally gratifying solutions, even if based on unrealistic desires, is within all of us. Our desires, ambitions and fantasies color the objective evidence of our world, of the space around us, according to our personal needs. They prevent the development of a reality that would be identical for all, unchanged and fixed.

10

The Structure
of Space

Reality is a term used with deceptive ease; yet it has no adequate definition. Its meaning is elusive (34) and has been the subject of dispute for centuries. Metaphysical philosophies offer a variety of idealistic "realities," while positivism admits no meaning to the term outside of sensory perception. We cannot attempt to find a definitive answer in this discussion; we can only deal with the functional aspects of its conception rather than with reality itself.

The conception of reality seems deduced from observable "behavior in an observed environment" (30), from its interaction within the surrounding space and interrelated in time. Its presence and being, anchored in a hierarchal order, must be agreed upon by others within their setting; without such agreement, events and experiences have no meaning. What is conceived as real undergoes scrutiny by society, which introduces the subjective values existing in that society. The ideational representation of interacting objects creates the structuring of space, forming the concepts of reality. Its comprehension is highly malleable, differing vastly as it is determined by prevalent beliefs. The accepted presence of spirit beings, of ancestral ghosts or the urbanized Western skepticism of such beliefs is reached by attitudinal and behavioral responses, but less by a conscious level of verbal accord. The reality of the medieval scientist, of Paracelsus, Galileo, Newton or Copernicus, was far more restricted and conceptually different than that of Pasteur, Planck or Einstein.

Conceptual reality is not limited to its scientific manifestation alone but involves the total conception of the internal and external world, of emotionally charged experiences as spiritual and ethical concepts. Reality, as it appeared to the Egyptian priest or medieval monk, was substantially different from the reality of today's Buddhist monk, a New Guinean village chief or the mayor of an American city. As man's physical and mental environment changes, the concepts of his world change. The interpretation of reality has not been a stable, unalterable concept throughout history. What seems constant is man's potential to adapt himself to inner and outer experiences, to the space around him and his ability to interact with such concepts. He possesses the integrative potential that enables him to adapt to his environment (32b).

The infant, the prehistoric man, and the psychotic all lack firm concepts of spatial direction. For them, the world exists only so far as they can reach—anything beyond that is of vague significance. As the infant matures, as the prehistoric man evolves, and as the psychotic reintegrates, they begin to structure the space around them according to their increasing awareness of coexisting events. They invest certain objects with psychic energy related to the significance of their experiences. Sociocultural factors, the intensity of relationships, feedback mechanisms, the possibilities of emotional gratification or rejection, the notions of past and present—all add to the concept of reality, and to the image of oneself.

Constant, unalterable universal forces affect the basic functions of all beings and form the roots of their behavior; as they cannot avoid these forces, they have to adapt to them. Even the most retarded individual and the most severely disturbed psychotic patient, who have lost conscious recognition of their surrounding *life space,* must still function in the gravitational field (30). Even the astronaut, temporarily removed to outer space where gravity ceases to exert its influence, maintains the accustomed spatial patterns. "Lifting the gravitational load from the otolith organs[1] did not cause disturbances of the central nervous system integrative processes" and did not alter the ingrained spatial orientation (6).

The constant presence of gravity affects men regardless of other influences; it transcends cultural and geographic boundaries. Even during prenatal life, gravitational forces exercise their influence, fixing the normal position of the fetus in the vertical direction, with the heaviest segment, the head, at the lower end. The gravitational system, being constant and acting perpendicularly, structures space vertically to the earth. The horizontal direction is added forming the base from which all action originates (134).

As gravity acts on all objects within its field, it structures internal and external space and regulates the basic biological patterns of human behavior and mental functioning (134, 123). Man cannot escape its influence, and he has evolved a structure responding to its field of energy. The human organism, by aligning itself not as a single, rigid unit but as an aggregate of structural segments (134), allows a flexible organization of its parts responsive to environmental changes. It adapts to the basic forces by erecting the principal segments—head, trunk and legs—in a vertical line balanced by the horizontal structure of the pelvis. The alignment of the segments of the human body not only stabilizes the body's bulk, but also allows it to move with minimal work and with the greatest conservation of effort (134). The gravitational controls seem to account for the earliest reflex action, the rooting reflex, that exists in man and animal alike. Coghill's observations (28) and Spitz's findings (137 a) indicate that the first activities of the newborn are undirected random movements that are apparently of genetic origin (56). They not only form the behavioral roots for the individual's functioning but they possess the potential to respond to internal and external forces that are essential for maturational growth. The capacity to react to stimuli and to incorporate them in the response patterns may become highly significant in the development of sophisticated and complex behavior.

The omnipresent forces, such as gravity, exert a constant control on the formation of structural concepts, and give them unavoidable spatial directions;

1. The otolith is a minute particle found in the inner ear. It is essential in maintaining equilibrium and participates in forming spatial concepts.

they form the universal foundation on which socialization processes actualize the development of specific cultural systems. Man operating within his functional space is constantly exposed to a continuous flow of stimuli, not only from his surroundings, but also from within himself. His needs to adapt to the space around him and to the events taking place therein motivate him in his actions. As he responds to his environment, it feeds back information, mostly in unspoken form.

The infant is born with a set of psychobiological functions and reflex movements (137 b) without which he would be unable to live. Out of such innate movements, essential emotional response patterns are shaped; the loud and prolonged expiration of breath results in the sigh, signaling exhaustion or despair; the cry of the newborn becomes a sign of anger, frustration, or need; out of the horizontal and vertical movements made in searching for the mother's nipple (the rooting reflex) develop the most basic language signs of *yes* and *no* (137 a), signals that are almost universally understood. These nonverbal gestures transcend the limitations of language and remain meaningful regardless of the degree of isolation or interrelation of the people concerned. The same basic gestures are understood by the New Guinea Highlander and the sophisticated Western executive alike.

From an *undifferentiated global state,* the infant develops patterns of coordinated motion by defining, differentiating and organizing his concepts. He must develop these patterns and direct them toward specific goals if he is to survive. The simple motions and response patterns become the universal building stones upon which further experiences construct more specific responses, that eventually become characteristic for a particular species (66). These patterns of response are anything but rigid. They enable the individual and the cultural group to acquire new, useable experiences, incorporating them into cohesive systems (22). But while a total personality or societal structure may be rigid, the series of response patterns must be sufficiently fluid and flexible to function adequately within the surrounding space. The extent and character of new encounters will fortify or discourage relationships, accommodating or terminating experiences. A stable environment furnishes support in establishing an inner structure that institutes priorities and preferences that depend on the significance and sequential importance of life experiences. Thus a hierarchal order of concepts is set up within the spatial structure (44). A successful, appropriate, well-integrated spatial structuralization is vital for the growth of the individual and the societal organization within which he functions. Most of this growth takes place when experiences are linked together into a dynamic system sufficiently stable to provide secure constancy. These structuralizations must withstand testing against proven and previously existing frames of reference. The adaptive potential in interaction between the individual and his sociocultural system advances societal growth; it forms an open system (11) of constant input and output, adjusting and evolving reality concepts while maintaining stable and appropriate reaction patterns (116).

The growth of concepts of reality and space is furthered by the socialization practices that exist in a specific group,[2] affecting the psychological development and the social adaptation of the individual. Early life experiences, determined by parental attitudes which in turn are controlled by the customs of the society,

2. The same technological practice connected with specific activities may have entirely different results in different societies. In New Guinea, copper was not mined until recently and it would have been outside the traditional practices; only in recent years have successful methods of exploring natural resources been introduced. Their development may cause considerable economic growth; some copper-rich areas, aware of their potential wealth, even consider seceding from the mainland. In contrast, mining of natural resources, long practices in Western countries, has made them aware of the danger in exhausting their resources, causing fears of eventual economic failure.

influence the responses of the individual within his cultural framework. Prevailing beliefs and the type of societal organizations—hunting, agricultural or industrial—shape the functioning of the individual and his relationship to his environment. His adaptation has to be flexible so that he can adjust to environmental changes and retain the ability to incorporate new, expanding concepts. The concepts that the individual has of himself must be in balance with those of his environment; marked discrepancies inevitably produce disturbances in the interactions between the individual and his surroundings. The two systems, the self-image and external space, are so closely interdependent that to change the society alters the lives of the individuals living in it, and to change a person's self-image will transform his vision of external space (44).

As man went forth into the space around him, he structured his concepts to meet the gravitational control that he encountered, expanding and moving horizontally. When he left his caves, he had to design shelters that would stand up. As he erected the walls of his huts, he had to align them vertically and stabilize them with horizontal restraining beams to prevent their collapse. When prehistoric man built important edifices, he often transported huge stones, megaliths, over long distances, erecting them against the forces of gravity. The significance of some of these monuments may be lost to us (60), but they bear witness to man's tremendous output of energy to overcome his restrictive environment. The basic designs of early dwellings were organized in the vertical and horizontal directions (50).

Only as civilizations reached higher levels of organization was the diagonal added to the two original directions; as that level was reached, the Egyptians and Babylonians began to build their pyramids.[3] Man's latent potential to organize and orient himself within his concepts of reality became activated; it enabled him to relate to the surrounding world and to bridge the gap between himself and the space outside him. He began to realize that he not only existed in space and time but that time and space existed within him (145); it enabled him to differentiate concepts, to separate objects in space, to define time; he became increasingly able to deal with such universal factors and realized that reality could not be conceived without them.

Increasing experience and the interaction between the individual and his environment circumscribe and define the early global concepts that lack differentiation. They shape the concepts of reality, separate objects in space, relate them in time, and position them within the spatial structure according to their significance. Only in severe psychosis, in infancy, and in mythology does a timeless Garden of Eden or "fool's paradise" exist, where spatial boundaries and temporal limitations are lacking and wishes are immediately fulfilled. Establishing conceptual boundaries in time and space drives man from his paradise of unlimited wish fulfillment into the harsh awareness of his limited power. As the infant reaches out, he begins to experience the boundaries of the world surrounding him; when he comes into bodily contact, his senses isolate objects from the unstructured background of his environment. Mythological man, the culture heroes of the aborigines and the Adam and Eve of Western religions, must forsake paradise when they abandon their unquestioning loyalty to the Divinity, become aware of

3. Mathematicians relate the length of the sides of the Cheops Pyramid to the longitudinal expanse of Egypt at its geographic center; in addition, its perimeter being supposedly in proportion to the circumference of the earth—it demonstrates an amazing mathematical and astronomical knowledge that had been apparently lost for thousand of years. The priests-scientists of ancient Egypt were committed to erect a spiritual center for their Pharaoh that would guarantee a continuum with the sun god in the sky—a life after death that insured Egypt the permanence of eternity (141a).

their separate existence, and seek to acquire knowledge that separates them from a previously satisfying unreality (30).

In prehistoric times, man was unaware of the continuum of his being. Even the members of societies such as the New Guinean clans, that had preserved their aboriginal Paleolithic state until fairly recently, dealt primarily with the problems of their immediate surroundings and the life space within which they functioned. They did not concern themselves with a future full of unknown factors. The Stone Age New Guinean observed closely what he could see, and he planned for imminent events, such as the next day's hunt; the exceptions were ceremonials that were often weeks or months away. As he did not abstract beyond simple images,[4] planning for the future fell outside his time-space framework. Nor was he concerned with events beyond the recent past; anything beyond that he considered insignificant, and he shrouded it in vague indifference.[5] His respect for his deceased ancestors and his fear of their retribution lasted only for a limited period of time, usually not more than three months; after that time, the spirits were dispatched to the island of the dead (136).

The Paleolithic hunter's concepts of the past remained vague and unrecorded except for the designs that he carved or painted on the walls of caves and rocks and on his tools. As man turned from hunting and gathering to planting food, he had to organize and plan for the future. His concepts of reality expanded; he formed new models built on past experiences, which he applied to his future planning. The question, What is? that had necessitated quick action when man hunted his prey, became replaced by What will be?

As man's experiences grew, he extended his conception of reality and began to record history. The ancient Egyptian began to single out and glorify the heroic deeds of the Pharaoh. He recorded the glorious history of his kings to inspire present and future generations. The admiration and respect of the society's past successes contributed to the Pharaoh's divine presence, and those successes became the foundation of the future. The Pharaoh was part of a dynasty that reached beyond his existence on earth; he formed a link with a structured totality. As the god-king, the Pharaoh was the visible incarnation of the gods; these gods were no longer the ghosts of the recent dead as were the spirit-beings of prehistory. The ghosts had been endowed with a circumscribed character; their role was highly individualistic and specific; as deceased ancestors, they dealt primarily with the affairs of the clan or moiety and with the immediate societal organization to which they belonged. Their function was often vengeful and capricious, often protective of their descendants in skirmishes with hostile neighbors. They became directly involved in the lives of the individual and the clan, but they were unconcerned with abstract ethical or moral values. They used trickery and cunning to annoy and punish those who offended them. In contrast, the gods of ancient Egypt and Mesopotamia performed a cosmic function for the entire kingdom and even for its vassal states.[6] They were created by abstracting and synthesizing qualities thought to be desirable, and they were sufficiently powerful to protect and to punish, to instill awe in their followers and fear in

4. The language of the Chimbu in the Highlands of New Guinea has no words for measuring the future; it has no expressions for time if counted in minutes or years; numerals beyond two are only called just "many" (21).

5. Beliefs and attitudes vary in different regions. But in some, the opinions of the old villagers are belittled and outdated (21).

6. One of the first signs of an existing religion lies in the attempt to establish "true gods" that are of cosmic significance and in the zeal to convert the heathenish unbeliever; personalized spirit-beings do not require converts.

those who opposed them. But the Egyptians gods had not freed themselves entirely from the Paleolithic belief in the supremacy of animals (50, 105); they had not yet become completely human images; their bodies were human, but they had animal heads.

Man's experience with reality exists in a continuum of time and space. Abrupt breaks with the past may produce major crises, as did the sudden impact of the twentieth century on the Stone Age culture of New Guinea. The social organization of the villages, composed of clans, moieties and kinships, was based on the rigid customs and rituals of their ancestors. The people were unprepared to deal with the onslaught of completely foreign experiences which they had no basis for understanding. Western technology proved overpowering; any form of resistance was in vain. It seemed futile to try to integrate their past practices into the new experiences. Therefore, the people reacted with helpless resignation—a reaction that was encouraged by their new masters, who not only ignored the existing traditional practices, but considered them inferior and barbaric. Many of the colonists interpreted the entirely unfamiliar culture according to Western cultural values.[7] The early colonial officers, not realizing how paralyzing the collision of values would be for the Melanesian, and considering him far beneath them, were puzzled that the natives did not accept their Western ways. It proved to be highly unrealistic to expect a society steeped in rigid tradition to adjust to the technology of the West in the span of a generation (106). The overzealous missionaries condemned the natives for their spiritual beliefs; they destroyed the men's houses, the social and cultural centers where the men gathered; their sacred images were burned as evil idols; the past lost all value and significance. The ties with the past were disrupted, leading to a disintegration of the people's spiritual values, with no opportunity to integrate the new experiences with past practices. Attempts to force entirely foreign life styles on them corrupted the New Guineans. Doubting the values of their own culture, unprepared to accept concepts which were strange to them, they became confused and eventually reacted with hostile antagonism (78, 127).

In recent years, a new breed of missionary, aware that a culture is only viable if it can maintain a continuity with the past, attempted to revive traditional art forms. Having been made to feel inadequate and ashamed of their past, many New Guineans had detached themselves from the previous cultural life, often denying any ties with the past. When some Melanesians were commissioned to carve plaques of traditional design, the revived patterns were not authentic—they lacked the force of the original concepts (7). Having lost contact with their own culture, New Guineans were able to produce only pleasing designs, cohesive in structure but of meaningless cultural value. The continuum with the past could not be successfully reestablished. In contrast, psychotic patients of moderate personality disintegration spontaneously painted plaques of traditional design (Case 506, 511). Their patterns were disorganized and lacking in cohesiveness, but the pathological regression had reactivated earlier conceptual patterns that corresponded to the patients' level of personality disintegration. Regressive mechanisms reduced the cultural veneer acquired in recent years. Concepts from the past were able to emerge into consciousness, illuminating a basic factor of psychopathology: psychiatric disintegration causes the patient to regress ontogenetically. The

7. The intolerance of the New Guinea traditions occurred mainly during the early days of colonization. The later penetration of the Highlands was led by informed government officials, creating far fewer conflicts (see Chapter 5).

cohesive, nonpsychotic carver of recent years does not have the option to return arbitrarily to earlier adjustment levels; his ties with the past have been disrupted and he has lost contact with his early life experiences.

The penetration of the highly developed technology of the West into countries that had been isolated from foreign influences, appeared, to people such as the New Guineans, to be magic. The only way to rationalize their impotence was to believe that their ancestors had failed to match the trickery of the Europeans in capturing material goods (77). They were not experienced in European ways, and they could only approach the unknown with the explanations at their disposal. It could not be expected that their magical way of thinking could assimilate the deductive logic of the European. Indigenes everywhere who were forced to find answers to new, unfamiliar problems, had to solve them with vague, incomplete ideas that could not be incorporated into their existing systems. The success and prestige of the foreign powers and the comparative powerlessness of their own systems rendered them ineffective and passive. The resentment provoked by their feelings of humiliation resulted in hostility, which they released through the familiar channels of magic; sorcery, an effective tool in the past, became far more significant than ever before (see Appendix).

Western society has been equally affected by the many crises disrupting the flow of its development in time and space; these have occurred when established institutions were threatened by new experiences and discoveries. The printing press, disseminating knowledge that had hitherto been reserved for a select few; the invention of gunpowder, making traditional warfare obsolete; and the discoveries of new continents, supporting Copernicus's theories, made man doubt entrenched tenets. Profound change may tempt man to free himself from the chains of traditional superstition, but often he is opposed by reactionary controls that may be temporarily successful in reversing advances. Blind and rigid adherence to the past or an unawareness of changing requirements may cause rebellion against the past and may disrupt the continuum of time. Not only did the French Revolution bring about a complete reversal of social and political conditions, but its most radical proponent, Robespierre, established a new "religion of reason." He attempted to break the French nation away from its historical roots by introducing a new calendar and planning a new era. Both attempts collapsed after a few months. Thus far in history, any attempt to isolate man from his past has met with failure. Many revolutions that rebel against the past initially attempt to deny their heritage, but after having established themselves, they become aware of the importance of their history, even if they distort some historical facts to justify the dogmas of the new society.[8]

The anxieties felt by prehistoric man as he attempted to step beyond his spatial boundaries are repeated in contemporary Western man. The wide dissemination of information of recent years has caused significant conceptual changes, forcing newly gained material to be grafted onto past experience more rapidly than the individual can assimilate it. The many new developments of the twentieth century have been overwhelming. Space travel has made us direct participants in events taking place halfway around the globe. Medical advances have removed the threat of death from many illnesses. In the past, such provocative discoveries primarily affected the scientific community, which served as a buffer to the public, sheltering it from the impact of new experiences, but the pace of

8. Soviet Russia denied her ties with any period of the Czarist Regime and denied that positive historical events had occurred prior to the revolution. Only after the government was firmly entrenched were heroes of her past recognized, even if they were noblemen such as Prince Alexander Nevsky.

technology and the effectiveness of the media now bring these discoveries to everyone.

Anxieties and apprehensions occur whenever man is confronted with infringements on the traditional limits of his power. Modern man finds some comfort in his sophisticated knowledge, but he reacts with great apprehension to the changes it has wrought in the spatial and temporal borders of his world. In his dismay, he suspects the scientific revolutions affecting his established concepts. He was awestruck when he discovered the destructive potential of the hydrogen bomb and a missile delivery system capable of inconceivable speeds. As the conventional space-time boundaries are violated, man seeks to hide as he did in the past, in the caves that are his bomb shelters, fearing that he cannot survive the holocaust that he could effect.

The basic conflict between progress and security goes on eternally. As in the myth of Prometheus being punished by Zeus for bringing fire to man, man's fear of his own power causes him to punish himself for transgressing the boundaries of the natural world, for splitting the atom and unleashing forces once thought inconceivable. These are fears that man has not yet stilled.

The development of spatial concepts reflecting man's ability to structure reality is visualized in his pictorial representations (112, 118). As prehistoric man moved out of his caves, his imagery became controlled by a more restrictive order, approaching a linear shaping of sequential thoughts.[9]

Linear thinking, a prerequisite for language, disassembles the many aspects of structural space (see Chapter 3) and orders them in sequence. It promotes additional links to build more complex structures. Being one-dimensional, it is highly effective for deductive logic and for stabilizing and preserving intellectual concepts (Table 1). Yet, the very accuracy of verbal language makes it restrictive and less able to convey information when dealing with multidimensional spatial structures; architectural designs, blueprints of even simple engineering charts, and geographic maps, illustrate the limitations of verbal language and the need for multidimensional presentations. Visual imagery translates the structure of objects and their interrelationships more effectively; it plasticizes and lends depth to the conceptual models within its external space (4 b).

The tribal artist[10] carves the ancestral figures and paints spirit-beings on the walls of his ceremonial houses, and brings the spirit world within the reach of those who share his beliefs. His art establishes links with the remote world of his forefathers by bringing them into the presence of the believers—he conquers space; the concepts of natural space are restricted in the indigene's mind, but beyond them lie the infinite "Gates of the Dream" (122 a). A rigidly enforced hierachic order bridges the gap between immediate and spiritual space, and secures the indigene's position within it. The order of his relationship to the supernatural is often strictly established by tradition and societal custom; only a narrow area of personal initiative is given to the individual. Its important aspect, the creation of sacred art, is for the most part under strict control, variations being sternly discouraged (98).

The designs of traditional art condense, elaborate, and distort; realistic details may be omitted, symbols indicating essential spiritual features added. Geometric

9. The change to abstractive thinking appears also in the development of religious attitudes. Spirit-beings and ghosts echo the personal immediacy of the spiritual needs of the Stone Age man. In contrast, the planter becomes dependent on gods lending him the required stability for meeting his present and future needs. His gods, compartmentalized and serving specific functions, as the gods of the winds, of rain and of the sun, are not however, temporary creatures, their significance lies in their permanency.

10. Most tribal societies, African or Melanesian, have a decidedly different societal structure and different art styles than prehistoric Stone Age man.

figures such as triangles, hatched lines indicating clouds, and ceremonial feathers, may be traditional parts of ancestral plaques, signifying that the spirit has power over the forces of nature, by adding them to the plaque in their abstract forms. The forms and shapes are not arbitrarily selected, but have been agreed upon by convention and maintained by the clan. They appear as distortions to the outsider, but they have communal significance and convey the very essentials of spiritual beliefs. Being of cohesive structure, they carry a message understood by the entire group. The visual message is understood with little verbal explanation; verbal meanings can hardly be ascribed to the primitive work. Specific meanings may be assigned to some of its parts—the circular center in Hohao plaques may represent the navel (illustration 6.3), symbolizing the spiritual center of the tribe; the border consisting of triangles may be indicative of clouds—but the total impact of the plaque goes far beyond such narrow meanings; the full significance of its power to instill fear and convey the might of its possessor cannot be understood in words. The image expresses the accumulated experiences of the artist who is part of the societal group within which the image functions (118).

The artist's ability to reveal the structure of man's inner world has, from its earliest beginnings in prehistory, responded to the need to cope with the unsolved riddles of existence. In all cultures, Western and non-Western, as man shaped his gods, he represented them in his art. When he was in danger of losing control of his destiny, he turned to external forces for help; he sought security in the control achieved by magic; he called on the spirits and gods to control his fate. When he was close to despair, he invoked the visible presence of his gods, carving idols that replaced the invisible, spiritual divinity. In tribal societies, the carving of ancestral figures brought the spirits within the reach of man and satisfied his close dependency on supernatural powers; the early Israelites worshipped the golden calf when it seemed their leader, Moses, had abandoned them in the desert.

The Greek and Roman sociocultural systems shaped the basis for Western thought and art. Greek art forms were adapted by Romans, whose invading legions propagated them throughout the major parts of Europe, reaching into Africa, where they built their classic temples. As the overexpanded empire collapsed, a void was left in place of a monolithic civilization; tribal bands from the east and north invaded large parts of the Roman territory, only to be pushed out by the next wave of pursuing barbarians. The constant changing of large population groups caused instability and a loss of order. It produced near-chaos, a climate highly unfavorable to the arts.

Artistic skills faltered, but did not cease. Isolated achievements continued to be made, fostered by the Catholic Church, which shifted its spiritual center from Rome to the East, establishing its capital in Constantinople, where Byzantine art flourished. There, a fervent spiritualism was born in an attempt to impose a rigid order on the threatening chaos. Its rigorous art forms forced a predominantly linear perspective that denied spatial depth onto the visual world (illustration 2.2-4). During subsequent periods, the sociocultural changes caused by the Crusades encouraged the widening of spatial horizons. The spiritualism of the early Middle Ages created artistic concepts in which the figures were projected vertically. Apparently unhampered by gravity, they floated upward toward Heaven.

As man develops increasing control over his destiny, art loses its spiritual power, and secular art, taking its place, presents more worldly subjects. The artist, as spokesman for society, shifts from dealing with invisible, divine forces to encounters between man and man. Man's moral impulses are no longer primarily devoted to his subservience to God, but, beginning with the Renaissance period, have become progressively humanized. The discoveries of the period and the increased dissemination of knowledge removed many mysteries from life, substituting empirical experience for the mysticism of the Middle Ages.

European paintings of the fourteenth and fifteenth centuries created a substantially complete integrated image. They are part of a culture aware of human values that had not been known since the fall of the Roman Empire. Broadened knowledge restored intellectual power to the Renaissance man, who still struggled with isolated cells of spiritual domination. Along with scientific knowledge, naturalism became increasingly important. Over the centuries naturalism became romanticized, culminating in the almost delusive aspects of some of Rousseau's philosophy. Ironically, the romanticizing of nature eventually corrupted its appearance, as in the allegorical paintings of Boucher and Frangonard and in the studied and artificial hamlet of Trianon (illustration 4.4) that stressed the elegance of the French court during the prerevolutionary days. Contrived rustic landscapes gave up their naturalistic character, substituting a suave treatment of their gallant themes, hiding from the political clouds. The English landscapes of Constable and Turner offer a strong contrast of the conceptual world of the early nineteenth century.

The industrial age reduced man's role from that of an artisan deriving satisfaction from his individual skills to that of a production man on the assembly line, who had lost his individuality. The computer age of the twentieth century makes of the human brain an electronic model; mathematical philosophies deemphasize the biological factors of vital growth, treating them as a predictable function that balances input and output with feedback reactions, giving man little credit for spontaneity. At mid-century, the exploration of space offered untold victories for man's mind. But after the first flush of success, he became aware that his triumph made him vulnerable to openings in his defensive borders, reducing the individual's securities and bringing a confused ambivalence.

Art that depicts man lost in the vast horizons of space and dwarfed by the new technology, confronts an unmanageable, almost infinite world; it retreats, in the paintings of De Chirico, Ernst, and Rouault, to a revival of supernatural mysticism. The landscapes of these artists are like jungles or deserts, space appears extended, and dehumanized mannequins replace human figures. The artist's use of fantastic symbolism expresses the apprehensions of living in a world where traditionally safe borders have become obsolete.

It has always been man's dream to overcome the forces of gravity but until fairly recently he has failed in his attempts. Even mythology, expressing the collective fantasies of men, has Icarus perish as he attempts to fly; Leonardo de Vinci was preoccupied with building a flying machine, but he never succeeded. Overcoming gravity was once thought to be evil sorcery; only witches were able to ride through the sky and return to earth. Man's beliefs allowed only those who were no longer earthbound—the saints and the dead—to float to Heaven; they were not of this earth, and were therefore beyond its control. It was not until the end of the eighteenth century that French balloonists overcame gravity and lifted themselves into the air. The successes of manned flight remained relatively limited until the Wright brothers had their first successful flight.

Marc Chagall was one of the first to explore the new structure of space artistically. Soon after the Wright brothers' flight, he developed his unrealistic style of garish colors, green cows, and people, houses and even villages that defied gravity. Man had begun to conquer gravity, and the artist now painted common mortals—no longer just beings with supernatural power—riding through the sky on sleighs, lovers flying through the room into the spacelessness and intimate close-

10.1. Birthday *by Marc Chagall.*
Collection, Museum of Modern
Art, New York.

ness of their ecstasy, as in the painting *Birthday* (illustration 10.1 [36]). Art had
transcended the limits of traditional spatial concepts, and the new technology
allowed their acceptance.

The scientific explosion, offering new options and opportunities, also brought
many perplexities and contradictions. The arts became deeply involved in the
many controverises, and supernatural mysticism was soon joined by a strong
adversary: harsh realism. One of the most popular expressions of the computer
age has been Pop Art, which utilizes commercial forms and eliminates any interference with its borrowings from mass culture, imprisoning the viewer by a slavish
adherence to its model. Warhol's famed *Can of Tomato Soup* reflects the computerized world in its managed clarity; the artist supplies the answers and
eliminates any personal commentary from the viewer. The other end of the scale
of contemporary art presents extreme abstractions; an oblique line with a few
barely perceptible dots, painted on the canvas in the same neutral color, offers
little guidance to the viewer, who is left alone to contemplate the artist's cryptic
message. Other artists, disturbed by the change of societal and spatial structure,
attempt to rehabilitate discredited values (5) by flouting standardized principles.
In seeking to express what has been repressed, the artist uses realistic details, presenting subject matter that is often explicitly sexual, leaving no room for interpretation. In attempting to free the viewer from tradition, the artist makes him a
captive of his zeal; he turns naked realism (illustration 10.2) into realism of the
naked (illustration 10.3). Artistic creativity, regardless of its style, is integrated
into the sociocultural world in which it is produced; it not only reflects the artist's view, but its meaning lies also in relating the artist's concepts of reality to
the existing sociocultural patterns. The structuralization of space (refer to Chapter 2) is not an unalterable fact, but seems to be regulated by the continuous
interaction between the individual and his society.

As in visual art, the graphics of the psychotic attempt to express a message, but theirs is a personal message, communicating the needs of their troubled inner world. The disintegrated concepts of reality that appear in the psychotic patient's graphics become increasingly controlled by the pathological process that affects his views of reality and of the spatial structure of its concepts. Often, patients talk with a strange emotional detachment about the disintegration or nonexistence of their future; there may be an empty smile on their faces, or they may speak in a monotonous voice, belying the distressing content of their words. One patient stated that she "has been dead, having died when I was born," expressing her conviction that one is alone after one is born, detached and isolated; her emotional emptiness made her feel that everything in life was cold and lifeless; there was no one alive. She seemed indifferent to her fate, only adding with a shrug, "I can't explain it."

The disintegrated personality becomes aware early of the first changes within himself, of the fragmentation of his thoughts and his feelings, and he projects them onto the surrounding world. It may be difficult for the nonpsychotic to understand the fears that overcome the psychotic when he perceives the transformation occurring around him. The psychotic feels, in his delusions, that he is

10.2. Ice *by Richard Lindner. Collection of the Whitney Museum of American Art, New York.*

enveloped by a vast desert (illustration 7.4) in which he feels isolated and frightened (130). His emotional detachment makes him feel lifeless and may make
other people appear to be faceless robots. Munch's paintings illustrate this point
with disturbing realism (illustrations 7.25, 26). Others, alarmed by the disruptions
within them, project their inner upheaval as a world breaking apart (illustration
7.2). The speech of the psychotic becomes vague, lacking coherence, alternating
from apparently meaningless verbiage to taciturnity. The disintegrated patient
often despairs of not being understood; his conviction that other people do not
care that he suffers from unbearable conflicts that are destroying him may
infuriate him. The futility of his attempts at verbal communication, the many
images pouring into his mind simultaneously, the fragmented, ever-changing
thoughts, may find a brief anchorage when he puts them on paper or canvas. As
he paints, he forces his images to come to a standstill. His attempts to stabilize
them make their forms appear increasingly rigid, contributing to a forced semblance of stability that he lacks otherwise (22). But he only succeeds for the
moment; because his concepts are unstable, their meanings escape again, becoming remote and detached whenever his level of integration becomes altered
(illustration 3.5).

10.3. 1970 Nude *by Tom Wes-
selman. Used by permission of
M. Knoedler & Co., Inc., New
York.*

The constancy of imagery in one's language is normally maintained by a *feedback mechanism* that is defective in the disintegrated personality. The lack of operative information leads to the disintegration of the spatial structure and to a disordered personality function. Constant images cannot be maintained, and they lack the stability to support the patient. The progressive levels of disintegration are evident in the spatial structure of patients' graphics (Table 2). Their imagery regresses from ghostly figures floating in space, threatening in their dissolution to an increasingly empty rigidity as the patients withdraw emotionally to protect themselves from experienced and anticipated emotional traumas. They react with a defensive withdrawal to latent early behavior patterns that are less complex and make fewer demands.

If the disintegrative processes are not too far advanced, the patient can make himself understood verbally, for the disintegration of his thought processes follows fairly specific rules (43); but his visual language may communicate more effectively (3, 14 b). This is illustrated by the schizophrenic patient who discovered on his own that a highly abstract painting was the portrait of a faculty member, painted two years earlier by a moderately disintegrated patient whom the first patient had never met (color plate 7). The earlier patient had been able to communicate through his imagery, in spite of its distortions, to another schizophrenic. It seems exceptional that the patient, who had no prior knowledge of the painting, recognized the portrait. However, as shown by past experiences, graphics

10.4. *At the beginning of reintegration, cultural characteristics reappear. The portrait, drawn by a mildly schizophrenic Japanese patient, retains oriental features.*

10.5. *This scene by a patient from Hong Kong has the flavor of Chinese art, in spite of a slight mixing of planes.*

by regressed patients express concepts often grasped by others who can respond to the disintegrative process of the patient.[11] Some of their symbols may have personal significance, but the basic conceptual structure that appears in their spatial representation has a common universal base. Beyond its basic universals, conceptual reality is a system that is susceptible not only to cultural and personal variables, but to the pathological process. Psychopathology creates unstable images; goal ideas are replaced by shifting, inconstant concepts. Fragmented, poorly structured elements reach conscious levels, and emotionally charged material, untested by experience, emerges (illustration 7.14). Socialization practices (32 a) that had contributed to the development of cultural variations lose more and more significance as the psychotic regresses. The changes in the spatial structure occur universally and become apparent in graphics by patients from entirely different sociocultural and educational backgrounds (14 a, 14 d, 15 b). A patient from a Western culture, a sophisticated college student,[12] shows essentially the same spatial structure (illustration 7.40) as a patient from rural Africa (illustration 7.46). Both patients organize their spatial concepts (trees erected on a baseline) vertically. Others show repeated elongations in their graphics; a graphic by a dis-

11. An outstanding proponent of this theory was Harry Stack Sullivan, who credited his understanding of the schziophrenic's language to his own personal conflicts.

12. The Western patient, a young American girl, had somewhat improved at the time and had developed some depth perception in contrast to the African patient who had shown less clinical improvement.

integrated patient from the Highlands of New Guinea (illustrations 8.56, 63) and one by a schizophrenic from Austria (illustration 7.7) offer such examples; in spite of their wide sociocultural differences, the structure of their spatial concepts show obvious similarities. The latent universal spatial structures had been repressed by their cultural development. Personality disorganization reactivates these early structures, and they appear in a preestablished pattern, corresponding to the level of disintegration (Table 2).

In the drawings of more regressed patients, considerable spatial distortions occur, overriding their cultural characteristics, as in a crayon drawing from Kenya (illustration 7.47); two-dimensional figures appear, their parts incompletely connected; the head is twisted to the front, while other parts of the body are viewed from the side.

The regression observed in the graphics is not, however, simply a regression to earlier levels of personality development. Experiencing pain and anxiety over the fragmentation of his ability to function, the patient concerns himself with ways to restore the fragmented world within him. Hampered by his inability to form cohesive thoughts, he projects his feelings of inadequacy; unable to accept his malfunctioning, he comes to believe that others conspire against him. In spite of the discomfort and defects of these delusions, they are the only defense that the psychotic patient can muster against the threat of personality disorganization.

TABLE 4

Cultural and Personality Functions in Tribal and Psychotic Art

	Tribal Art	Psychotic Graphic Expressions
Ego Structure	Integrated	Disintegrated
Ego Boundaries	Intact	Dissolved
Concept Formation	Stable, often rigid, cohesive, well delineated	Unstable linkage, vague, overlapping, fragmented
Defense Mechanisms	Goal directed, adapted to cultural group images; Magical thinking; Rigid; Omnipotence	Lacking goal ideas; Unconscious mechanisms overwhelm the poorly integrated ego; Magical thinking; Omnipotence
Symbolism	Culturally determined; Societal values	Solipsistic
Relation to External Reality	Societal organization may disregard individual needs; Stylistic characteristics often developed due to societal needs	Individual may sacrifice external reality
Summary	Shared, common reality within which the individual functions	Common reality is reduced

These changes have greater significance when observed during the progress of a patient's clinical condition, as he reintegrates from early levels of spatial organization to the integrational patterns prevailing in his society. Such reintegration was followed during the clinical recovery of several of our patients (illustrations 7.38–41). But the process of reintegration can only progress to the spatial structure existing in the patient's own culture. As the patient from the Papuan Gulf region reintegrates, he paints plaques (illustrations 8.17–24) very similar to those of his own region (illustration 8.13), while the Highlander paints anthropomorphic figures (illustration 8.63) similar to drawings by New Guinean nonpsychotics (illustration 8.66). Even if reintegration is still somewhat incomplete, cultural characteristics reappear, as seen in a portrait by a young Japanese patient that maintained its Oriental facial features (illustration 10.4); the facial elongation indicates an early level of personality disintegration. In the watercolor of a Chinese fisherman painted by a patient from Hong Kong (illustration 10.5), the mixing of perspective planes indicates moderate spatial disintegration. A patient who has reached adulthood maintains some of his acquired life experiences as long as he is not fully regressed; acquired life experiences are included in the restitutive process. The simultaneous presence of regressive and restitutive mechanisms contribute to unstable images and to a partial breakdown of the structure of the visual world. The ability to stabilize the self by relating it to an ordered structural space becomes impaired, and one loses the ability to function adequately in time and space. As the regression advances, sociocultural factors appear to exert diminishing influence, and the restitutive abilities likewise diminish; concepts revert to early spatial patterns (Table 4).

In spite of essential differences, the graphics of schizophrenics all reveal a conceptualization of space that is related to children's drawings and prehistoric cave paintings (50, 14 a). The small child's scribbles (illustrations 2.12, 7.60), the multidirectional space of primitive art (50), and the highly disorganized and *dedifferentiated* drawings of the mentally ill are not formed by chance. The attempts to structure space advance from a state of undifferentiated chaos, to building a spatial framework on a baseline (illustration 2.13), and further to a subjective interpretation of reality (Table 3). On that level, the customary limitations of concepts and their interrelationships have not yet developed; the intrinsic boundaries delineating objects have not adequately formed; objects may appear transparent, and their spatial arrangements may be seen as an arbitrary placing of one on top of the other in vertical projection (illustration 2.14); or the various views of figures in the same paintings may not appear in their customary relationship—mixing the geometric planes (illustration 2.15). Further growth eliminates the subjective aspects of spatial structure and establishes the conceptual limits of the viewed objects as they are perceived by the eye; they lose their transparency and are arranged without mixing perspective planes; some distortion may occur in the form of elongation (illustration 2.16). Eventually, as the conceptual integration progresses, a level of three-dimensional perspective is reached.

The psychotic cannot produce significant art. When he draws, he seeks to control his multitudinous thoughts, but without success—he shapes images without cohesion. He can only arrest the flow of the many concepts in his mind by putting them on paper or on the canvas. Often he draws and paints on any surface that he can find. Even if he had never shown any interest in art prior to his illness (14 a), he becomes possessed by the need to communicate his thoughts and his feelings in hope of making himself understood; the results are of minimal artistic value (14 c). The magic of the psychotic may be similar to that of primitive man (122 b), but he is alone, without the support of his community; his magical thoughts cannot reach beyond himself. His ill-defined concepts readily accept similes and approximations as identities permeating all his life functions. In New Guinea where the unknown affects the actions of villagers, the uneasiness and guilt connected with unexpected events, particularly tragic incidents, provoke the use of magic to neutralize what happened. But magic and spiritual beliefs are compartmentalized and restricted to specific circumstances, and the natives draw a clear line between their ritual magic, and the thinking of the psychotic.

Magic beliefs are not limited to the psychotic or to primitive society; it seems that magic stirs all of us. It is there when we ardently pursue distant goals (122 b) and when we hope against hope (147 a). If a Westerner believes in spiritualism, he may turn to astrologers or clairvoyants for solutions to problems that perplex him. He may seek quick answers for crises that affect not only him but also his community or his nation. As the compulsive personality finds release by performing rituals to soothe his conscience (38), substitutive action offers relief from anxieties that threaten the noncompulsive individual and his society in periods of crisis. Attacking a single issue may seem a remedy for complex social problems; it often sways public opinion by providing an outlet for the inablility to deal with the problem as a whole.[13] Magic thinking finds social acceptance when it is based on value systems specific for the sociocultural group (Chapter 9).[14] We defend our failures in meeting our difficulties by attempting to *encapsulate* them and to restrict them to unsubstantiated, hasty rationalizations.

Psychopathological behavior is perceived as aberrant when the group to which the disintegrating individual belongs cannot tolerate his disturbing actions or his bizarre conduct. While the Indian village in Guatemala could absorb the disturbed personality of its medicine man (16), the violent acts of patients from New Guinea make them unacceptable to their community. The disintegrated personality's magic thinking and ritualistic behavior arouses perplexity and uneasiness among the villagers because it falls outside their established norms.

As our study progressed, it confirmed our view that we should avoid the uncritical application of Western standards, including diagnostic labels, to non-Western cultures (Chapter 4). The ritualistic behavior and delusions of magic and sorcery of the psychotic are often interwoven with other forms of psychopathological symptoms, making it important to separate pathological mechanisms from culture-bound material. The pathological process, the patient's illness, does not depend solely on biological factors (11); man exists within an environment that exerts inescapable controls. He has to be endowed with mechanisms that enable him to adjust to environmental influences, both physical and psychological. Some influences are constant but indiscernible forces that dominate the formation of man's orientation to the earth, not just to the actions of men. Gravity, for instance, governs the structuralization of space; it forms a universal base on which all human action is built (14 a, 50, 134). The developmental stages of spatial structure follow patterns that are predetermined by the individual's level of personality integration and by the societal organization within which he functions (44). Spatial structure conveys the potential growth of reality concepts over which the individual has limited control, being forced to operate within his framework (44, 50). He cannot reach beyond the structure that corresponds to his sociocultural level; this restricts a reintegrated Melanesian patient to using the traditional designs of his region (illustration 8.15), while a Western patient structures her reality concepts in the three-dimensional perspective (illustration 7.41) used since the days of the Renaissance.

Socialization practices establish controls that define the prevailing attitudes and behavior patterns of a culture (32 a); they exert a significant impact on the individual and his society, requiring him to adapt to environmental circumstances. As his personality develops, his interaction with the surrounding world establishes his role and social status within a hierarchical order.

By producing a disintegration of the personality structure, mental illness interferes with the socialization practices. As these practices are responsible for cultural patterns, the disintegrative and regressive mechanisms of the psychotic

13. A local spiritual debacle existing in Salem, Massachusetts, brought on the witchhunt of 1692, ending in the execution of thirty-two people condemned for witchcraft. Far more recently, in 1955, when juvenile delinquency was recognized to be a far-reaching social problem, oversimplified solutions were sought to deal with the issues. Many thought that by outlawing cartoons of violence (its visual representation) violence itself

reduce their significance. Their loss parallels the regression to earlier levels of personality organization; the disintegrated personality is no longer capable of interrelating the multiple determinants of human behavior, and it regresses to universal factors of behavior. The "universals" appear crossculturally—they are psychobiological, genetically transmitted structures common to all (32 a). They form a living system with a constant flow of input and output (116) interacting ceaselessly with their environment, coordinating, organizing and structuring experiences. Gravity, the essentials of the earth's atmosphere, light and its velocity and the near constancy of time, exert an unchanging control requiring an adaptation to their influences over which there is no effective deviation possible. They are rooted in the cumulative cultural heritage, internalized in the individual, and they carry with them the potentials of maturation. They originate in a state of relative globality as universals in all cultures, forming the building blocks for the development of human behavior. Their innate capacity for maturation leads to increased differentiation and articulation of their conceptual structures (28, 56).

Severe psychotic regression to the level of universal, unstructured concepts modifies the simple regressive behavioral patterns by the psychopathological processes and by the continuous attempts at restitution. As pictorial imagery corresponds to the psychic life of those who produce it (50), graphics by psychotic patients not only facilitate the recognition of regressive spatial patterns but they confirm the parallels existing between the various levels of personality disintegration and spatial structure (see Table 2).

When the disintegrated personality loses his ability for verbal communication, he begins to paint; he paints his message of the disintegrating world around him with undisguised, stark directness (color plate 3). While the artist, Western or non-Western, has an understandable and readable message to convey (13, 14 b), the painted message of the psychotic remains a personal communication. His failure lies in the lack of cohesiveness, frustrating the subliminal impact of his art, and in his inability to communicate the underlying structure of the world, the motif that the artist and viewer normally share. Visual expressions, being more than a symbolic language, become a primary system of communication, giving insight into the world of feelings, desires and concepts that are beyond verbalization (118).

---

could be outlawed (Hearings for U.S. Senate Resolution 62, 1955). The substitutive action against a single facet was believed to remove the entire problem; this is a persuasive example of magic thinking.

14. Individuals making borderline adjustments who had been ignored by their country in the past and who may have lived in obscurity may be suddenly elevated to prominency by socio-economic or historical changes. Many historians attribute the rise of Hitler to the distressing political conditions of the 1920's; the leaders of the French Revolution, as of other uprisings, were mostly unknown personalities. They became effective by their unscrupulous dogmatism that omittted essential links in the sequence of their thought processes, another characteristic of magic thinking (Table 1). It is only rarely that theoreticians rise to political leadership, their deductive thinking precludes magic solutions desired by an impatient revolutionary public.

A.1. *In a dramatized performance, a sorcerer kills his victim. Copyright by the* Post Courier, *Port Moresby, and reprinted with permission.*

Appendix

In the appendix, we shall supply additional information from nonprofessional sources about present day New Guinea. We shall include official reports by two Australian patrol officers[1] who were called for help in transporting patients to the hospitals; they give us some insight into the home environment of the patients and the attitudes of their families, and add a somewhat different slant to the understanding of the villagers' way of life. The local newspaper supplies further information about a wide range of events taking place in the country. Not all news items report unusual and outstanding events; some tell of practices that were daily occurrences in the past and are unique only as they are still practiced at present. Some of the incidents also occur in other countries, but are called by different names—"street riots," or "gang wars"—which are not unusual in explosive areas of the West. If they take place in New Guinea, they conjure up romantic images to the outsider; they become tribal wars and their participants are warriors instead of rioters. It is true, however, that such incidents have cultural roots, for they are founded in the traditions of the past; the weapons being used are bows and arrows instead of Saturday night specials.[2] Other events are of far greater importance to the future of the country as it deals with the expansion and the development of its economy and resources.

Before citing the news reports, we shall reproduce the official accounts given by patrol officers who investigated the incidents leading to the hospitalization of the patients. The reports may convey the climate that still exists in rural areas of New Guinea. The reporting officer was stationed in the Eastern Highlands; he investigated the accusations brought against a mental patient who supposedly shot arrows at the animals and people in his village (Case A570). The patient's village could only be reached by a twenty-to-thirty-minute walk from the district road; only a narrow foot path connected it with the outside. As customary, the village was located on a mountain ridge; this gave it a strategic position when head-

---

1. The patrol officer was an administrative officer in charge of a patrol post that usually covered an area of several square miles. At one time, the station was on the edge of an unexplored area. The officer was usually the only European in the area. The local people were hostile considering the post as an intrusion into their country. The officer was in charge of a few Melanesian policemen, a medical orderly and a few workmen; he policed the area, held court, provided health care and advised on improving farming methods. The patrol posts were bases for exploring untouched wilderness (106). In most cases the duties of the patrol officer became far less adventurous during the years before independence.

2. Saturday night specials are cheap guns sold in the United States of America. Easily obtainable, they are the most commonly used illegal weapons.

235

hunting raids terrorized the villagers. They built their homes in clusters (illustration 5.4) to force a potential enemy into a disasvantageous position. About fifteen to twenty small round huts encircle a central opening (illustration 4.2) where most of today's communal activities take place, replacing the ceremonial houses.

The patient's home was built in the traditional manner. It had *pitpit* (mud) and bark walls inside; the roof was made of kunai grass. A fireplace placed in the center of the floor had blackened the roof and the supporting rafters with smoke. Upon entering, the officer cataloged the contents of the hut as follows:[3]

> Black palm bow with many arrows
> 9 bush material containers of Karuka, nuts extracted from the fruit of the
>   Pandanus palm
> Several bottles and boiling pots for cooking
> Many blankets
> Several wooden suitcase style boxes
> Coffee drying plastic
> Coffee sacks
> Pillow, tin boxes, plates, mugs
> 3 cheap kerosene lanterns
> 1 broom, 1 shopping basket
> 1 hammer
> 2 iron axes
> 1 Roman Catholic rosary[4]
> 1 headdress of Cassowary feathers (no other traditional Sing Sing decorations
>   visible, though these Cassowary feathers often used by him during normal
>   times)

The patient owned land several miles away from his home. His wife tended the gardens and cooked his food; before his illness, he used to clear and fence large gardens.

> The first changes noted in the patient (O.)[5] occurred in 1953. He had gone to ——— [halfway between Watabung station and Chimbu border] where he shot two dogs without apparent reason. Police from Chuave caught him and hat him taken to Kundiawa, where it was decided to send him to Goroka Base Hospital for possible treatment. From Goroka, he was sent to a hospital for psychiatric treatment in Port Moresby. He was there for six months, so I have been informed, before he was returned to his village.
>
> O. was a loner and also a traveller. He was forever going over to the ——— Pass and could be seen all over the Watabung Census Division, or Asaro or Goroka, particularly when there was a dispute, celebration or village quarrel.
>
> He was apparently attracted to Europeans whom he knew, for instance, in the former D.C.'s [District Commissioner] and A.D.C.'s [Assistant District Commissioner], Europeans working for PWD [Public Works Department] on the Pass and other sections of the Pass. When I first came to live in Watabung, he was a frequent visitor, often bringing presents of fresh vegetables when he knew me.
>
> Villagers said that although he wouldn't listen to them and their suggestions, he would

---

3. The report is reproduced verbatim except that some parts are omitted for brevity.

4. The simultaneous possession of a headdress used in traditional ceremonies and of a rosary reflect the ambiguous attitude toward spiritual life of the New Guineans. Most have been converted by missionaries to Christianity; they attend church services on Sundays, but otherwise continue to believe in their traditional spirit-beings. Most other items found in the hut, except the bow and arrows, and possibly the blanket, are Western-made products. Even the iron axes (probably made of steel) are not of traditional origin.

5. We are withholding the name of the patient and of his home village in order to protect his rights of privacy.

listen and at least start to comply to what someone in authority had directed him to do, Policemen, Teachers, Administrative Officers, etc. O. would not sit down in the "haus-man" [Communal house for all villagers and sleeping house for men] these days and talk to everyone, so said other villagers when asked about his conduct.

The Europeans treated him paternalistically to the extent that they were not quite sure if he would carry out threats of shooting local people and often, like a child, given [sic] money and presents to go away and not bother anyone. Over a period of many months in 1972, one would know that O. was approaching from a long distance away, by the continual blowing of a police whistle given to him by a previous District Commissioner.

O. liked to see people laughing at his "Sing Sing" antics and this seemed to make him carry on more. I remember on one Saturday morning, whilst the market was in progress near the river and a large audience was present, O. rushed to the top of the ridge leading to his village, but overlooking the market, and grabbing his bow and arrows gave a solo sing-sing [sic] and dance for everyone down below.

Local people from his "haus-lain," as well as others about the station have treated him for a long time with a kind of mixture of amusement, tolerance as well as contempt, never listening to anything he had to say. They were always wary of him though, if he carried his bow and arrow with him.

To fellow villagers outside his own immediate family, O. would repeat instructions heard from people in authority; Administration Officers, Police, Europeans, Ministers or Priests of Religion, etc.; he used to go around the villages for instance telling everyone to get rid of pigs from inside/underneath houses and away from "haus-lains," to fence in village pigs and clean the "haus-lain" (from the time he was a young man, he would remember administration officers, patrolling in the area, instructing villagers to do this).

O. was baptised as a Catholic in 1964 at the age of 35. Apparently he was a regular church attendant at the Catholic Church. He gave, for a local man, huge sums of money at the collection during the service—as much as 50 cents or $1.00. He used to go around the village telling everyone that they should go to church and become Christians, that the church was a good thing and people should not forget it during the week. When he was really agitated and having one of his "fits" he informed everyone he was "Jesus" or "God."

Since 1953, he has been sent to Goroka many times by the police for various offences. He once shot two pigs at his "haus-lain," I was informed. The villagers were very tolerant, only cut them up and everyone ate them, even though it was not for a particular occasion.

Once in 1972, O. shot a pitpit arrow at the driver of a "Roka" truck because he would not give him a lift to the top of the —— Pass. O. spent two days in the Goroka Police "lock-up" for this offence. He has shot arrows at many local people, generally missing them, whether intentionally or not, is not known. O's wife apparently was scared that her husband would one day shoot someone and bring trouble to them from the village of O's future victim. She wished that the family would cut off some of his fingers, so he could not tighten the string of the bow. His brothers would not agree to this finally as it would mean that he could not work in the garden either. The people of the village believed that a "Masalai" (feared spirit) inhabited a small area above his garden and whenever he came back to the village after having visited this particular garden for collecting new tangets [for clothing] or cutting wood, the "masalai" had affected him and he showed signs of "strangeness."

O. has always been treated tolerantly by his own family until they became unable to control his impulsive behavior. During the week preceding Sunday 25th of March, when I drove him to Goroka Hospital, I had heard reports of his misdemeanours, trying to burn down a house and shoot village pigs, etc. Nothing could be done about this, as the —— Pass had been blocked for the previous four days (due to rains) so a police car could not get through. On 25th March, O's family themselves brought him down to Watabung station, not without much struggling, I gather. He began shouting out and trying to break down the door of the "lock-up" at the station, something he could easily have done given a little time. Due to his struggling, his hands had to be fastened and he was driven to Goroka in the back of a car in a horizontal position, held down by his brothers.

The increasing understanding of mental illness appears in the short report made by the Assistant District Officer to the Laloki Psychiatric Center on the admission of a patient from his district.

Case 506: On the second of this month, I was called to the patient's village where he was alleged to have run amok with an axe. Fortunately nobody was injured, but some damage had been done to houses and personal possessions of other village people. As I was aware of his history (previous hospitalizations), I did not proceed on criminal charges, and after consultation with the District Health Officer, his movement was arranged back to Laloki.

The Port Moresby newspaper makes interesting reading, acquainting the reader with current, often contrasting accounts of life in New Guinea and attesting to the rapid transition taking place in the country during the last thirty to forty years. In the same issue a headline may report on sorcery still being practiced, frightening and intimidating the people by inflicting pain and death, while a news story on another page may announce the visit by a foreign opera company to the capital or the educational or economic development taking place in rural areas. Tribal wars resulting in the death of six warriors made headlines in the international press. At another time, two people were killed as "payback" when they were involved in an unavoidable traffic accident. Their deaths paid for the deaths of the victim, carrying out traditional justice; but today's courts no longer tolerate such local customs, severely punishing the avengers, often by life imprisonment.

Since cannibalism and headhunting expeditions have been outlawed, sorcery has taken their place and has become increasingly widespread. The Papua New Guinea *Post Courier* carried a story on August 14, 1974, headlined "Highland Leader Exposes Magic and Sorcery." (We are quoting most of the news story verbatim.)

Mr. A., a local councilman claims that superstitious practices—poison and evil power and other acts of the sorcerer and magic man are still a fear and a problem in the Highlands.

"They are the greatest human killers and the people in the village communities are so scared that they are becoming enemies with those who perform such things. I have always thought that the practice of these things would be buried away for good, but instead they are improving their rotten technology."

Mr. A. said, nowadays, the magic makers and sorcerers were far more active with the use of improved tools and many people were dying every day through their activities. He continues, "Before the white man came, their tools for magic and sorcery were as primitive as themselves, but now, with the introduction of modern things like knives, razor blades, batteries and other poisonous chemicals, they are putting in new ideas and improving their primitive technology and tools. When the magic makers and sorcerers hear a rumor that a certain means of magic or sorcery is active and popular in an area, they can either buy the magic power or the owner can teach them how to make it and its principles and application for what they offer to him."

The councilman continued, "In my area there is no one except myself who has the kind of power to locate and pinpoint a sorcerer or magic man. This power was given to me in my dreams, the night before I stood for the by-election last year and it is this inner power that directs me to pinpoint a man who has the magic tools. I can then tell him to bring it out to the open and give it to me, and that man will obediently do it. It is because of this power that I have been able to get many varieties of magic and sorcery things from the sorcerers and magic makers and these are kept in my house."

He had brought one of them, "Afa" to the Area Authority meeting and passed it on to the head of the police in the Eastern Highlands, Inspector ——. However, he said the police had very little or no chance at all to stop the practice of magic and sorcery.

"The sorcerers use an implement that consists of a tiny cane and razor blades. The cane is curved into a horseshoe shape and sharp razor blades are fastened closely together around it. In "Afa," the sorcerer hides and when he sights his victim he says his magic words and performs other related procedures to knock the victim into an unconscious and helpless state. He then forces the tool down the victim's throat. Then as he works the implement up and down, the blades rip off the internal organs including the intestine and stomach" (illustration A1).

Another story is reprinted from the *Post Courier,* dated November 3, 1975.

Lovers Spark Tribal Combat in New Guinea

More than 1,000 warriors from two rival tribes donned war paint and went into battle yesterday wielding axes, spears and arrows over a forbidden love affair. Six tribesmen died from arrow and spear wounds, police said. The battle broke out at "first light" in the Western Highlands of Papua New Guinea.

A forbidden love affair between a man from one tribe and a girl from the other triggered the fighting, according to police reports. . . . The lovers broke "inter-tribal taboos" a police spokesman said. . . . The rival tribesmen, glistening with war paint, clashed at dawn in the Wapenamanda area, about 360 miles northwest of Port Moresby. In the course of the bitter, hand-to-hand combat, he said, the shouting warriors ripped down and burned at least 40 homes and uprooted nearly 400 coffee trees.

Two and a half years earlier, a short lived tribal war had occurred in the Chimbu District. The front page story of the *Post Courier* of May 23, 1973, reports:

60 Charged After Fight

Sixty Chimbu warriors have been charged with carrying weapons in public following a 400-man fight on Monday. The clash started with a Sunday card game. A fight followed the game and a man was killed.

A mobile squad and four other police were rushed to the area, outside a regular police zone, when the fight was re-kindled on a larger scale the next day. Food gardens were destroyed and three men were taken to the hospital with arrow wounds. Sixty warriors were arrested. They were charged in the Kundiawa Local Court yesterday with carrying weapons in a public place. . . . Another man, (M. N.) has been charged with unlawful killing of a man at the K. village.

The transition taking place in New Guinea today is nowhere better evidenced than in its legal procedures. Tribal law required misdeeds, even unavoidable accidents to be paid back quickly—often on the spot and with force. Updated procedures require patient investigation and delays, depriving those who are affected of immediate satisfaction; they eliminate the element of revenge and often appear inadequate as retaliation for the harm experienced. People still practicing payback and intertribal fights cannot accept the government's attempts to introduce an impartial court system and an effective law enforcement body. The new independent government has not only required consultants in agriculture and economic techniques, but they also sent their policemen to other countries to study their police systems. This article appeared in the *Post Courier* of July 12, 1974:

Study of Police Techniques

Police techniques in South-east Asia can easily be adopted in Papua New Guinea. . . .

Mr. A., aged 26, a subinspector with the Royal Papua New Guinea Constabulary said this after returning from a three month overseas study tour; he studied police systems used in Singapore, Malaysia and Hong Kong.

He said he was impressed with the methods of crime investigations, patrol and policing methods used in densely populated areas and the "jungle warfare system." He said the system was used to make sure that no secret armed forces should occupy any part of the jungle. He said jungle warfare teams had also helped improve local conditions in the area.

It would be highly slanted to emphasize violent acts as a predominant problem of the New Guineans. Many New Guineans are proud of their cultural heritage and recognize it as an important link with their past on which a solid future is to be built. It has led to a revival of national consciousness that brought village chiefs to Port Moresby. The *Post Courier,* August 9, 1974, carried this story:

The Chiefs Coming for Festival

Arrangements have been made to fly about 20 village chiefs from the Highlands to visit Port Moresby and perform at the Fourth Papua New Guinea Arts Festival. The chiefs and their wives will fly to Port Moresby early next month.

"They will be helping to keep our valuable traditional customs by practicing the regional dances, myths and legends," their spokesman said. "By doing this, we will be restoring and practicing some aspects of our culture and not just simply talking or writing about them.

The main reason behind the chiefs' trip to Port Moresby is to give them the opportunity to explore the outside part of the world. . . . These people are isolated out in the bush. They are the traditional village people with no idea about the urban life and what's going on outside the other parts of the country and the outside world. I'm sure none of the men and women have left the area and this will be their first time to visit the big city and, of course, see the sea for the first time."

In the last few years, according to their spokesman, the mountain people bombarded their fellow countryman with questions like, "What sort of place is Moresby, what kind of people live there and what do the people grow and eat?

By treasuring their traditional customs, the people do not want to isolate themselves from the outside world; many are eager to learn about other countries. Some had an occasion to visit parts of Southeast Asia.

From the *Post Courier,* August 5, 1974:

Visiting Their Friends

The ordinary folk of Eastern Highlands are visiting the ordinary folk of Singapore and Malaysia.

Aim: To see a post-independent country and find out from the village people what THEY think of independence.

The significance of the exchange of information is that our ordinary folk are actually local government leaders, and their impressions could count for a lot in the future attitude of Eastern Highlanders.

Eight leaders were selected from the district's area authority and they left Goroka on Thursday, for Port Moresby and flew to Singapore on Saturday. . . . They hoped to see examples of village and cottage industries, both primary and secondary, that could be tried in their home areas. They hope to widen their total outlook so they can be better leaders in their own areas. . . . They will be able to speak to national, local and village leaders and to ordinary village people. (illustration A2)

But not all New Guineans agree on the importance of their cultural heritage. In regions that have submitted to foreign influences for many years, they have often lost contact with their traditional background; as a consequence, they have attempted to detach themselves from their past; they believe that their own and their country's future lies in a hasty Westernization. Being aware of the economic plight existing in many new nations, Australia, when it surrendered its protectorate, guaranteed substantial support to Papua New Guinea, but the action did not solve financial problems. A large number of people, particularly from the Highlands, would have preferred to postpone the country's independence (attained in 1974).

From the *Post Courier,* November 4, 1975:

Cash Problems Now True: Abal

The Opposition Leader, Mr. Abal has criticized the Government for rushing into political independence before economic independence has been achieved. He said predictions by people outside the Government that the country would face financial problems after Independence had proved to be true. He said many Parliamentarians were confused about

A.2. *Papuans await the arrival of their plane. Copyright by the* Post Courier, *Port Moresby, and reprinted with permission.*

self-reliance. "We (the Opposition) feel Papua New Guinea should be economically self reliant before being politically independent," Mr. Abal said during the Budget debate yesterday.

But the government is aware of the need to develop the country's economy and its natural assets. An important resource can be developed from the use of hydroelectric power; the many rivers may become a significant factor in supplying the energy for future projects. On August 6, 1974, the Courier reported on the yet-unharnessed reserves.

More Purari Talks

More talks on the proposed Purari hydro-electric scheme are expected to be held soon.
The Ministers hoped that officials of their Governments and the Japanese Government could meet as soon as possible to discuss cost allocation and responsibilities among the three Governments together with administrative arrangements for studies of the scheme.
Mr. Whitlam [the Australian Prime Minister at that time] said that Australia was ready to co-operate with PNG on the second investigating stage of the Purari project.

New Guinea's new leaders recognized the necessity to foster economic development by a large building program. Other countries, particularly Australia, offered technical advice. The *Post Courier* wrote on July 12, 1974:

Army Helps to Develop Mendi

A handful of Australian Army engineers in Papua New Guinea is handling a civic action budget that would be the envy of a dozen such units in Austalia.
This year it has a works budget of $3.5 million to spend on highways and roads, bridges, hospitals, schools, airfields, a rural improvement program, housing and a score of less projects.
The 25 officers and men form the District Engineers Office at Mendi, in the Southern Highlands. The office operates in a civil role as part of the Public Works Department, and is the only long-term Australian Army commitment to a large scale overseas civic action program. Some of its projects include the Mendi to Poroma highway, 18 miles of road cutting through tortuous terrain, at a cost of $1.4 million; the 17 mile Ialibu to Kagua

road, $1/2 million; construction of a police mobile squad, $160,000; and the first stage of a high school at Ialibu, $52,000.

At times, foreigners become overzealous in introducing Western ways—particularly religious values—to the New Guineans. As in the past, missionary activities may challenge the culture and traditions, to the dismay of some of the local people. A letter to the Editor of the Courier on July 8, 1975, carries this story.

Destroying Culture and Tradition

The Minister of Culture and Recreation would be shocked if he came to the mid-Wahgo area of the Minj sub-district of the Western Highlands, and saw some of the activities of this religious group. He would be greatly tempted to deport the leader and his so-called disciples the next day. I am convinced that the mission is destroying some of our most traditional, beautiful and respected customs, and at the same time is spoiling the people. The restrictions it places on its followers are such that it cuts them off from the rest of the community and communal activities. I have never heard it preached, where Christ says, "You shall not practice your traditional customs if you want to be my followers."

Before preceeding [sic] any further, let me mention some of our traditional customs that the mission has told the people not to practice. The mission forbids its members to take part in our Highlands most traditional, beautiful and respected pig-killing Sing Sing that goes on for three or four years at a time. The mission has gone as far as telling the people not to watch the Sing Sing when performed by others and not to partake of any food and drinks shared during the Sing Sing break. As far as the mission is concerned, the Sing Sing is "devil or evil-spirit-oriented" and members of the mission are to keep away from it. "Em samting bilong Satan" (the Sing Sing is Satan's work) as they put it.

Besides not taking part in the traditional Sing Sing, young boys and girls are told not to date in our traditional customs—expressed in Pidgin as "Karim Leg," a custom whereby boys and girls meet each other and which enables them to find their future partners. The mission considers this an unworthy practice and children of the members are to have no part of it.

It is customary for my people to hold a gathering after somebody dies to show that they share the sorrows of the family and relatives of the departed. In this gathering they kill pigs and share them with everyone present with plenty of food. The mission, once again, sees this custom as somewhat "Satan-oriented" and its members are told to stay away. Surely we have freedom of religion in this country, but that doesn't give them the liberty to stop people from practicing traditional customs.

Signed_____
Minj

In reading the reports about the present activities and life in New Guinea, it becomes clear that the clash between traditional values and new experiences is often puzzling not only to the individual but also to the local governments. There is often talk of seceding from the union of the central government. But the country's leaders realize that an operable solution has to be found; values of the past should be preserved and incorporated into the present way of life. A complete rupture of the historical continuum must be avoided at all costs.

Glossary

Acephalous: A societal organization without a clearly defined leader; there are no hereditary leaders.

Affect: Feeling tone attached to a mental concept or idea.

Affect, labile: Unstable emotional feeling tone attached to a mental concept. It often results in difficulties in interpersonal relations. It may cause comparatively mild emotional disturbances, or the intensity may increase to severe pathological states during which behavior becomes uncontrolled.

Ambivalence: The coexistence of opposing feelings, emotions, concepts, or wishes. Opposing feelings and thoughts expressing insoluble conflicts and interfering with decisive action—a principal symptom of schizophrenia.

Autonormal: Behavior considered normal for a given individual within his own society.

Autopathologic: Behavior considered abnormal or unacceptable within one's own society.

Big men: Successful and respected leaders who are convincing orators and who have accumulated wealth that they share with others by giving festivals; the term is particularly used in the Western Highlands.

Bullroarer: A ceremonial wooden paddle, often decorated with traditional designs. As it is twirled, it emits a warning sound to prevent any unauthorized or uninitiated person from seeing the sacred object.

Cassowary: A flightless bird of New Guinea with powerful claws; plays an important role in the mythology of the area.

Catatonia: A condition, especially in schizophrenia, characterized by muscular rigidity and mental stupor, at times alternating with great excitement and confusion.

Compulsion: A seemingly meaningless act that has to be repeated, often against the patient's conscious wishes, and that does not resolve the underlying anxiety.

Couvade: "Men's childbed," imitation by the father of childbirth at the time of his wife's delivery in order to avoid injuring the child by sympathetic magic.

Culture-bound illness: Mental illness or symptom formation controlled by sociocultural factors.

De-differentiation: A regressive mental process involving disintegration of the personality, occurring in psychotic states, primarily in schizophrenia. The patient's vague, poorly shaped concepts are in a state of flux, and there is severe emotional detachment alternating with uncontrollable outbursts of intense feeling. (*See also* 146.)

Defenses, defense mechanisms: A variety of mental mechanisms that offer protection against overwhelming anxieties or guilt. The personality has no willful choice or control over them. Some are problem-solving and do not have to be repeated; others do not relieve the underlying anxieties or guilt and have to be continually repeated.

Denial: An unconscious mental mechanism used by the individual to protect himself by rejecting disturbing experiences by denying their existence. The term is often extended to include the replacement of unacceptable experiences by wish-fulfilling fantasies.

Disintegrated: The pathological personality function, often found in serious mental disorders in which various aspects of the personality can no longer function harmoniously—in an integrated manner; not meant in the literal sense of separating into component parts.

Dream time: A concept used among the Melanesian people particularly the Australian aborigines; but it is also operable in New Guinea and refers to the mythological past of the aborigines. It speaks of the time when the world was created and of the origin of man. The period is part of the historical past which is transmitted to his children.

Dysphoria: Depressive mood combined with some anxiety.

Ego boundaries: Allow the personality to extend as far as functional unity can be extended; they are a dynamic, not a static, force separating the image of oneself from external experiences. An essential concept in establishing one's identity and forming concise boundaries of objects appearing in the environment.

Ego control: Control mechanisms exercised by the total personality; some result in pleasurable aspects, such as aesthetic reactions; others are highly restrictive, as in obsessive-compulsive patterns.

Ego rhythm: Used by Ehrenzweig (35) as a mechanism that swings between unconscious undifferentiated states and integrated concepts. It differentiates and merges images as they evolve from unconscious levels and reach consciousness. The mechanism plays an important role in the process of creation.

Encapsulate: To segregate emotionally disturbing experiences, avoiding anxieties by detaching them from the conscious functioning of the personality.

Enculturation: Adaptation to one's own culture and fulfilling one's role in the social order.

Espanto: Soul loss, occurring in Central America. Manifested by depression, apathy, loss of appetite, and diarrhea, and resulting from a sin committed against the saints or God.

Feedback mechanism: Complex mechanisms taking place on various levels of psycho-physiological functions. In our presentation, we restrict the use of the term to socio-cultural factors essential in the communication process. It includes verbal and non-verbal forms essential for the interaction between the individual and a group of people.

Folded over: A form of perspective in which objects are projected in both a vertical and a horizontal plane.

Fox possession: Severe disturbances related to delusions of the penis disappearing into the patient's own body, reported primarily in rural Japan.

Gates of the Dream: Psychoanalytic classic by Geza Roheim (122a), an early anthropologist, on the psychological aspects of the spiritual life in Melanesia and its implications for the universal aspects of the unconscious.

Ghost dance: A ceremonial dance among the Paiute Indians of western Nevada (1870's) to induce a new Messiah to restore the world to the Indian and to them from the control of the white man.

Global, globality, undifferentiated global state: Lacking differentiation of concepts; diffuse imagery; due in early phases of personality development to regression.

Goal-directed: Striving toward a specific aim, often determined by an emotional charge.

Horror vacui: Fear of empty space, frequently resulting in a pathological need to fill all the space in a drawing.

Hysterical convulsions: Convulsions similar (not identical) to epileptic attacks; due to emotional disturbances.

Imunu: Life source, the spirit of the dead. Headhunting expeditions had been often launched to acquire the imunu.

Inarticulate concepts or structures: Vague and poorly circumscribed concepts, overlapping, unstable, and continuously fluctuating (35).

Intrapsychic: Taking place within the mind.

Kiap: New Guinea placetalk for district officer.

Lap lap: A piece of clothing wrapped around the lower part of the body.

Laughter, objectless, uncontrollable: Laughter without apparent cause; disproportionate and loud, often produced by internal delusionary thoughts indicating a disconcern with external control; a frequent symptom of schizophrenia.

Life space: The totality of experiences and facts determining an individual's behavior. (*See* Lewin, 88).

Masalai: An English Pidgin word for a superhuman being; a feared spirit (77).

Neologism: A new word or phrase coined by a patient, notably a schizophrenic. It is made by condensing parts of two words or ideas together.

Obsession: A thought or idea which forces itself on the individual, often producing anxiety.

Oceanic feeling: A feeling of oneness; incomplete separation of the self from the environment, being one with God or the universe. It reflects an early state of personality development, or regression to a level on which early images, feelings and vague memories are merged.

Omak: String of bamboo sticks, each indicating that the wearer has sponsored a feast; therefore reflecting his wealth and his influence.

Organic brain syndrome: Pathological disturbances in brain functions such as memory, concentration, judgment, orientation, impairment of intellectual functioning, affect disturbances without psychotic manifestations (delusions, hallucinations, etc.).

Organic psychosis: A mental disease caused by physical damage to the brain, which may be due to senility, arteriosclerosis, or ingestion of toxic substances.

Pathognomonic: Diagnostic of a specific disease.

Payback: A widespread custom in New Guinea where destructive action, particularly sudden or unexplainable death, has to be avenged to placate the spirit of the dead who cannot rest until the deed has been avenged.

Perseverated, perseveration: A continuous, repetitious act, gesture, or verbal phrase; often characteristic of schizophrenic disintegration or organic brain damage.

Perspective tordue: Twisted perspective, presenting various views of the same object. A figure is painted in Egyptian art by showing the head in profile, the body in a frontal view, and the limbs in a side view.

Phylogenetic: Pertaining to the development of a species; in contrast to *ontogenetic,* which pertains to the development of the individual.

Reality testing: A function of the integrated personality (ego function); evaluation of the external world and new experiences against the internal world of accumulated past experiences; differentiation between the self and the non-self.

Regression, regressed: Reversion to earlier levels of personality functioning, particularly due to schizophrenia.

Rooting reflex: A reflex movement in which an infant turns the head and opens the mouth.

Rorschach technique: A psychological procedure, originated by the Swiss psychiatrist Hermann Rorschach, published in 1922. It consists of ten standardized ink blots. The intent of the procedure is to gain an insight into the total functioning of the personality and the patient's reaction to stress.

Running amok: Originally described in Malaya, a period of excitement with undirected homicidal attacks following a period of brooding or depression.

Schizophrenic, paranoid type: Mental illness resulting in the inability to coordinate one's thoughts and feelings; significant in its emotional detachment and withdrawal from personal relationships.

Sing sing: Ceremonial festival in New Guinea.

Socialization practices: Social institutions by which the individual internalizes the culture of his society and integrates its value system into his personality.

Undoing: An unconscious defense mechanism of the individual, consisting of a positive act, actually or magically replacing unacceptable, disturbing experiences or feelings, often of guilt. Rituals, attempts to expiate guilt, compulsive ceremonials, and obsessive counting are considered mechanisms of undoing.

Vertical projection: Projection of concepts along a vertical plane.

Xhosa Cult: A reaction of the Bantu people of South Africa to restore their rights against the invading Boers.

References

1. Abramson, J. A. and Holst, R. *Hewa Sacred Bark Paintings*. Records of the Papua, New Guinea Museum, no. 3 (April 1973): 17-62.

2. Ackerknecht, E. H. "Psychology, Primitive Medicine and Primitive Culture." *Bulletin of the History of Medicine* 14 (June 1943):30-67.

3. Arieti, S. *Interpretation of Schizophrenia*. New York: Brunner, 1955.

4a. Arnheim, R. *Art and Visual Perception*. Berkeley: University of California Press, 1954.

4b. ——. *Visual Thinking*. Berkeley: University of California Press, 1969.

5. "Art and Confrontation." *Collected Essays*. Greenwich, Connecticut: New York Graphic Society, 1968.

6. Graybiel, A., et al. "Vestibular Experiments in Gemini Flights V and VII." *Aerospace Medicine* 38, no. 4 (April 1967): 360-370.

7. Beier, U., and Kiki, A. M. *Hohao*. Melbourne: Thomas Nelson, Ltd., 1970.

8a. Belshaw, C. S. *The Great Village: Hanuabada*. Melbourne: Routledge & Kegan Paul, 1957.

8b. ——. "Recent History of Mekeo Society." *Oceania* 22, no. 1 (September 1951): 1-23.

9. Berndt, C. H. "Ascription of Meaning in a Ceremonial Context in the Eastern Highlands of New Guinea." In *Anthropology of the South Seas,* edited by J. D. Freeman and W. R. Geddes, pp. 161-183. New Plymouth, New Zealand: Thomas Avery and Sons, Ltd., 1959.

10a. Berndt, R. M. *Excess and Restraint*. Berkeley: University of California Press, 1962.

10b. ——. "Some Methodological Considerations in the Study of Australian Aboriginal Art." In *Art and Aesthetics in Primitive Societies,* edited by Carol F. Jopling, pp. 99-126. New York: E. P. Dutton & Co., 1971.

11. Bertalanffy, Ludwig von. *General Systems Theory*. New York: George Braziller, 1968.

12. Biderman, A. D. and Zimmer, H. *The Manipulation of Human Behavior*. New York and London: E. P. Dutton & Sons, 1961.

13. Biebuyck, D. *Tradition and Creativity in Tribal Art.* Los Angeles: University of California Press, 1969.

14a. Billig, O. "Structures of Schizophrenic Forms of Expression." *Psychiatric Quarterly* 44 (1970): 187–222.

14b. ——. "Is Schizophrenic Expression Art?" *Journal of Nervous and Mental Disease* 153 (1971): 149–164.

14c. ——. "Representation of Motion in Schizophrenic 'Art.' " Paper read at World Congress of Psychiatry, 1971, Mexico City.

14d. ——. "Socio-Cultural Roots of Psychopathological Expression." *Japanese Bulletin of Art Therapy* 6 (1975): 89–95.

15. Billig, O., and Burton-Bradley, B. G. "Psychotic Indigenous Painters from New Guinea." *International Journal of Art Psychotherapy* (1973): 315–328.

15a. Billig, O. and Burton-Bradley, B. G. "Cross-Cultural Studies of Psychotic Graphics from New Guinea." *Psychiatry and Art* 4 (1975): 18–47.

15b. ——. "Psychotic 'Art' in New Guinea." *The Journal of Nervous and Mental Disease* 159 (1974): 40–62.

16. Billig, O., and Gillin, J., et al. "Aspects of Personality and Culture in a Guatemalan Community." *Journal of Personality,* vol. 16, part 1, December 1947, pp. 153–187; part 2, March 1948, pp. 326–68.

17. Blackwood, B. *Both Sides of Buka Passage.* Oxford: Clarendon Press, 1935.

18. Bleuler, E. *Dementia Praecox or the Group of Schizophrenics.* New York: International Universities Press, 1950.

19. Brandle, M. M. Personal communication.

20. Brinton, C., et al. *A History of Civilization.* Englewood Cliffs, New Jersey: Prentice-Hall, 1955.

21. Brown, P. *The Chimbu.* Cambridge, Massachusetts: Schenkman Publishing Co., 1972.

22. Burnham, D. L. and Burnham, A. L. *Schizophrenia and the Near-Fear Dilemma.* New York: International Universities Press, 1969.

23. Burridge, K. O. L. in *Gods, Ghosts and Men in Melanesia.* Edited by P. Lawrence and M. J. Meggitt. Melbourne: Oxford University Press, 1972.

24a. Burton-Bradley, B. G. "The Amok Syndrome in Papua and New Guinea." *Medical Journal of Australia* 1 (1968): 252.

24b. ——. "Human Sacrifice for Cargo." *Medical Journal of Australia* 2 (1972): 668–670.

24c. ——. *Stoneage Crisis.* Nashville, Tennessee: Vanderbilt University Press, 1975.

24d. ——. "Mixed Race Society in Port Moresby." *New Guinea Research Bulletin,* no. 23 (1968): 1–51.

25. Carpenter, W. T. "Cross-Cultural Evaluation of Schneider's First Rank Symptoms of Schizophrenia." *The Journal of the American Psychiatric Association* 131 (1924): 682–687.

26. Clark, K. "Landscape in Art." *Encyclopedia of World Art,* vol. 9, pp. 10–38. New York: McGraw-Hill, 1963.

27. Clearhout, G. H. "The Concept of Primitive Applied to Art." *Current Anthropology; World Journal of the Sciences of Man* 6, no. 4 (1965): 432–38.

28. Coghill, G. E. Quoted by D. Hooker in *Evidence of Prenatal Functioning of the Central Nervous System.* New York: American Museum of Natural History, 1958.

29. Dark, Philip, J. C. "Study of Ethno-Aesthetics: The Visual Arts." From *Proceedings of the 1966 Meeting of the American Ethnological Society,* edited by June Helm, p. 132. Seattle and London: University of Washington, 1967.

30. Deutsch, M. "Handbook of Sociology." In *Field Theory in Social Psychology,* edited by Gardner Lindzey, vol. 1, pp. 181–222. Cambridge, Massachussetts: Addison–Wesley, 1954.

31. Devereux, G. "Art and Mythology: A General Theory." In *Art and Aesthetics in Primitive Societies,* edited by Carol F. Jopling, pp. 193–224. New York: E. P. Dutton & Co., 1971.

32a. DeVos, G. A. "Transcultural Diagnosis of Mental Health." In *Transcultural Psychiatry,* edited by A. V. S. DeReuck, pp. 328–353. Boston: Little, Brown and Co., 1965.

32b. ———. "Cross-Cultural Studies of Mental Disorder." *American Handbook of Psychiatry,* edited by S. Arieti, pp. 535–550. 2nd ed. New York: Basic Books, 1974.

33. Dynes, W. "Gothic Art." *Dictionary of Art,* vol. 2. Edited by B. S. Myers. New York: McGraw-Hill, 1969.

34. Edel, A. "Psychiatry and Philosophy." In *Handbook of Psychiatry,* edited by S. Arieti, vol. 1, pp. 961–965. New York: Basic Books, 1974.

35. Ehrenzweig, A. *The Hidden Order of Art.* Berkeley and Los Angeles: University of California Press, 1969.

36. Erben, W. *Marc Chagall.* New York: Frederick A. Praeger, 1957.

37. Faille, J. B. de la. *The Works of Vincent Van Gogh.* Amsterdam: Reynal & Co., 1970.

38. Federn, P. *Ego Psychology and the Psychosis.* New York: Basic Books, 1952.

39a. Firth, R. *Art and Life in New Guinea.* London: Studio, 1936.

39b. ———. *Elements of Social Organization.* London: Watts and Co., 1951.

40a. Forge, A. "Art and Environment in the Sepik." In *Art and Aesthetics in Primitive Societies,* edited by Carol F. Jopling, pp. 290–314. New York: E. P. Dutton & Co., 1971.

40b. ———. *The People and the Culture in Papua New Guinea,* edited by Peter Hastings, pp. 60–73. Sydney: Angus and Robertson, 1971.

41. Francastel, P. "Space and Time." *Encyclopedia of Art,* vol. 13, pp. 182–203. New York: McGraw-Hill, 1958.

42. Fraser, D. *The Many Faces of Primitive Art.* Englewood Cliffs, N.J.: Prentice-Hall, 1966.

43. Freedman, B. J. "The Subjective Experience of Perceptual and Cognitive Disturbances in Schizophrenia." *Review of Autobiographical Accounts: Archives of General Psychiatry* 30 (March 1974): 333–40.

44. Freedman, S. J. "Sensory Deprivation: Facts in Search of a Theory." *Journal of Nervous and Mental Disease* 32, no. 1 (1961): 17–21.

45. Freud, S. *The Future of an Illusion.* London: Hogarth, 1928.

46. Frizzi, E. *Ein Beitrag Zur Ethnologie Von Bougainville und Buka.* Bessler Archiv., Leipzig, 1914. Reprinted by Johnson Reprint Corp., New York, 1968.

47. *Fulcher of Chartres: Chronicle of the First Crusades.* Translated by M. E. McGinty. Philadelphia: University of Pennsylvania, 1941.

48. Gebrands, A. "The Concept of Non-Western Art." In *Tradition and Creativity in Tribal Art,* edited by D. Biebuyck, pp. 58–70. Berkeley: University of California Press, 1969.

49. Gehlin, R. *The Service.* New York: World Publishing Co., 1972.

50. Giedion, S. *The Eternal Present: The Beginning of Art.* New York: Random House, 1962.

51. Glasse, R. M. "The Huli of the Southern Highlands." In *Gods, Ghosts and Men in Melanesia,* edited by P. Lawrence and M. J. Meggitt, pp. 27–49. Melbourne: Oxford University Press, 1972.

52. Goethe, J. W. *Faust, part 2.* Translated by G. M. Priest. New York: Knopf, 1941.

53. Gombrich, E. H. *Meditations on a Hobbyhorse.* London and New York: Phaidon, 1959.

54. Grabar, A., et al. *Romanesque Painting.* New York: Skira, 1958.

55. Grimm, H. *Leben Michelangelo's.* Berlin: W. Speman Verlag, 1909.

56. Hallowell, A. I. "Hominid Evolution, Cultural Adaptation and Mental Dysfunctioning." In *Transcultural Psychiatry,* edited by A. V. S. DeReuck, pp. 26–54. Boston: Little, Brown and Co., 1965.

57. Hanneman, E. F. *Grass Roots Art of New Guinea.* Sydney: Pacific Publications, 1969.

58. Hartmann, Eduard von. *Philosophie des Unbewussten.* Berlin: Duncker Verlag, 1869.

59. Hauser, A. *The Social History of Art,* vol. 1. New York: Vintage, Knopf, 1957.

60. Hawkins, G. S. *Stonehenge Decoded.* Garden City, New York: Doubleday and Co., 1965.

61. Held, R. "Exposure-History as a Factor in Maintaining Stability of Perception and Coordination." *The Journal of Nervous and Mental Disease* 132, no. 1 (1961): 26–32.

62. Heller, R. *Edvard Munch: The Scream.* New York: Viking Press, 1973.

63. Hinsie, L. E., et al. *Psychiatric Dictionary.* New York: Oxford University Press, 1960.

64. Hocke, G. R. *Die Welt als Labyrinth.* Hamburg: Rohwolt, 1957.

65. Hodin, J. P. *Edvard Munch.* New York: Frederick A Praeger, 1972.

66. Hooker, D. *Evidence of Prenatal Functioning of the Central Nervous System.* New York: American Museum of Natural History, 1958.

67. Huizinga, J. *The Waning of the Middle Ages.* Garden City, New York: Anchor Books, Doubleday and Co., 1954.

68. Inkeles, A. "The Fate of Personal Adjustment in the Process of Urbanization." Quoted by G. A. DeVos in *American Handbook of Psychiatry,* 2nd ed. Edited by S. Arieti. New York: Basic Books, 1974.

69. Jacobus, M. W. et al. *New Standard Bible Dictionary.* Garden City, New York: Funk and Wagnalls, 1936.

70. Johnson, Ellen. "Edvard Munch." *Dictionary of Art,* vol. 3. Edited by B. S. Myers. New York: McGraw-Hill, 1970.

71a. Jung, C. G. *The Psychology of Dementia Praecox.* Nervous and Mental Disease Monograph Series, no. 3. New York and Washington: Nervous and Mental Disease Publishing Co., 1936.

71b. ——. *Picasso in the Spirit in Man, Art and Literature.* Bollingen Series, vol. 15, pp. 135–41. New York: Pantheon Books, 1966.

72. Kasanin, J. S. *Language and Thought in Schizophrenia.* Berkeley: University of California Press, 1944.

73. Klossowski, D. S. *Alchemy.* New York: Bounty Books, 1973.

74. Kremitske, J. "Images and Iconoclasm." *Encyclopedia of World Art,* vol. 7, p. 811. New York: McGraw-Hill, 1963.

75. Kris, E. *Psychoanalytic Exploration in Art.* New York: International University Press, 1952.

76. Lambo, T. A. "Schizophrenic and Borderline States." *Transcultural Psychiatry.* Ciba Foundation Symposium. Boston: Little, Brown and Co., 1965.

77. Lawrence, P. *Road Belong Cargo.* Victoria, Australia: Melbourne University Press, 1964.

78. Lawrence, P. and Meggitt, M. J. *Gods, Ghosts and Men in Melanesia.* Melbourne: Oxford University Press, 1972.

79a. Leach, E. R. "A Trobriand Medusa?" In *Art and Aesthetics in Primitive Societies,* edited by Carol F. Jopling, pp. 45–54. New York: E. P. Dutton & Co., 1971.

79b. ——. In *Dictionary of Social Sciences.* Edited by J. Gould and W. L. Kolb. New York: Free Press, 1965.

80. Leach, M., ed. *Dictionary of Folklore, Mythology and Legend.* New York: Funk and Wagnalls, 1950.

81. LeBon, G. *The Crowd.* London: F. Unwin, Ltd., 1903.

82. Jeanneret-Gris, C. E. [Le Corbusier]. *New World of Space.* New York: Reynal and Hitchcock, 1948.

83. Lee, D. N. and Woodhouse, H. G. *Art of the Rocks of Southern Africa.* Cape Town, South Africa: Purnell Sons, 1970.

84. Legge, J. D. *Australian Colonial Policy.* Sydney: Angus and Robertson, 1955.

85. Leighton, A. H. et al. *Psychiatric Disorders Among the Yoruba.* Ithaca, New York: Cornell University Press, 1963.

86. Lenneberg, E. H. *Biological Foundations of Language.* New York: Wiley and Sons, 1967.

87a. Levi-Strauss, C. *Structural Anthropology,* pp. 245-269. New York: Basic Books, 1963.

87b. ——. "The Science of the Concrete." In *Art and Aesthetics in Primitive Societies.* Edited by Carol F. Jopling. New York: E.P. Dutton & Co., 1971.

88. Lewin, B. D. *The Image and the Past.* New York: International Universities Press, 1968.

89. Lidz, R. W., Lidz, T., and Burton-Bradley, B. G. "Culture, Personality and Social Structure." *The Journal of Nervous and Mental Disease* 157 (1973): 370-388.

90. Linton, R. *Primitive Art in the Sculpture of Africa.* Edited by Eliot Elisofon and William Fagg. New York: Frederick A. Praeger, 1958.

91. Loeb, F. F., Jr. "A Frame by Frame Film Study of Rooting-like Movements in an Adult Human." Presented at the American Psychiatric Association Meeting, 1968, Boston.

92. Loewenfeld, V. *The Nature of Creative Activity.* London: Paul, Trench & Trubner, 1939.

93. Lombroso, C. *Genie und Irrsinn.* Leipzig: Reclam Verlag, 1910.

94. Lyons, J. *Noam Chomsky.* New York: Viking Press, 1970.

95. Maher, R.F. *New Men of Papua.* Madison, Wisconsin: University of Wisconsin Press, 1961.

96. Margetts, E. L. Personal Communication.

97. Maudsley, H. As quoted by E. D. Wittkower in *American Handbook of Psychiatry.* Edited by S. Arieti. 2nd. ed. New York: Basic Books, 1974.

98. Mead, M. "The Bark Paintings of the Mountain Arapesh of New Guinea." *Technique and Personality.* Lecture Series, no. 3. New York: The Museum of Primitive Art, 1963.

99. Menninger, K. A. *A Manual for Psychiatric Case Study.* New York: Grune and Stratton, 1962.

100. Morgenthaler, W. *Ein Geisteskranker als Kuenstler.* Bern: Ernst Bircher, 1921.

101. Morrison, J. R. "Changes in Subtype Diagnosis of Schizophrenia." *The Journal of the American Psychiatric Association.* 131 (1974): 674-677.

102. Mountford, C. P. "The Artist and his Art in an Australian Aboriginal Society." *The Artist in Tribal Society.* Edited by M. W. Smith. New York: The Free Press of Glencoe, 1961.

103. Mueller-Braunschweig, H. "Psychopathology and Creativity." *Psychoanalytic Study of Society* 6 (1975): 71-99.

104. Muensterberger, W. "Art and Aesthetics: Some Elements of Artistic Creativity Among Primitive People." In *Art and Aesthetics in Primitive Societies,* edited by Carol F. Jopling, pp. 3-10. New York: E. P. Dutton & Co., 1971.

105. Myers, B S. *Art and Civilization.* New York: McGraw-Hill, 1967.

106. McCarthy, J. K. *Patrol Into Yesteryear.* Melbourne: Cheshire Publishing Proprietary, Ltd., 1963.

107. Nagera, H. *Vincent Van Gogh.* New York: International Universities Press, 1967.

108. Nashville *Tennessean.* 7 September 1971.

109. Navratil, L. *Schizophrenie und Kunst.* Munich: Deutscher Tachenbuch Verlag, 1965.

110a. Newton, D. *Art Styles of the Papuan Gulf.* New York: The Museum of Primitive Art, 1961.

110b. ——. *New Guinea Art in the Collection of the Museum of Primitive Art.* Greenwich, Connecticut: New York Graphic Society, 1967.

110c. ——. "Oral Tradition in Art History in the Sepik District, New Guinea." *Proceedings of the American Ethnological Society* 168 (1966): 125-200.

110d. ——. Personal Communication.

111. Nijinski, R. *The Diary of Vaslav Nijinski.* New York: Simon and Schuster, 1936.

112. Onions, C. T. et al. *The Oxford Universal Dictionary.* 3rd ed. Oxford: Clarendon Press, 1955.

113. *Districts of Papua and New Guinea.* Port Moresby: Department of Information and Extension Services, 1970.

114. *Papua-New Guinea Post Courier,* 23 May 1973.

115. Peck, H. T. *Harper's Dictionary of Classical Literature and Antiquities.* New York: Copper Square Publishers, 1963.

116. Peterfreund, E. *Information, Systems and Psychoanalysis.* New York: International Universities Press, 1971.

117. Prinzhorn, H. *Bildnerei der Geisteskranken.* Heidelberg: Springer Verlag, 1922.

118. Read, H. "Art in Aboriginal Society: A Comment." *The Artist in Tribal Society,* edited by M. W. Smith, pp. 14-22, 124-134. New York: The Free Press, 1961.

119. Rennert, H. "The Prognostic Significance of 'Horizon-Dislocation' in Schizophrenic Drawings." *Confinia Psychiatrica* 12 (1969): 23-27.

120. Reitman, F. *Insanity, Art and Culture.* New York: Philosophical Library, 1954.

121. Riesen, A. H. "Studying Perceptual Development Using the Technique of Sensory Deprivation." *The Journal of Nervous and Mental Disease* 132, no. 1 (1961): 21-25.

122a. Roheim, G. *The Gates of the Dream.* New York: International Universities Press, 1969.

122b. ——. *Schizophrenia and Magic.* New York: International Universities Press, 1955.

123. Rolf, I. P. "Structural Integration: Gravity, an Unexplored Factor in a More Human Use of Human Beings." Quoted in Sobel, D. S. Reference number 134.

124. Rosenblatt, P. C., Walsh, R. P. and Jackson, D. A. "Breaking Ties with Deceased Spouse." Paper read at the Ninth International Congress of Anthropological and Ethnological Sciences, Chicago, 1973, in press.

125. Roszak, T. *The Making of a Counter Culture.* Garden City, New York: Doubleday Books, 1969.

126. Ruesch, J. "Non-Verbal Language and Therapy." *Psychiatry* 18 (1955): 323–330.

127. Ryan, J. *The Hot Land, Focus on New Guinea.* Melbourne: MacMillan Company of Australia, 1971.

128. Schilder, P. "Psychoanalysis of Space." *International Journal of Psychoanalysis* 16 (1935): 274–295.

129a. Schmitz, C. A. *Oceanic Art.* New York: Harry N. Abrams, 1969.

129b. ———. *Wantoat.* The Hague, Paris: Morton and Company, 1963.

130. Sechehaye, M. *Autobiography of a Schizophrenic Girl.* New York: Grune and Stratton, 1951.

131. Selz, P. *The Work of Jean Dubuffet.* New York: The Museum of Modern Art, 1962.

132. Smith, K. V. and Smith, W. B. *Perception and Motion.* Philadelphia: W. B. Saunders Co., 1962.

133. Smith, M. W. *The Artist in Tribal Society.* Proceedings of a symposium held at the Royal Anthropological Institute. New York: The Free Press of Glencoe, 1961.

134. Sobel, D. S. "Gravity and Structural Integration." In *The Nature of Human Consciousness,* edited by R. E. Ornstein, pp. 397–407. New York: The Viking Press, 1974.

135. Soby, J. T. *Giorgio DeChirico.* New York: Arno Press, 1966.

136. Somare, M. *Sana.* Port Moresby, Papua New Guinea: Niugini Press, 1975.

137a. Spitz, R. *No and Yes.* New York: International Universities Press, 1957.

137b. ———. *Genetic Field Theory of Ego Development.* New York: International Universities Press, 1959.

138. Steinberg, S. et al. "The Art of Edvard Munch and its Function in his Mental Life." *Psychoanalytic Quarterly* 23 (1954): 409–423.

139. Storch, A. *Primitive Archaic Forms of Inner Experiences and Thought in Schizophrenia.* New York: Nervous and Mental Disease Publishing Co., 1924.

140. Straker, M. "Schizophrenia and Psychiatric Diagnosis." *Journal of the American Psychiatric Association,* 131, no. 6 (June 1974): 693–4.

141a. Strathern, A., and Strathern, M. *Self-Decoration in Mount Hagen.* Toronto: University of Toronto Press, 1971.

141b. Thompkins, Peter. *Secrets of the Great Pyramids.* New York: Harper and Row, 1971.

142. DeReuck, A. V. S. and Porter, R., eds. *Transcultural Psychiatry.* CIBA Foundation Symposium. Boston: Little, Brown and Co., 1965.

143. Van Gogh, V. *The Complete Letters of Vincent.* Three vols. Greenwich, Connecticut: New York Graphic Society, 1959.

144. Wassing, R. S. *African Art.* New York: Harry N. Abrams, 1968.

145. Weizsacker, V. von. *Wahrheit und Wahrnehmung.* Leipzig: Weizsacker, 1943.

146. Werner, H. *Comparative Psychology of Mental Development.* New York: International Universities Press, 1957.

147a. Williams, F. E. *Drama of Orokolo.* Oxford: Clarendon Press, 1969.

147b. ——. *Orokaiva Magic.* Oxford: Clarendon Press, 1969.

147c. ——. *Papuans of the Transfly.* Oxford: Clarendon Press, 1969.

148. Wittgenstein, O. G. "Gruppenbildung und (oder) Isolierung." *Psychother, Psychosom* 14 (1966): 264-281.

149a. Wittkower, E. D. and Weidman, H. D. "Magical Thought and the Integration of Psychoanalytical and Anthropological Theory." Reviewed in *Transcultural Psychiatry Research Review* 10 (April 1973): 16-18.

149b. Wittkower, E. D. et al. "A Review of Transcultural Psychiatry." In *American Handbook of Psychiatry,* edited by S. Arieti, pp. 535-50. 2nd ed. New York: Basic Books, 1974.

150. Wynne, L. C. "The Transcultural Study of Schizophrenics and Their Families." *Transcultural Research* 15 (1963): 10-13.

151. Zimmer, H. *Myths and Symbols in Indian Art and Civilization.* New York: Pantheon, 1946.

152. Zubeck, J. P. *Sensory Deprivation.* New York: Appleton-Century-Crofts, 1969.

153. Zubin, J. "A Cross-Cultural Approach to Psychopathology and its Implications." *The Classification of Behavior Disorders,* edited by L. D. Eron, pp. 45-85. Chicago: Aldine Publishing Co., 1966.

Index

Page numbers for illustrations appear in boldface type.
Titles of works of art are given in italics.

Art, traditional. *See* Art, New Guinean, traditional; Designs, traditional
Art, Tribal, 67, 75, 160–61, 195–96, 197, 212–13, 222, 230
Art, Western, 29, 74, 106, 197, 198–99. *See also* Art, Contemporary
"Art on the Rocks," 70
Art therapy, 5, 6, 172, 178
Artist, 29, 30, 32, 37, 39, 51, 69, 78–79, 82, 95–97, 98, 105, 124, 125, 128, 131–32, 185, 196, 212–13, 222–23; and mental illness, 95–97, 105, 213; in New Guinea, 29, 57, 69, 131–32, 185, 196; in primitive society, 78, 124, 125, 128, 212–13, 222; relationship to culture and society, 30, 32, 51, 69, 78–79, 223; relationship to schizophrenic, 37, 39, 82, 96. *See also* Art
Artist-priest, 69
Asoro, 68n
Astrology, 207, 213
Astronauts, 25
Astronomy, 72
Aurignacian Period, 139n
Auto-da-fé, 28–29

"Baby garden," 156–57
Bahasia Indonesian, 56
Bakota, 68
Bakuba cup, 77
Bambara mask, 77
Bantu, 47
Baseline, 11, **12**, 18 table 2, 20, 22, **33**, **93**, 94, 95 table 3, 117, **118**, 120, **122**, 135, 137, 153, 184, **189**, 191, 229, 231; as concept foreign to New Guinean art, 153; in children's drawings, **20**, 22; in New Guinean schizophrenics' graphics, 135, 137; in schizophrenics' graphics, 94, 120, 122
Beaumarchais, Pierre Augustin Caron de, 79
Bedroom (Van Gogh), 98
Bergman, Ingmar, 100
Berndt, C. H., 73, 195n
Bias, diagnostic, 5, 48
Big men in New Guinea, 43, 57–58, **58**, 68, 209, 210
"Bigpela," 157
Birth of Venus (Botticelli), 95
Birth of Venus, The (Bouguerau), 95, **97**
Birthday (Chagall), **225**
Bleuler, Eugen, 48
Body painting, 167, **168**, 169–70, 185
Bomana, 5, 6
Bomana prison, 130, 148
Book of Revelation, 94
Bosch, Hieronymus, 28, 30, 95n; *Vanity*, **31**
Botticelli, Sandro, *Birth of Venus*, 95
Boucher, Francois, 29, 224
Bougainville, 165
Bouguerau, A. W., 95; *The Birth of Venus*, **97**
Boundaries, conceptual: of primitive

Boundaries (cont.)
artist, 124; of schizophrenic, 91, 94, 115, 122, 125, 160
Brahma, 17, 126
Braque, Georges, 95n
Brecht, Bertolt, 79
Breton, André, 104
Breughel, Pieter The Elder, 28, 30, 95n
Bride price, 46, 140
Buddhism, 49
Buka Island, cases from 156–66
Bullroarers, 58, 68, 164
Burial of Count Orgaz (El Greco), **89**, 93
Burton-Bradley, B. G., 5
Bushmen, South African, 196
Byzantine Period, 11, 223

Calle d'Avignon, 35
Can of Tomato Soup (Warhol), 225
Cannibalism, 41, 46, 53, 59, 60, 62–63, **62**, **63**, 64, 65, 66, 78, 130, 132, 134, 138, 140, 164, 169, 182, 238
Cargo cult, 48, 65, 66, 137, 156, 157, 158, 159, 161, 165, 190, 209, 210
Carolingian Empire, 10
Cassowary feathers, 178
Castration, fear of, in schizophrenic, 112–13
Catatonic stupor, 45, 49
Catholic Church, 11, 91, 128, 164, 177–78, 203, 223; in New Guinea, 164, 177–78, 203. *See also* Christianity, in New Guinea; Missionaries in New Guinea
Cave paintings, 22, 23, 70, 129n, 212
Central District, cases from, 133–39
Ceremonial houses, 9, 10, 140
Cervantes Saavedra, Miguel de, 13
Chagall, Marc, 224; *Birthday*, **225**
Chalmers, Reverend James, 53
Chant of Creation; 69
Charlemagne, Charles the Great, 10
Chemotherapy, 148, 172, 178, 179, 189
Chevrons, 145–46, 147, 148
Children's drawings, 20, 22, 76–77, 117, 120, 231
Child's Brain, The (de Chirico), 100–101, 103, 104
Chile, 3
Chimbu, District, 168, 169–75, 181, 219n; cases from, 169–75
Chirico, Giorgio de, 3, 89, 96, 97, 100–107, 114, 224; *The Child's Brain*, 100–101, **103**, 104; *Enigma of the Hour*, **102**, 104; *Nostalgia of the Infinite*, **103**, 104; *The Square*, **106**; *Troubador*, **103**
Christ: as cult hero in New Guinea, 64, 140; New Guinean schizophrenic's delusions of being, 153 (*see also* Delusions); New Guinean schizophrenic's identification with, 190
Christian Science, 91
Christianity in New Guinea, 64–65, 134, 138, 140, 164, 210, 236n, 242. *See also* Catholic Church, in New Guinea;

Christianity (cont.)
Missionaries in New Guinea
Clans in New Guinea, 57, 59, 157, 212
Coghill, G. E., 8, 216
Colors in New Guinean art, 132, 185, 195
Communication: lack of, with outside world in New Guinea, 42, 166 (*See also* New Guinea, isolation of); nonverbal, 2, 29, 129; verbal, 129, 131, 227. *See also* Language
Constable, John, 129, 224
Constancy, lack of, 83
Constantinople, 223
Convulsions, schizophrenic, 34, 49
Copernicus, Kopernik, 13, 215, 221
Council of Hieria, 128, 129
Councils, local, 175
Couvade, 206–7
Creation myths, 17, 58, 59, 78, 113, 191; in New Guinean culture, 58, 59, 191
Creative Arts Centre, 176, 195
Creativity, 3, 27, 33–34, 39, 69, 74, 81, 82, 105, 213, 214, 225; of artist and schizophrenic compared, 27, 39; and mental illness, 3, 81, 105, 213; stages of, 33–34
Cronos, 113
Crosland, Mary, 102
Cross, design of, 147, 159, 163
Crows in the Wheatfields (van Gogh), **80**, 100
Crusades, 11, 127, 223
Cubism, 34
Cult hero: Christ as, in New Guinea, 64, 140, 210; in New Guinean culture, 60; in primitive art, 73. *See also* Cargo cults
Cult leader, 47, 48, 207. *See also* Cargo cults
Cults, function of, in New Guinean culture, 60. *See also* Cargo cults
Cults, Millenarian, 210

Dada Movement, 28, 105
Dali, Salvador, 18 table 2, 28, 89
Death, 24, 61, 78, 141, 201, 202; attitudes concerning, in New Guinea, 61, 141, 202
De Chirico, Giorgio. *See* Chirico, Giorgio de
Dedifferentiation, 231
Delusions, schizophrenic, 5, 45, 83, 84, 126, 134, 137, 153, 155, 158, 178, 190, 204–5, 237; of being Jesus, 153, 178, 237; of grandeur, 155; of thought control, 83, 134; of world destruction as imminent, 126, 137
Demoiselles d'Avignon, 34
Depth: in history of art, 11, 13, 15; in schizophrenic art, 21, 88–89, 106, 114, 135 (*See also* Perspective tordue). *See also* Perspective; Space
Designs, geometric, 18 table 2, **36**, 73, 95 table 3, 105, 120, 155, **169**, 174, 181, 185–86; in art cross-culturally, 73, 120, 181, 185–86; in schizophren-